Research on Technology Use in Multicultural Settings

A Volume in:
Research in Educational Diversity and Excellence

Series Editors
Yolanda N. Padrón
Hersh C. Waxman

Research in Educational Diversity and Excellence

Series Editors

Yolanda N. Padrón
Hersh C. Waxman
Texas A&M University

Latinos/as and Mathematics Education
Research on Learning and Teaching in Classrooms and Communities (2011)
Edited by Kip Téllez, Judit N. Moschkovich, and Marta Civil

Educational Resiliency
Student, Teacher, and School Perspectives (2006)
Edited by Hersch C. Waxman, Yolanda N. Padron, and Jon P. Gray

Research on Technology Use in Multicultural Settings

Edited by

Tirupalavanam G. Ganesh
Anna W. Boriack
Jacqueline R. Stillisano
Trina J. Davis
Hersh C. Waxman

INFORMATION AGE PUBLISHING, INC.
Charlotte, NC • www.infoagepub.com

KH

Library of Congress Cataloging-in-Publication Data

The CIP data for this book can be found on the Library of Congress website (loc.gov).

Paperback: 978-1-62396-825-0
Hardcover: 978-1-62396-826-7
eBook: 978-1-62396-827-4

Printed in the United States of America

11/17/16

CONTENTS

Preface.. vii

1. Introduction and Overview 1
   Anna W. Boriack and Hersh C. Waxman

2. Interactive and Traditional Books: Literacy Beliefs and
   Practices in Latino Families 11
   Deanne R. Pérez-Granados and Lynne C. Huffman

3. Integrating and Adapting an Inquiry Technology-Rich
   Curriculum in the Context of a Latin American Science
   Methods Course.. 45
   M. Elizabeth Gonzalez and Barbara Hug

4. Integrating Flexible Language Supports within Online
   Science Learning Environments....................................75
   Douglas Clark, Brian Nelson, Robert Atkinson,
   Frank Ramirez-Marin, and William Medina-Jerez

5. Case Studies of Online Testing in Multicultural School
   Districts 107
   Brooke Kandel-Cisco, Jacqueline R. Stillisano,
   Trina J. Davis, and Hersh C. Waxman

6. Deconstructing the Digital Divide in Research: Moving From
   a View of the Poor as "Other" to the Poor as "Us" 121
   Cecelia Merkel

7.   **Supporting Reading-to-Learn in Science: The Application of Summarization Technology in Multicultural Urban High School Classrooms**..139
     Kimberley Gomez, Samuel Kwon, Louis Gomez, and Jennifer Sherer

8.   **Building Capacity in Community Context: Studying the Impact of Technology on Low-Income Immigrant Spanish-Speaking Families**..159
     Hector H. Rivera and David J. Francis

9.   **Strategies to Engage Female and Hispanic Youth in Robotics in the Southwestern United States**...............................177
     Tirupalavanam G. Ganesh

10. **Understanding the Shape of Learning in the Context of Technological Innovation**..195
     Finbarr Sloane, Jennifer Oloff-Lewis, and Anthony E. Kelly

11. **Alternative Models for Evaluating Technology Use in Schools**...209
     Jacqueline R. Stillisano, Danielle B. Brown, and Hersh C. Waxman

12. **Future Directions for Improving Technology Use in Multicultural Settings**...225
     Anna W. Boriack, Tirupalavanam G. Ganesh, and Hersh C. Waxman

     Editor and Author Biographies...237

PREFACE

This volume is intended for an audience of researchers, educators, and policy-makers who are interested in the integration of technology in multicultural educational settings. As we point out in the initial chapter of the book, developing students who can participate in a global economy that is increasingly more focused on technology is one of the greatest challenges facing educators today. We hope that this book will serve both as a resource and as a motivator to make changes necessary to support the integration of technology in schools.

Our intention was always for the volume to be an interdisciplinary collection. While all the authors are scholars in the field of education research, several bring expertise in fields other than instructional technology. This mingling of expertise was a purposeful choice because we believe that improving integration of technology is a challenge that requires a wide range of voices and perspectives.

As readers will notice, many of the chapters acknowledge the support of the Education Research Center (ERC) at Texas A&M University. For the past several years, the ERC at Texas A&M has been involved in a number of state and national research projects that focus on science, technology, engineering, and mathematics (STEM) integration. Several of these projects specifically focused on the integration of technology in multicultural settings. The ERC brought together researchers from several disciplinary backgrounds such as mathematics, science, technology, bilingual education, and literacy and provided opportunities for faculty,

Research on Technology Use in Multicultural Settings, pages vii–viii.

doctoral students, and post-doctoral researchers to consider the ways in which research could inform what we know and need to know about improving STEM education for students from multicultural settings. Collaborations across institutions included research symposia and presentations at national and international conferences.

Although the ERC was a galvanizing organization for many of the authors in the volume, we are confident in the authors' research and attention to improving the integration of technology in multicultural schools and classrooms. If this volume motivates other researchers to join in the effort, then it will have been a great success.

We would like to thank the authors in this volume for their commitment and patience. We would also like to thank Hersh Waxman and Yolanda Padrón for their series' editorship. We are also indebted to Anna Boriack, whose skillful and careful editing, proofing, and formatting contributed much to the accuracy and coherence of the book.

T. Ganesh
A. Boriack
J. Stillisano
T. Davis
H. Waxman

CHAPTER 1

INTRODUCTION AND OVERVIEW

Anna W. Boriack and Hersh C. Waxman

ABSTRACT

This chapter begins with a brief overview on the importance of using technology in the classroom but also the challenges that are faced when implementing technology. The remainder of the chapter provides an overview of the chapters that are included in the book.

INTRODUCTION

Developing students who can participate in a global economy that is increasingly more focused on technology is one of the greatest challenges facing educators today. Several recent reports highlighted the need for federal, state, and local policymakers to use technology comprehensively to: (1) develop proficiency in 21st century skills, (2) support innovative teaching and learning, and (3) create robust education support systems (National Academies of Sciences, National Academy of Engineering, and Institute of Medicine, 2007; National Research Council, 2011; President's Council of Advisors on Science and Technology, 2010). This new emphasis on 21st century skills suggests that in order to successfully compete

Research on Technology Use in Multicultural Settings, pages 1–10.
Copyright © 2015 by Information Age Publishing

in today's global economy, "districts need to integrate new technologies, online learning, and interactive software to enhance student achievement and personalize instruction" (Gayl, 2007, p. 4). If technology is properly introduced, it can change everything in the school and classroom (Salomon, 1992). Technology can fundamentally change the nature of student-teacher interactions because it alters the ways that information can be obtained, manipulated, and displayed. As Judson (2006) puts it "the use of technology may very well enable the dynamics of students constructing personal meaning, learning from one another, learning from experts, and creating unique interpretations" (p. 592). Technology-based learning environments can help replace the learning of facts with exploration, and direct instructional approaches with intensive interaction among students (Salomon, 1992). Technology can be the catalyst that helps teachers shift from traditional lecture and drill approaches to more student-centered, authentic approaches that emphasize teaching for understanding. Technology has the potential for deepening classroom instruction, making it more meaningful, and assisting the learning of higher-order thinking skills (Niemiec & Walberg, 1992). When technology is used in all these ways, it can promote high performance and provide *all* students with the opportunity to develop the 21st century skills that they will need to be successful.

Research has indicated that the use of educational technology as a learning tool can increase student learning (Hattie, 2009; Lee, Waxman, Wu, Michko, & Linn, 2013; Reimann & Aditomo, 2013; Walberg, 2011). Furthermore, there is substantial evidence that indicates that technology-enhanced instruction is an effective teaching practice for students in urban schools, especially for English language learners (ELLs) and students from high-poverty urban schools (Padrón & Waxman, 1996; Park, 2008; Waxman & Padrón, 2002; Waxman, Padrón, & Arnold, 2001; Waxman, Padrón, & García, 2007). The use of technology for students with various cultural and linguistic backgrounds offers teachers the ability to individualize instruction so that it can focus on students' interests and respond to their individual learning needs.

Although technology has been found to be a strategy that improves students' academic achievement, there are many studies that have found that technology is not being integrated in schools, especially into the teaching and learning process (Cuban, 2001, 2013; Padrón, Waxman, Lee, Lin, & Michko, 2012; Waxman, Evans, Boriack, & Kilinc, 2013; Waxman & Huang, 1995, 1996). In other words, research has found that educational technology is not being integrated into the delivery of instruction in most schools and classrooms. These findings are similar to other studies that have also found that the quantity of computers in the classroom does not appear to be a key factor that affects teaching and learning, but rather it is the way computers are used in instruction that appears to makes a difference (Lei & Zhao, 2007; Lowther & Ross, 2003). The potential benefits of technology often go untapped in schools for a number of reasons. Some of the important factors that negatively impact technology's potential are: (1) teachers are not well prepared for using the computer or Internet; (2) technology is intimidating to some teachers; (3) there is a lack of coordination between curriculum developers and technology coordinators; (4) technology is often used for teaching lower-order skills; (5) teachers need extensive training, planning time, and technological support; (6) there is not a clear focus about the role of technology in the school or classroom; (7) there needs to be a lower student to computer ratio; (8) the school climate does not support technology; and (9) the school and classroom Internet connections are not robust or high-speed (Collins & Halverson, 2009; Fouts, 2000; Okojie, Olinzock, & Okojie-Boulder, 2006). Furthermore, technology integration in schools and classrooms is often viewed very narrowly, which consequently hinders teachers' understandings of the role of technology (Okojie et al., 2006). In order to effectively use technology in classrooms, teachers need to understand how various instructional activities and technology are interconnected. In addition, school administrators need to be aware of other issues (e.g., school infrastructure, equity, professional development, and teachers' attitudes) that impact the integration of technology in their schools.

More research is needed to understand how these factors specifically impact the integration of technology into schools and classrooms in multicultural settings. The present book focuses on critical issues related to the integration of technology in schools. In particular, this book focuses on three key questions related to issues of technology integration in schools in multicultural settings: (1) How is technology being used in schools? (2) How can technology be used to facilitate student learning? and (3) What are some of the key concerns related to integrating technology?

OVERVIEW OF THE BOOK

This book is the third volume in the series on *Research in Educational Diversity and Excellence*. The goal of this series is to bring issues of diversity and educational risk to the forefront of national attention in order to assist the nation's diverse students at risk of educational failure to achieve academic excellence. This series focuses on critical issues in the education of linguistic and cultural minority students and those placed at risk by factors of race, poverty, and geographic location.

The purpose of the present book is to summarize and discuss recent perspectives, research, and practices related to educational technology use in multicultural settings. Technology that is already perpetuated in our daily lives brings up a myriad of issues to the area of education. While educational systems should be geared to address challenges appropriately, the systems should also be designed and developed to provide opportunities to take advantage of technology use. This book is noteworthy in that it presents a variety of theoretical and practical considerations for technology use in diverse multicultural contexts. This book consists of 11 chapters, which (a) propose theoretical concerns for understanding technological learning environments today and envision the potential impact of future technology use and (b) examine technology tools and models that have been used for interventions, programs, and projects, and measure and document specific outcomes and challenges involving complex interactions within low-income and language-minority families and students.

The second chapter, "Interactive and Traditional Books: Literacy Beliefs and Practices in Latino Families" by Deanne R. Pérez-Granados and Lynne C. Huffman, describes a home-based literacy intervention program that was conducted with low-income, Latino families. Half of the families (eight) were recent immigrants (had been in the U.S. five years or less), and half of the families had been in the U.S. for more than five years. The families were provided with traditional and interactive storybooks. Surveys and interviews were conducted to determine family background, family characteristics, literacy beliefs, and literacy practices. Book-sharing activities between parents and children were videotaped at the end of the intervention program to determine what types of interaction occurred during book sharing. Both traditional and interactive storybook activities were taped for further analysis. The results showed no significant differences between the two groups (immigrant and resident) on parent literacy practices, language use, and duration of the book-sharing activity. There were also no significant differences found between book type (traditional and interactive) for any of the categories, although child and child/mother off-task behavior was approaching significance. This study implies that providing low-income Latino families with books (traditional and/or interactive) may increase book-sharing with toddlers, which could increase their readiness for school.

In Chapter 3, Elizabeth Gonzalez and Barbara Hug discuss the adoption and adaptation of a technology-rich science inquiry curriculum. This exploratory study took a piece of software that had been developed in the United States and integrated it into a science methods course at an Argentinean college. The teacher and students were then observed and interviewed to determine what modifications were made in the curriculum in order to adapt it to the new context. It was determined that the instructor's previous experiences, pedagogical content knowledge, and understanding of the students influenced how the curriculum was adapted for use in the science methods course. The students (pre-service teachers) had many misconceptions about the collection and analysis of data, which the teacher was able to address through the use of the new curriculum. The results of this exploratory study provide insight into how a teacher adapts a technology-rich curriculum for a new, multicultural context. Further studies have been planned to see if the results can be generalized.

The fourth chapter, "Integrating Flexible Language Supports within Online Science Learning Environments," describes how multilingual scaffolding was developed and used in an online science project. The scaffolding allowed English language learners (ELLs) to switch between Spanish and English for both written and spoken text in order to help them make sense of both science concepts and academic English. The results indicate that students used Spanish to help them understand unfamiliar English terms, but they still engaged in the activity mostly in English. This implies that computer-supported learning environments could provide support for ELLs to learn academic English by providing scaffolding in their primary language. While this study used only Spanish and English, future programs could include scaffolding in other languages so that ELLs from multiple linguistic backgrounds could be accommodated in a single classroom. Computer-supported learning environments that include these types of scaffolding could increases ELLs' access to concepts that are on grade level while also helping them learn academic English, which is important for their success in school and the future.

Chapter 5 uses a case study approach to examine the challenges faced by multi-cultural school districts when implementing large-scale online testing. Interviews with over 75 district and school personnel found that inequitable access to technology, lack of resources, and alignment between classroom instruction and online tests are challenges that need to be considered and addressed before online testing can be fully implemented. Additionally, more specific concerns (e.g., technology infrastructure) varied by location of the schools (urban, suburban, rural). This implies that a single solution of online testing is not going to be adequate, and several solutions will need to be offered. The schools and districts felt that online testing should be phased in, so that they could have an adequate amount of time to prepare both their teachers and resources.

Cecelia Merkel discusses deconstructing the digital divide in research in the sixth chapter. The chapter used an ethnographic perspective in order to study technology use among low-income families that participated in a computer training and distribution program. Through interviews, focus groups, and observations, the study revealed that participants integrated technology into their lives and addressed technical issues in a variety of ways. Participants also faced barriers, such as problems connecting to the Internet and older computers, when trying to use technology in their daily lives. Merkel suggests that researchers and policy makers should not remove the details of people's lives from discussions about technology use. Instead, a situated approach should be used that examines how marginalized groups integrate technology in their lives when given the opportunity and what barriers they face. Research should be conducted in which marginalized families are treated as experts in their own lives and on the issues that are important to them.

Chapter 7, "Supporting Reading-to-Learn in Science: The Application of Summarization Technology in Multicultural Urban High School Classrooms," examines the use of a technology summarization tool, Summary Street, in urban high school content area classrooms. The use of summarization in content area classrooms may increase reading comprehension, especially for second language learners. The study examined two content area classrooms (science and social studies) that integrated Summary Street for their ninth-grade students. The findings indicated that students were engaged with the technology and revised their summaries several times in order to improve their scores. Teachers also felt that Summary Street was useful and encouraged students to read and re-read the text more carefully. The teachers had concerns that the tool did not enable students to learn content area knowledge; however, a multiple-choice exam showed that students were learning the content. Additionally, Summary Street scored students on content, not on grammar and syntax, so the teachers were concerned that students were getting the impression that poor grammar and syntax were okay. Future research is needed to adequately address this concern. The results from this study suggest that technology summarization tools, like Summary Street, might be able to increase reading comprehension for students, especially struggling readers and second language learners.

The eighth chapter, by Hector Rivera and David Francis, discusses a community technology intervention program designed to assist Spanish-speaking parents in learning technology for work and family advancement. The results indicated that participants perceived that the program had a positive impact on their lives. They also believed that the technology skills that they learned would be useful for helping their children with schoolwork at home. Additionally, pre- and post-test results revealed that participants significantly increased their technology skills with programs like Microsoft Word, PowerPoint, and Excel. This increase in technology skills lead to some participants being able to advance in their current employment or obtain new employment. Some participants also chose to continue their education by taking further technology classes (such as web page design), health-related classes, and basic statistics. The findings from the study suggest that community-based technology programs may be able to help Spanish-speaking immigrants increase their technology skills, which in turn affects both their lives and the lives of their children.

Tirupalavanam Ganesh explores the use of robotics in an informal learning environment to engage female and Latino youth in science, technology, engineering, and mathematics (STEM) problem-solving in Chapter 9. Participants studied an endangered or protected species and designed a robot that behaved similarly to the species. Art and cultural contexts were used to make the problem engaging and applicable to participants. Pre- and post-surveys revealed that participants' attitudes about women and minorities doing well in science increased. Additionally, participants' self-efficacy with "tinkering" (ability to take things apart and put them back together) improved. At the end of the program participants expressed in-depth knowledge of both the science content and robotics. The results indicate that combining robotics with real-life problems that are applicable to participants may increase their interest in STEM fields.

The tenth chapter, "Understanding the Shape of Learning in the Context of Technological Innovation," discusses the features of change that guide researchers as they study student growth over time. The chapter authors raise concerns with the current methods that are being used to analyze longitudinal studies. They suggest that hierarchal linear modeling (HLM) is a better way to analyze longitudinal data in order to study the changes that might be occurring both within groups and within individuals. The usefulness of HLM is explored both graphically and algebraically. The discussion in the chapter indicates that researchers should consider using HLM to provide a more accurate picture of the changes that occur during longitudinal studies.

Stillisano, Brown, and Waxman explore alternative models for evaluating technology use in schools in Chapter 11. This chapter discusses five evaluation models (experimental, CIPP, logic, AEIOU, and classroom observation) and their appropriateness for evaluating technology use in classroom settings. The strengths and weakness of each model are included along with examples from research studies when available. The use of these alternative evaluation models may improve our understanding of technology use in classrooms, which could then be applied to current and future programs.

In the concluding chapter, Anna Boriack, Tirupalavanam Ganesh, and Hersh Waxman discuss future directions for research on educational technology. They discuss needed research in the field as well as new areas that present opportunities for further research.

SUMMARY

The purpose of this book is to make available information for improving our understanding of some new directions for research on technology use in multicultural settings. The book describes some of the conceptual and research-based approaches that successfully work in improving technology use in schools. This book also illustrates several ways we can promote educational technology to improve teaching and student learning. We maintain that conceptual and empirical work on technology use can be a critical component for improving the role of teachers and administrators, policymakers, parents, and other educators. Although recognition of the uniqueness of each school and classroom situation will always need to be considered, the accumulation of research evidence over time and across studies provides consistent findings that enhance our understandings of improving student learning. In other words, more conceptual work and research on technology may allow us to change and improve the education of teachers and consequently improve the education of students.

There are, of course, many unanswered questions about promoting technology over the long term. We hoped to be able to provide a synthesis both of what we think we know and what we need to know. We were probably less successful in developing this synthesis, not because of the quality of the chapters, but because of the lack of information that can be brought to bear. As we will point out in the conclusion (Chapter 12), there is much work to be done. We hope that these chapters will encourage others to join us in the continuing search to answer some of the interesting questions related to promoting technology use in schools.

We want to thank the Education Research Center (ERC) at Texas A&M University that provided support for our technology research. During the past eight years, we have conducted extensive research on technology use in schools. Our ERC research has included descriptive and correlational studies, using both qualitative and quantitative research methods (Brown, Alford, Stillisano, Rollins, & Waxman, 2013; Davis, Stillisano, & Waxman, 2012; Padrón et al., 2012; Waxman, Boriack, Lee, & MacNeil, 2013; Waxman et al., 2013). This research has helped us formulate many of the ideas, perspectives, and findings that we describe in this book.

While the term *research* often has a negative connotation for educational practitioners and policymakers, it is the best criterion we have for determining effective practices in education. The conceptual work and research presented in this book suggest several consistent relations among technology use and improved teacher and student outcomes. We are confident that the research shared in this volume will inspire additional researchers to conduct investigations that will yield new practices and policies to improve technology use in multicultural settings.

We also would like to thank all the authors who gave generously of their time to the chapters in this volume. We chose many individuals who were prominent in the area of technology use in schools. We gained knowledge from reading their current thoughts about technology as well as a renewal of energy and enthusiasm about the potential benefits of continuing to promote technology use in multicultural settings. We also gained a sense of direction about what questions need to be answered next, and we hope that others who read these chapters will share these outcomes.

REFERENCES

Brown, D. B., Alford, B. L., Stillisano, J. R., Rollins, K. B., & Waxman, H. C. (2013). Evaluating the efficacy of mathematics, science, and technology teacher preparation academies in Texas. *Professional Development in Education, 39*(5), 656–677.

Collins, A. & Halverson, R. (2009). *Rethinking education in the age of technology: The digital revolution and schooling in America.* New York, NY: Teachers College.

Cuban, L. (2001). *Oversold and underused: Computers in the classroom.* Cambridge, MA: Harvard University Press.

Cuban, L. (2013). *Inside the black box of classroom practice: Change without reform in American education.* Cambridge, MA: Harvard Education Press.

Davis, T. J., Stillisano, J. R., & Waxman, H. C. (2012). A statewide evaluation of districts' readiness for large-scale online testing: Unique perceptions and challenges from diverse school districts' lenses. *Journal of Texas Alliance of Black School Educators, 4,* 33–54.

Fouts, J. T. (2000) *Research on computers and education: Past, present and future.* Seattle, WA: Bill and Melinda Gates Foundation.

Gayl, C. L. (2007). *Global competitiveness in the 21st Century* (National School Boards Association Policy Research Brief). Retrieved from http://www.nsba.org/Advocacy/Archives/PolicyResearchBriefsArchive/NSBAPolicyResearchBriefGlobalCompetitivenessinthe21stCentury.pdf

Hattie, J. A. C. (2009). *Visible learning: A synthesis of over 800 meta-analyses relating to achievement.* New York, NY: Routledge.

Judson, E. (2006). How teachers integrate technology and their beliefs about learning: Is there a connection? *Journal of Technology and Teacher Education, 14,* 581–597.

Lee, Y.-H., Waxman, H. C., Wu, J.-Y., Michko, G., & Linn, G. (2013). Revisit the effect of teaching and learning with technology. *Educational Technology and Society, 16*(1), 133–146.

Lei, J. & Zhao, Y. (2007). Technology uses and student achievement: A longitudinal study. *Computers & Education, 49,* 284–296.

Lowther, D. L. & Ross, S. M. (2003, April). *When each one has one: The influence on teaching strategies and student achievement of using laptops in the classroom.* Paper presented at the meeting of the American Educational Research Association, Chicago, IL.

National Academies of Sciences, National Academy of Engineering, and Institute of Medicine. (2007). *Rising above the gathering storm: Energizing and employing America for a brighter economic future.* Washington, DC: The National Academies Press.

National Research Council. (2011). *Successful K–12 STEM education: Identifying effective approaches in science, technology, engineering, and mathematics.* Washington, DC: The National Academies Press.

Niemiec, R. P. & Walberg, H. J. (1992). The effects of computers on learning. *International Journal of Educational Research, 17,* 99–108.

Okojie, M., Olinzock, A. A., & Okojie-Boulder, T. C. (2006). The pedagogy of technology integration. *The Journal of Technology Studies, 39*(2), 66–71.

Padrón, Y. N. & Waxman, H. C. (1996). Improving the teaching and learning of English language learners through instructional technology. *International Journal of Instructional Media, 23,* 1–13.

Padrón, Y. N., Waxman, H. C., Lee, Y.-H., Lin, M.-F., & Michko, G. M. (2012). Classroom observations of teaching and learning with technology in urban elementary school mathematics classrooms serving English language learners. *International Journal of Instructional Media, 39*(1), 45–54.

Park, H. S. (2008). The impact of technology use on Hispanic students' mathematics achievement within family and school contexts: Subgroup analysis between English- and non-English-speaking students. *Journal of Educational Computing Research, 38,* 453–468.

President's Council of Advisors on Science and Technology. (2010). *Prepare and inspire: K–12 education in science, technology, engineering, and math (STEM) for America's future.* Washington, DC: Author.

Reimann, P. & Aditomo, A. (2013). Technology-supported learning and academic achievement. In J. Hattie & E. M. Anderman (Eds.), *International guide to student achievement* (pp. 399–401). New York, NY: Routledge.

Salomon, G. (1992). The changing role of the teacher: From information transmitter to orchestrator of learning. In F. K. Oser, A. Dick, & J. L. Patry (Eds.), *Effective and responsible teaching* (pp. 35–49). San Francisco, CA: Jossey-Bass.

Walberg, H. J. (2011). *Improving student learning: Action principles for families, schools, districts, and states.* Charlotte, NC: Information Age Publishing.

Waxman, H. C., Boriack, A. W., Lee, Y.-H., & MacNeil, A. (2013). Principals' perceptions of the importance of technology in schools. *Contemporary Educational Technology, 4*(3), 187–196.

Waxman, H. C., Evans, R. T., Boriack, A. W., & Kilinc, E. (2013). Systematic observations of the availability and use of instructional technology in urban middle school classrooms. *Journal of Contemporary Research in Education, 1*(3), 104–113.

Waxman, H. C. & Huang, S. L. (1995). An observational study of technology integration in urban elementary and middle schools. *International Journal of Instructional Media, 22*, 329–339.

Waxman, H. C. & Huang, S. L. (1996). Classroom instruction differences by level of technology use in middle school mathematics. *Journal of Educational Computing Research, 14*(2), 147–159.

Waxman, H. C. & Padrón, Y. N. (2002). Research-based teaching practices that improve the education of English language learners. In L. Minaya-Rowe (Ed.), *Teacher training and effective pedagogy in the context of student diversity* (pp. 3–38). Greenwich, CT: Information Age Publishing.

Waxman, H. C., Padrón, Y. N., & Arnold, K. A. (2001). Effective instructional practices for students placed at risk of failure. In G. D. Borman, S. C. Stringfield, & R. E. Slavin (Eds.), *Title I: Compensatory education at the crossroads* (pp. 137–170). Mahwah, NJ: Erlbaum.

Waxman, H. C., Padrón, Y. N., & Garcia, A. (2007). Educational issues and effective practices for Hispanic students. In S. J. Paik & H. J. Walberg (Eds.), *Narrowing the achievement gap: Strategies for education Latino, Black, and Asian students* (pp. 131–151). New York, NY: Springer.

CHAPTER 2

INTERACTIVE AND TRADITIONAL BOOKS

Literacy Beliefs and Practices in Latino Families

Deanne R. Pérez-Granados and Lynne C. Huffman

ABSTRACT

Parent reports of literacy beliefs and practices, and observations of parent-toddler book-sharing interactions were used to investigate the effectiveness of a home-based intervention using traditional books and interactive books with low-income Latino families, half recent immigrant parents and half long time residents. Results showed that all parents had positive orientations toward child-centered literacy activities but low numbers of children's books and frequency of book-sharing in the home. Compared to interactive books, parents used greater language quantity and diversity for the traditional books. There were no differences based on book type for family time spent in various participation patterns; for both book types, more time was spent in collaborative and negotiation participation patterns, and less time spent in asynchronous and off-task participation patterns.

INTERACTIVE AND TRADITIONAL BOOKS: LITERACY BELIEFS AND PRACTICES IN LATINO FAMILIES

Learning to read is an essential early academic skill that is related to a child's future academic experiences, particularly for children from low-income families (Snow, Porche, Tabors, & Harris, 2007). The 2009 Nation's Report Card on

Research on Technology Use in Multicultural Settings, pages 11–44.

Reading (National Center for Education Statistics [NCES], 2010) revealed that although low-income children's fourth and eighth grade reading scores have improved compared to 2003 and 2005 scores, their scores have consistently lagged behind their higher income counterparts by 12–13% (28–30 points). This report also showed a similar literacy achievement gap for African-American and Latino children compared to European-American children (NCES, 2010). National educational policy and intervention initiatives have focused on closing these kinds of reading achievement gaps.

While educational policy such as the No Child Left Behind (NCLB) Act emphasized educational accountability in K–12 schools, it also channeled resources toward initiatives such as the Early Reading First Program that was designed to improve the quality of early childcare programs that serve preschool aged children (George W. Bush White House Archives, 2002). However, a research summary report produced by the National Institute for Literacy suggested that interventions focused on either specific emergent literacy skills such as the alphabetic code and language enhancement, or specific literacy-related activities such as shared book reading and parent involvement in literacy-related instructional approaches were as effective as preschool and kindergarten programs (National Institute for Literacy, 2008). More recent educational policies under the Obama administration target both early home and schooling experiences, such as the Preschool for All initiative and the Maternal, Infant, and Early Childhood Home Visiting Program, both of which emphasize the development of school readiness such as emergent literacy skills (Early Learning, n.d.). Hence, efforts to address achievement gaps in low-income and minority populations have been extended into the first five years of life and acknowledge the need to target children's earliest learning experiences.

Research suggests that the home literacy environment in the years before elementary school, parent-child interactions with high quantities and qualities of talk with their children, and activities such as storybook reading play an important role in children's early literacy development (Griffin & Morrison, 1997; Jordan, Porche, & Snow, 2000). In addition to parental involvement, it is suggested that technological advancements, via computer-based educational tools, can support early literacy development (Hutinger et al., 1998). However, there also are claims that reliance on technology-based learning tools like computer software may place children's learning and development at risk (Armstrong & Casement, 2000).

In this chapter, we will address some of the important issues that surround the use of technologically-enhanced interactive books in efforts to promote emergent literacy skills in young children from low-income immigrant households. To this end, we first review scientific literature addressing three salient areas of inquiry:

1. What are the critical components of emergent literacy in toddlers and young children?
2. What are characteristics of interactive books, and how have these computer-based educational tools intended to support emergent literacy?

3.   In what ways do family background (e.g., socioeconomic level, cultural-linguistic factors, and immigration experiences) play a role in young children's emergent literacy?

This literature guided the questions and design of the research study described in this chapter.

Next, we describe a research project that investigates the impact of a multifaceted home-based intervention incorporating traditional books and interactive books on child emergent literacy and parent-child interactions in a sample of low-income Latino families. Finally, we briefly address the implications of our initial research findings for future applied research and for emergent literacy intervention programs.

Background and Literature Review

Education and psychology research indicates that there are multiple influences on emergent literacy. Some factors considered in this study are connections between language and literacy development, early language and print-related experiences, the linguistic and literacy environment facilitated in the home context, and potential discontinuities or "mismatches" between home and school cultures (Azmitia, Cooper, García, &, Dunbar, 1996; Beals, 2001; Beals & Snow, 1994; Hart & Risley, 1992; Heath, 1983, 1986; Laosa & Henderson, 1991; Sigel, Stinson, & Flaugher, 1991; Snow, 2001; Walker, Greenwood, Hart, & Carta, 1994). Research highlights the value of reading aloud with young children for promoting language development (Chomsky, 2001). Furthermore, there is evidence that literacy practices vary across families of varied cultural and SES backgrounds (Bradley & Caldwell, 1984, 1986; Bradley et al., 1989). Others have found differences in parent-child interactions during book reading activities across groups (McNaughton, Phillips, & MacDonald, 2003; Phillips & McNaughton, 1990), as well as across individuals (Haden, Reese, & Fivish, 1996).

Components of Emergent Literacy Skills

Proficient reading is the result of developmental processes with roots in infancy (learning to understand and speak language) and into the toddler years (making connections to the symbols of language). Three specific practices or skills in early childhood have been linked to later reading abilities: oral language, phonological processing abilities, and print knowledge (Dickinson, McCabe, Anastasopoulos, Peisner-Feinberg, & Poe, 2003). The connection between oral language and later literacy skills is supported by studies showing a strong relationship between vocabulary skills and children's decoding skills early in the process of learning to read (Wagner et al., 1997). There are also strong connections between preschoolers' vocabulary skills and their phonological sensitivity. In addition to oral language and phonological sensitivity, aspects of children's print knowledge seem to be important in emergent literacy skills (Burgess & Lonigan, 1998; Chaney,

1992). For preschoolers, understanding the rules of print (e.g., left-to-right and top-to-bottom print orientation, the difference between pictures and print; Clay, 1979) and the functions of print (e.g., that the print tells a story or gives directions; Purcell-Gates, 1996; Purcell-Gates & Dahl, 1991) seems to aid in the process of learning to read. Given the strong link between language development and reading, researchers have suggested that parents and programs should encourage the fullness of children's verbal experiences and early language environment via conversation and book-sharing (Kuo, Franke, Regalado, & Halfon, 2004). Reading aloud with young children creates rich learning opportunities for children's language and emergent literacy development (Chomsky, 2001).

Educational Technologies and Literacy Development

Technological advancements have led to the innovative design and development of computer-based educational tools that support children's literacy development (Bransford et al., 1996; Pinkard, 1999). However, while some applaud these trends, welcoming technology into educational contexts around literacy (Hutinger et al., 1998; Labbo & Ash, 1998), others caution that reliance on technology-based learning tools, such as computers, places children's learning and development at risk (Armstrong & Casement, 2000). New technologies are quickly becoming an integral part of many everyday activities. Thus, contextual artifacts, such as books, are being adapted to integrate these new technologies. It seems likely that these interactive books create a new kind of book-reading experience. However, it has not been determined yet how interactive books change, diminish, or enhance the book-sharing experience.

Before we can address the questions concerning the potential impact of interactive books on parent-child book-sharing experiences, it is important to explore what an interactive book has to offer that is different from traditional books. Interactive books, often referred to as "talking story books," qualitatively change the nature of literacy practices, whether it is independent child engagement or parent-child dyadic engagement with the interactive book. The multimedia design of interactive book platforms creates a dynamic learning context vis-à-vis design features that have three important affordances for learning:

1. a user-driven learning environment, either teacher-controlled or learner-controlled, that allows for navigation through rich, dynamic, and interactive information resources (e.g., verbal, visual, auditory—text, images, sound) and learning activities;
2. multi-layered content material that allows the user to engage with cognitively complex material at age-suitable and developmentally-appropriate levels (e.g., labeling object images, decoding phonics, blending, reading text aloud, defining key vocabulary terms); and,
3. a flexible interface that allows users to explore text material, in detail, through interactive games that engage the learner with concepts (for ex-

ample, involving number, color, and letter recognition) embedded in images (Kamil, Intrator, & Kim, 2000; Leu, 2000).

There is evidence that use of interactive books enhances literacy skill development, including comprehension and decoding, for beginning readers and for older children experiencing reading difficulties (Kamil et al., 2000). For instance, the auditory function of interactive books can be helpful as responsive and supportive text by sounding out letters and words and providing vocabulary and comprehension aids (Kamil et al., 2000). Further, the heightened user control made available through the affordances of the technology result in a corresponding increase in the level of user engagement and motivation (Leu, 2000).

Research exploring the potential literacy learning benefits of interactive books has focused on children's engagement with computer-based systems such as the Living Books® CD series developed by the Learning Company. The interactive book system used in its study is not computer-based, but offers many of the same design features of computer-based counterparts. This interactive book system developed by LeapFrog Enterprises Incorporated is a commercial product in which the "learning experience is brought to life" through "the use of technology that is intuitive, invisible, and engaging" (Leapfrog Enterprises, Inc., n.d., p. 1). There were originally two lines of these literacy learning products that were developmentally appropriate for young children: the LeapPad Learning System© (for preschool children, 3–6 years of age) and the Little Touch Learning System© (for infants and toddlers, 12–36 months of age). The original LeapFrog learning systems included a portable, durable platform to which a variety of books and cartridges could be added. The most recent versions of the LeapFrog literacy learning systems are now the stylus based Tag™ (ages 4–9 years) and Tag Junior™ (ages 1–4 years) Reading Systems that work with a Leapfrog library of print books for preschool children and board books for toddlers. Both the original and the new Tag™ designs of Leapfrog literacy products allow children to read the book as they might any other kind of book, but the technology creates opportunities to hear the book read aloud and to play interactive games that focus on phonics, vocabulary, and basic concepts such as numbers, colors, and shapes.

Leapfrog Enterprises Incorporated has also developed a successful school-based market. LeapFrog SchoolHouse offers a variety of programs, including the Literacy Center®, which addresses literacy skills such as print awareness, phonemic awareness, and understanding of the alphabet principle (LeapFrog SchoolHouse, n.d.). The Literacy Center® targets a range of grade levels from Pre-K through elementary school. LeapFrog SchoolHouse programs have been adopted by school boards in states across the country, including Utah and Texas. Effectiveness studies by independent researchers provide evidence that the students using LeapFrog SchoolHouse Literacy Center® over the course of one school year outperform control groups on key reading predictor tests that focus on skills such as phonemic awareness and decoding skills (LeapFrog SchoolHouse, n.d.).

The LeapPad Learning System® was designed as a tool for literacy development to be used by preschoolers typically during independent, solitary book-reading activities rather than socially collaborative parent-child book-sharing activities. However, the Little Touch Learning System© was designed to be developmentally appropriate for infants and toddlers. Thus, it integrates many of the design features of the LeapPad Learning System®, but it emphasizes adult-child book-sharing rather than independent book reading. The design features of the Little Touch Learning® are intended to support children's early literacy experiences from the "first [parent-child] reading experience together to the independent toddler years," emphasizing the socially collaborative book-sharing activity between parents and children that will enhance opportunities for early literacy skill development.

There is evidence that computer-based interactive books are useful and effective literacy tools for early readers and for children experiencing reading difficulties. The success of the computer-based LeapFrog SchoolHouse programs, used in classroom settings as material that complements traditional reading curricula (LeapFrog SchoolHouse, n.d.), raises the possibility that literacy skill development also may be enhanced by using non-computer-based interactive book platforms. However, much less is known about the potential benefits of home use of these types of products for school age children, and even less is known about the potential benefits for very young children (under age 5) who are not yet in school.

Literature on emergent literacy development points to a clear connection between early literacy experiences at home, like book reading or book-sharing, and children's language development and later school achievement (Hutinger et al., 1998). An essential aspect of these early, at-home literacy experiences in which young children are involved is that parents, or older social partners, are necessary participants in fostering learning opportunities. However, many of the interactive book products available for children are specifically designed for independent use rather than as part of a shared activity with a parent or older social partner who can facilitate the potential learning opportunities. Thus, the critical question that needs to be addressed is how do interactive books change, diminish, or enhance the book-sharing experience for very young children? The short-term longitudinal design of this research study aims to address this question. Participant families experienced an intervention that integrated the use of the Little Touch product into their family literacy practices. Post-intervention assessment compared parent-toddler language and participation patterns when book-sharing the Little Touch interactive book to book-sharing with traditional books.

Family Factors that Impact Emergent Literacy

Entry into formal schooling is a key transitional period for most children. There is substantial and compelling evidence that learning to read in school is easier for children with higher levels of emergent literacy skills (Chomsky, 2001; Hutinger et al., 1998; Whitehurst & Lonigan, 1998). Entering formal literacy education contexts, typically in kindergarten, is a transitional period that can make some children vulnerable to what has been referred to as "discontinuities," but it also can be a period in which children's future educational experiences are enhanced, particularly with regard to literacy development (Clay, 1979). The literacy achievement gaps revealed by the 2009 Report Card on Reading (NCES, 2010) described above might suggest that the literacy development of children in families of low socio-economic status (SES) and minority status (i.e., African-Americans, Latinos) does not adequately prepare them for literacy practices in schooling contexts. However, González (2002) points out that achievement differences that are often attributed to SES, especially for Latino children, may also reflect other important parent and family factors. Such factors include "levels of education, social status of occupation, degree of acculturation, English language proficiency....levels of stress and distress, number of children, and the presence of mental and health problems" (González, 2002, p. 57). These factors affect families by placing them at risk for or vulnerable to difficulties that impact children's development. The discontinuities or mismatch perspective needs to be explored in greater depth in order to understand how literacy practices in homes and schools might or might not correspond with one another.

McDonnell, Rollins, and Friel-Patti (2003) explored patterns of discourse during mother-child storybook readings and found that highly engaged mothers who were perceptive and responsive, via labeling and discourse, to their children's participation and changing nature of the task provided a model for "intervention with at-risk populations." These research projects included only European-American middle-class mothers. It often is assumed that these labeling and discourse strategies are the optimal ways by which children from minority group cultures, low socioeconomic strata, and other at-risk groups will learn word meanings from book-sharing; however, this assumption remains to be tested. In California, Texas, and a growing number of other states, children from immigrant families, including Spanish-speaking Latino families, often encounter cultural and language barriers when entering school. These children's unique cultural and linguistic everyday experiences may not fit the design and goals of traditional school readiness programs that promote emergent literacy development. Movements for educational access and equity have begun to target preschool and young children from poor immigrant communities, seeking to provide early access to the services, experiences, and supplies needed for school readiness. Some teacher-focused intervention efforts involving book-sharing activities with Latino toddlers in childcare settings have met with some success (Valdez-Menacha & Whitehurst, 1992). However, the field is missing answers to major questions concerning what minority immigrant children need to develop, thrive, and, specifically, develop literacy skills for school success. Furthermore, the availability of culturally and linguistically appropriate family-focused outreach and intervention strategies is limited, especially for parents of infants and toddlers.

Intervention Research: The Technology, Literacy, and Caring (TLC) Project

This research project explores the complex processes of literacy development in the context of book-sharing activities in the homes of low-income Latino children and their parents. This study departs from traditional literature exploring young children's emergent literacy development in family contexts in two important ways. First, rather than focus on preschool age children close to entering formal schooling experiences in elementary school, we targeted infants and toddlers, noting an increasingly articulated community emphasis on intervention and outreach programs to reach families when children are very young, preferably at birth. Second, rather than focus only on book-sharing with traditional story books, we examined the potential impact that a technological literacy tool, like the Leapfrog Little Touch Learning System®, would have on parent-child book-sharing activities and sought to understand how such a literacy tool might provide parents with an additional resource they could use to engage their young children in literacy practices. In this study, the following questions are explored:

1.   For the low-income Latino families in this study, what are parent-reported beliefs concerning child literacy development and technologically enhanced books? What are parent-reported practices concerning book-sharing? What is the relation between parent beliefs and parent practices around literacy?

2.   How do parent-reported literacy beliefs and parent-reported book-sharing practices vary for low-income Latino families who are recent immigrants compared to those who have lived in the U.S. for a sustained period?

3.   How do parent-child book-sharing activities with traditional books compare to book-sharing activities with a technological, interactive storybook, such as Leapfrog's Little Touch Learning System®?

4.   How do parent-child book-sharing activities vary for low-income Latino families who are recent immigrants compared to those who have lived in the U.S. for a sustained period?

METHODS

Study Design

This study employed a short-term longitudinal design, utilizing multiple methods including: (a) parent interviews and questionnaires focusing on family background, activities, and literacy practices; (b) child language and early literacy skill assessments; and (c) videotaped observations of parent-young child interactions during book-sharing activities. The goal of these combined methodological approaches was to unravel the complex processes of literacy development in the context of low-income families as they utilized both low-technological (traditional) and high-technological (interactive) books as educational tools. Because low-income Latino families may not be as familiar with technologically enhanced interactive books as they may be with traditional books, this longitudinal design allowed a consideration of how that familiarity develops over time.

Parents and children were visited in their homes on two separate occasions over the course of a year, the visits occurring six to seven months apart: once before the intervention was introduced, and again after the intervention period ended. All families were allowed to keep the Little Touch platform and books and also were given some traditional board books at the post-intervention visit.

Study Sample

Participants included 16 families recruited from different community outreach programs. These programs were targeted because they serve low-income children and families. All families were Latino (mostly Mexican descent). In most families, Spanish was the dominant language used by parents and children (13, or 81%), while in some families, parents were Spanish-English bilingual, but with a preference for or dominant use of English (3, or 19%).

Intervention

Families were provided with a combination of two literacy programs for the duration of the intervention period. The first program, Raising a Reader (RAR) program (http://www.pcf.org/raising_reader/), provides parents with board books that offer engaging artwork, age-appropriate language, and multicultural themes. The RAR program is designed to engage parents in a routine of daily book-sharing with their children by providing them with a regularly rotating supply of high-quality picture books in bright red bags that are brought to children's homes. The program also provides parents with an informational video about the developmental benefits of regular home literacy activities for children and the ways parents and children might share books together (e.g., dialogic book-sharing, child-centered book-sharing). Finally, the RAR program provides information about the use of local public libraries as a cost-free and readily available resource of children's books, supporting parents as they sustain the book-sharing practices beyond the duration of the program. The RAR program was made available to families through a variety of community outreach programs targeting low-income families that included: subsidized childcare programs, home visitation child health education programs, and subsidized housing programs. The principal investigators of this study collaborated with the RAR program developers. The investigators invited RAR-eligible families to participate in this research study, and after completing the pre-intervention data collection, the investigators offered and started the RAR program for participant families.

The second intervention program, the Little Touch (LT) program, provided families with the Little Touch Learning System® and a library of six Little Touch books; three Little Touch books were given at the onset of the intervention period, and three were given at the halfway point of the intervention period. This product is designed for children between nine and 36 months of age, and features one critical design feature that is an important departure from most of the other LeapFrog products: the potential to create opportunities for, and encourage, socially collaborative book-sharing between parents and young children rather than independent child book use. Manufacturers of the Little Touch product invite parents to engage in literacy activities with their infants and toddlers with statements like: "Welcome to a reading experience that's designed to let you and your child embark on a magical story-time journey of exploration, discovery and fun!" Other important design features of the Little Touch product that differ from the preschool products include: (a) instead of a stylus to activate functions, everything is finger touch-activated, such that very young children as well as adults can quickly and easily activate the many functions with a finger touch; (b) it is smaller and lighter than the LeapPad platform, and includes a soft pillow on the bottom of the platform so that it can easily sit on an adult's or child's lap with the goal that parent and child engage in book-sharing together rather than the child engaging with the book independently; and (c) in addition to the narration mode included in LeapPad products, it also includes different interactive functions designed to encourage parent-child engagement at three different developmentally appropriate settings, starting with "Music and Soundscapes," in which touching images on the page activates rhythmic music, songs, and sounds for the youngest users, followed by "Word Play," in which touching images provides corresponding object labels and short phrases for slightly older users, and the "Laugh and Learn" setting for the oldest users that includes interactive games encouraging parents and children to identify colors and shapes, and other important concepts (e.g., emotions, sequences, and patterns).

Parents were given an extensive demonstration regarding how to activate the different functions of the learning system (e.g., turn the machine on/off, adjust volume, activate different settings, use narration mode) and basic maintenance of the platform (e.g., where and how to install batteries, how to remove and clean the pillow, how to clean books). After the demonstration, they were given the opportunity to use the Little Touch Learning System with their child while the researchers were present to field any questions regarding use of the product. When the second set of books was delivered midway in the intervention period, they were asked if they been able to use the product regularly and if they had any questions or problems using the product.

Measures

The selected measures focus on three groups of data: (1) parent interview and survey data of family background, family characteristics, daily activities, and literacy beliefs and practices; (2) video-taped observation data of parent-child participation in videotaped book-sharing activities with traditional and interactive books; and (3) parent survey data of family expectations concerning technology and interactive books. Parent interviews were conducted in either Spanish or English based on parent preference. Parent surveys were available in both Spanish and English. When a parent's literacy skills made it difficult to complete the surveys independently, a bilingual research assistant read the questions aloud to the parent and wrote down the parent's responses.

Family Background, Characteristics, Literacy Beliefs, and Practices

Before the start of the intervention, parents participated in an interview session and were asked to complete several questionnaires and surveys gathering information about their family's background (e.g., education, income, immigration experience); family characteristics (e.g., family environment, parental stress, child behavior difficulties); and parent orientation toward literacy and literacy-related practices at home.

Family Demographics Interview

This interview followed a pre-established protocol and included closed- and open-ended questions about family demographics and background information (e.g., family structure, number/sex/age of parents, number of siblings, number of other individuals in household, family income, level of parent education, parent age and occupation, race/ethnic group identity, post-immigration generational status, length of time in the United States, and primary language(s) spoken in home).

Family Background and Home Literacy Activities Interview

This interview followed an established protocol based on the Head Start Family and Child Experiences Survey (FACES) and included closed- and open-ended questions that addressed the following topics: (a) parent ideologies about child roles in the family and how children learn in the context of the family; (b) parent and child daily routines and activity schedules; (c) parents' educational, occupational, familial, and cultural goals for their children; and (d) family literacy activities such as visits to libraries, museums, zoos, aquariums, religious events, and engagement with books and other reading materials in the home (Office of Planning, Research, and Evaluation, 2000).

Family Environment Scale (FES)

The FES is a 90-item true-false self-report questionnaire that assesses three dimensions of family environment: (1) interpersonal relationships within the family (relationship), (2) activities and interests within the family (personal growth), and (3) structure and organization of the family (system maintenance) (Moos & Moos, 1981). Ten subscales are generated; six of those 10 were selected for this study: cohesion, conflict, and expressiveness (reflecting relationship); achievement orientation and intellectual-cultural orientation (reflecting personal growth); and organization (reflecting system maintenance) (Moos & Moos, 1981, 2009). Raw scores were converted to T-scores, which are based on a heterogeneous sample of 1,432 families. T-scores above 60 (i.e., conflict) or below 40 (i.e., cohesion, expressiveness, achievement orientation, intellectual-cultural orientation, and organization) are considered clinically significant.

Parenting Stress Index—Short Form (PSI/SF)

The PSI/SF, a 36-item abbreviated form of the well-validated long form of the PSI, provides a short but accurate assessment of self-reported parenting stress. The PSI/SF has 36 items with three main subscales: parental distress (PD), parent-child dysfunctional interaction (P-CDI), and difficult child (DC). A total stress score indicates an overall level of parenting stress (Abidin, 1990). Raw scores above 33 on the PD and DC sub-scales and above 27 on the PCDI subscale are considered clinically elevated. Raw total scores above 90 indicate a clinically significant high level of stress.

Brief Infant-Toddler Social and Emotional Assessment (BITSEA)

This measure is designed to detect social-emotional and behavior problems and delays in the acquisition of competencies in children 12–48 months old. This 31-item measure focuses on three problem domains: externalizing (i.e., activity/impulsivity, aggression/defiance, and peer aggression scales); internalizing (i.e., depression/withdrawal, general anxiety, separation distress, and inhibition to novelty scales); and dysregulation (i.e., sleep, negative emotionality, eating, and sensory sensitivity scales). The indices yield clinical (extreme 15% of a normative sample) and of concern (extreme 25% of a normative sample) cut scores. These scores were defined in a national standardization sample of 12- to 36-month-olds and an epidemiologic sample of 37- to 48-month-olds (Briggs-Gowan, Carter, Irwin, Wachtel, & Cicchetti, 2004).

Parental Literacy Orientation and Family Literacy Practices

The following two questionnaires were used to ask parents about their every day child-centered literacy beliefs and practices:

1. Before and After Books and Reading questionnaire (BABAR). This is a 10-item parent-report measure of child-centered literacy orientation (e.g., Is reading aloud a favorite child activity and a part of child's daily routines?) (Needlman, 2001).
2. Raising a Reader questionnaire (RAR). This is a 23-item parent report measure of child-centered literacy orientations, like the BABAR, but also includes other learning activities (trips to library, songs, and games) and parent's feelings when reading to his/her child (e.g., When I read to my child, I feel happy, bored, worried) (SRI International, 2003).

Parent-Child Book-sharing Activities

Videotaped observations of book-sharing sessions with a traditional storybook and a LittleTouch storybook were conducted with each family after the completion of the intervention period. Families were presented with a traditional pre-selected storybook (*The Run Away Bunny*), and then were given the LittleTouch platform with one pre-selected storybook (*Guess How Much I Love You*). Order of book presentation was the same for all families. Books were selected to be as close in length and complexity as possible, but the content varied to keep children engaged over successive books. All activities sessions involved the target child, parent(s), and any other family members included by the parent. Researchers set up the camera and microphone, but left the room once the activity had begun. Parents were instructed to share the books with their child. They were welcome to look at the pictures, talk about the pictures or story, read the book, or share the book in whatever way they preferred. Parents were also asked to inform the researcher when they were done with the book.

Videotaped observations were coded along two dimensions: (1) complexity and quantity of parent and (when present) child language, and (2) interactive nature of parent-child participation.

Language Coding

The focus of the language coding was on *extra-textual talk*, including verbal statements by either the parent or child that went beyond direct reading of written text. This particular kind of language has been identified as an important part of the book-sharing experience, as it offers young children opportunities to participate in discourse with frequent and diverse language exchanges (Haden et al., 1996). Extra-textual talk has also been related to parent and child engagement during book-sharing activities, and high levels of engagement over repeated book-sharing sessions were related to increased rates of discourse behaviors such as initiations, responses, and book related comments (McDonnell et al., 2003). The language coding scheme developed for this study was informed by dialogic reading research (Huebner, 2000; Whitehurst, 1994) and was designed to capture the quantity, diversity, and complexity of both mother and child extra-textual language use during book-sharing interactions (Hammett, VanKleeck, & Huberty, 2003). In addition, a second set of codes was developed exclusively for the Little Touch book-sharing to capture the language generated by the Little Touch software. See Table 2.1 for a description and example of each coding category.

Four researchers (three of whom worked on establishing the original coding scheme) coded the book-sharing sessions using the coding categories described, tallying the frequency of each of the possible codes listed above for consecutive 10-second intervals covering the entire book-sharing activity. Researchers regularly consulted with each other when questions arose during coding sessions.

Participation Coding

This coding scheme focused on *organized patterns of participation* and viewed the book-sharing activity as embedded in the broader parent-child relationship. It was designed to capture the differences in the engagement and emotional levels (e.g., enjoyment/happiness or frustration/anger) of children and parents, how the variation in parent-child interactive experiences affect the quality of the book-

TABLE 2.1. Language Coding Category Descriptions

Coding category	Description
Label	Speaker provides label, identifying and/or naming a specified object/image on the page (e.g., "That is a bunny.")
Question	Speaker asks the other person a question relevant to the book-sharing activity (e.g., "Where's the caterpillar?")
Definition	Speaker provides definition phrase; providing the meaning or significance of a person, place, or thing (e.g., "A cocoon is where the caterpillar lives before he becomes a butterfly.")
Explanation	Speaker provides explanation, perhaps clarifying a situation in the book (e.g., "The mother bunny wants to change herself into a tree to be close to the baby bunny.")
Elaboration	Speaker provides an elaborative phrase, extending the topic of discussion (e.g., "There are three strawberries. Let's count them: One, two, three.")
Description	Speaker provides a descriptive phrase that extends beyond a label, typically using adjectives and adverbs (e.g., "That bunny is so cute.").
Correction	Speaker uses a corrective word/phrase; reprimanding or correcting the other participant for giving or using the wrong word or providing the wrong information. (e.g., Child labels the bunny as a puppy, and mother responds "No, that is a bunny.")
Reading	Parent reads the text, verbatim, off page.
Setting	Parent or child activates or changes setting (Settings 1, 2, 3); book announces setting.
Activities	Parent or child activates/uses activity setting; book introduces activity.
Object	Parent or child touches object on the page to activate sound/label/activity relevant to that object; book makes sound, labels the object, or suggests an activity related to the object.
Narration	Parent or child activates/uses narration mode; book narrates text.

sharing session, and the dyad's success in creating an interaction context that fosters the child's engagement and enjoyment. Research has shown that children's participation in home literacy activities that are rich with cooperative engagement and positive socio-emotional quality is predictive of their success in early reading (Leseman & de Jong, 1998). This coding scheme emphasized the contribution of both partners in the social processes of interaction, negotiation, and communication; it focused on organized patterns of participation in order to capture the dyadic dynamics of the interaction rather than the individual behavioral contributions of parent or child alone (Latzke, 2002; Mejia-Arauz, Rogoff, Dexter, & Najafi, 2007).

The coding scheme included a particular focus on parent-child interactions, contrasting collaborative, synchronous, and joint endeavors from asynchronous ones. The primary goal was to differentiate instances when both participants were actively engaged with the other person around and within the book-sharing activity from instances in which each participant had a separate, independent agenda that did not correspond with the goals of the other person. There are two superordinate patterns of participation that reflect this contrast; each pattern represents a very different focus on "who is leading" or "controlling" during dyadic engagement (Latzke, 2002; Mejia-Arauz et al., 2007). The first is a collaborative/negotiated pattern of participation in which the interactions between parent and child involve shared coordination and mutuality in collaborative, horizontal interactions that develop into a pattern of mutual responsiveness. These patterns of participation are characterized by a fluidity and flexibility in parent-child roles and leadership and in parent-child input or responsibility, and tend to be enjoyable and engaging for both participants. They are also characterized by active, flexible, and non-coercive negotiation efforts to encourage the other participant's engagement or re-engagement in activity. The second is an asynchronous, vertical, or hierarchical pattern of participation involving either overt tutorial or didactic interactions between parent and child or interactions in which the parent or the child is taking the lead and controlling the activity. Asynchronous parent-child interactions are characterized by parental interventions to control the child's behavior to increase the child's attentiveness and responsiveness, with characteristic child behaviors reflecting lack of interest in and lack of attentiveness to the book-sharing activity, and even child distress responses (e.g., crying, whining) or child aggressive responses toward the parent (e.g., hitting, pushing away) or the book (e.g., throwing book away). The specific coding categories are described in Table 2.2.

The participation coding scheme was built on a foundation of research (Latzke, 2002; Mejia-Arauz et al., 2007) and adapted to reflect not only the nature of the

TABLE 2.2. Participation Coding Category Descriptions Coding

Category	Description
Collaborative	Participation is characterized by high proportion of smooth, mutual exchanges with joint attention, mutuality, and synchronous interactions. Parent equalizes asymmetry in adult-child competence, offers support that facilitates child's involvement, invites and sustains child's attention and participation, responds to what child says and does, and adapts the book-sharing activity to child's interests, motives, and understandings. Child reciprocally takes initiative, contributes to shared endeavor, and sometimes offers leadership in the process. Talk is used for the purpose of engaging social partner in book-sharing activity, either by augmenting and/or guiding engagement (e.g., "Let's turn the page, and see what happens to the little bunny.").
Negotiation	One participant (usually child) shows slight disinterest or disengagement from shared activity; other participant (usually parent) makes active, flexible, and non-coercive efforts to encourage other's engagement or re-engagement in activity.
Asynchronous—Child Distressed	Parent engaged in book-sharing activity, but child is not, because she/he is whining, crying, or struggling to get away. Parent's book-sharing is not contingent or response to child's state of distress.
Asynchronous—Child Off-task	Child is not participating in book-sharing activity, while parent continues to engage in one-sided, didactic approach with no attempts to re-engage child.
Parent & Child Off-task	Both parent and child are not engaged in the book-sharing activity.

book-sharing interaction compared to activities in other research (e.g., structured imaginative play), but also to reflect parent and child participation goals and agendas as interpreted by their behaviors while engaged in the activity. Researchers coded each book-sharing session, deciding on which coding category captured the pervasive pattern of participation that took place within consecutive 15-second intervals over the entire duration of the activity. Two researchers viewed several videotaped book-sharing sessions, both independently and jointly, and through iterative discussions, reflections, and versions of the coding descriptions, collaboratively developed the coding scheme. These two researchers independently coded a small subset of sessions and discussed their coding agreements and disagreements, resulting in further refinement of the coding scheme.

Family Beliefs Concerning Technology and Interactive Books

Parents were asked to complete two questionnaires that were developed by researchers in collaboration with a LeapFrog representative. The first, the Little Touch pre-intervention survey, was given to parents after their initial introductory overview of the product and first opportunity to use the product with their child. Questions in the Little Touch pre-intervention survey focused on the child's interest in books and book-sharing, and their initial impressions of the product's educational and entertainment potential (e.g., What is good or difficult about using Little Touch? Do you think using Little Touch will be fun, enjoyable, educational for your child?). The second, the Little Touch post-intervention survey, was given to parents at the second home visit, once the intervention period was complete. About half of the questions in the post-intervention survey focused on who used the Little Touch with the child (e.g., Besides yourself, who else uses Little Touch with your child?), how often it was used, and which books were favored. The remainder of the survey focused on the Little Touch functions (e.g., Which setting have you used most? How often have you used the narration?) and parents' perspectives on the ways Little Touch enhanced the parent-child book-sharing activity (e.g., Using Little Touch helped keep my child interested, helped my child pay attention, gave me new ideas of things to do during book-sharing; agree or disagree).

Statistical Analysis

Descriptive analyses were conducted for the basic demographic variables (e.g., child age, maternal education level, etc.) and family characteristics (e.g., parenting stress, child behavior problems, child competence, and family characteristics). Means are reported for the entire sample (16 families), as well as for each family subgroup based on immigration experience (eight recent immigrant families and eight long-term resident families). Mean values for independent variables are reported for the total sample and for each immigrant group. Comparative analyses conducted for this study include one-tailed, dependent t-tests for comparisons across book type (traditional book and interactive book), independent samples *t*-tests for comparisons across family immigrant groups (recent immigrant and resident), and Pearson product correlations to test for relations between the number of years the mother has lived in the U.S. and independent variables.

RESULTS

Sample Description

All 16 families in this study were classified as low socioeconomic status, as indicated by family income and parent education levels. Toddlers were two-thirds male and approximately 14 months old at the start of the intervention (see Table 2.3). In order to consider acculturation effects, the sample was divided into two groups, using a median split based on the number of years the mother had spent in U.S.. Half the sample was placed in the recent immigrant group, who had come to the U.S. within five years or less ($M = 2.8$ years, $SD = 0.9$). The second half of the sample was placed in the resident group, having lived in the U.S. for longer than five years ($M = 15.7$ years, $SD = 6.2$). These two groups also had statistically significant differences with regard to child gender (37.5% male vs. 87.5% male) and to maternal education level in years ($M = 6.6$, $SD = 4.5$ vs. $M = 13.4$, $SD = 2.1$).

Family characteristics included measures of family environment, parental stress, and child behavior competencies and problems. Table 2.4 provides a summary of these data for the entire sample and each group. A significant proportion of families showed indicators of particular risk with clinical levels of total parenting stress (43.8%) based on the Parental Stress Index (PSI) measure, and child behavior problems (50.0%) and child lack of competence (31.3%) based on the Brief Infant Toddler Social Emotional Assessment (BITSEA) measure. However,

TABLE 2.3.   Socio-demographics for Total Sample and Immigration Groups

Socio-demographics Variables	Immigrant ≤ 5 years in U.S., n = 8 M (SD)	Resident > 5 years in U.S., n = 8 M (SD)	t-test (p-value)	Total Sample n = 16 M (SD)
Maternal time in U.S. (years)	2.8 (0.9)	17.0 (7.2)	− 5.6 (p=.000)	9.9 (8.8)
Family income, monthly ($)	1333.33 (422.69)	1841.67 (687.32)	− 1.54 (p=.15)	1587.5 (605.3)
Maternal education level (years)	6.6 (4.6)	13.4 (2.1)	− 3.81 (p=.002)	10.0 (4.9)
Child gender (n; % male)	n=3 37.5%	n=7 87.5%	1.9 (p=.04)	n=10 62.5%
Child age at Time 1 (months)	14.4 (5.3)	15.9 (4.4)	− 0.62 (p=.55)	15.5 (4.7)
Child age at Time 2 (months)	22.5 (4.7)	23.5 (4.0)	− .46 (p=.65)	22.8 (4.1)

TABLE 2.4.   Indicators of Family Psychosocial Risk

Study Participants	Immigrant ≤ 5 years in U.S. (n = 8)	Resident > 5 years in U.S. (n = 8)	p-value	Total Sample (n = 16)
Family Environment Scale (FES)	M (SD)	M (SD)	t-test (p-value)	M (SD)
Cohesion	53.9 (9.4)	52.6 (18.0)	– 0.09 (p=.93)	53.2 (13.2)
Expressiveness	46.7 (7.4)	51.3 (8.3)	– 1.25 (p=.23)	47.2 (9.2)
Conflict	40.1 (6.0)	41.7 (9.3)	– 0.54 (p=.60)	41.5 (7.7)
Achievement Orientation	48.9 (11.0)	46.1 (6.4)	0.16 (p=.88)	49.8 (10.6)
Intellectual-Cultural Orientation	45.9 (10.3)	49.0 (9.6)	– 0.88 (p=.39)	47.3 (9.3)
Organization	59.6 (7.1)	52.3 (10.3)	0.97 (p=.35)	54.3 (10.0)
Parenting Stress Index (PSI)—% Standard Scores in Clinical Range				
Total Parenting Stress	50.0%	37.5%	p=.61	43.8%
Parental Distress	37.5%	25.0%	p=.59	31.3%
Parent-Child Dysfunctional Interaction	25.0%	0.0%	p=.13	12.5 %
Difficult Child	25.0%	37.5%	p=.59	31.3%
Brief Infant-Toddler Social Emotional Assessment (BITSEA)—% Sum Scores in Clinical Range				
Bahavior Problems	62.5%	37.5%	p=.31	50.0%
Lack of Competence	12.5%	50.0%	p=.11	31.3%

results from the Family Environment Scale showed that many families had positive family characteristics, particularly with higher degrees of cohesion and organization, and with lower degrees of conflict. No significant differences in family psychosocial risk were noted when comparing the recent immigrant subgroup to the resident subgroup.

Parent Literacy Beliefs and Practices

Parent interview and questionnaire data were explored to address the following questions:

1.   What are parent beliefs about child-centered literacy practices and technologically enhanced interactive books? What are the parents' child-centered literacy practices and feelings about book-sharing?

2.   For the families in this study, how are parent beliefs about child-centered literacy practices and technologically enhanced interactive books related to the parents' child-centered literacy practices and feelings about book-sharing?

3.   How do parent literacy values, beliefs, and practices vary for low-income Latino families who are recent immigrants compared to those who have had lived in the U.S. for a longer time?

Parent interviews and questionnaires were analyzed to explore these research questions.

Parent Literacy Practices and Beliefs about Traditional Book and Interactive Book-sharing

Interview and questionnaire data revealed that families in this study reported very positive literacy beliefs concerning both traditional and interactive books (see Table 2.5). With regard to literacy practices, families reported high levels of happiness and low levels of boredom and frustration during book-sharing. However, the number of children's books in the home was low (approximately six books), and the frequency of book-sharing was limited (3.8 days out of seven, on average).

Correlation analyses showed some relations between parent-reported literacy beliefs and practices. As Table 2.6 shows, there were significant positive correlations between parent beliefs about the child's interest in reading/book-sharing

TABLE 2.5.   Parent Reported Literacy Beliefs and Practices

	M (SD)	Possible score range
Parent Literacy Beliefs		
Child interest in reading/book-sharing	3.60 (1.45)	1–5
Book-sharing important for child's future development/learning	8.94 (1.98)	1–10
Interactive books fun for child	4.69 (0.48)	1–5
Interactive books educational for child	4.69 (0.60)	1–5
Parent Literacy Practices		
Number of children's books in home	6.00 (5.18)	0–20
Number of things child does with books	1.75 (0.58)	0–2
Weekly book-sharing frequency (# days)	3.77 (1.83)	1–7
Parent feels happy and close to child during book-sharing	4.70 (0.60)	1–5
Parent feels bored during book-sharing	1.50 (0.76)	1–5
Parent feels frustrated during book-sharing	1.27 (0.70)	1–5

TABLE 2.6.   Correlations Between Child Behavior and Parent-Child Interactions

	Parent Literacy Beliefs			
	Child's interest in reading/ book-sharing Pearson's r (p-value)	Book-sharing important for future Pearson's r (p-value)	Interactive books fun for child Pearson's r (p-value)	Interactive books educational Pearson's r (p-value)
Parent Literacy Practices				
Number of children's books in home	.19 (p=.56)	.20 (p=.52)	−.06 (p=.84)	.12 (p=.69)
Number of things child does with books	.70 (p=.004)	.39 (p=.13)	−.06 (p=.82)	.34 (p=.20)
Weekly book-sharing frequency	.34 (p=.29)	−.12 (p=.70)	−.46 (p=.11)	−.22 (p=.47)
Parent feels happy during book-sharing	.62 (p=.02)	.35 (p=.20)	−.25 (p=.36)	.28 (p=.31)
Parent feels bored during book-sharing	−.73 |(p=.005)	.06 (p=.85)	.51 (p=.06)	−.24 (p=.41)
Parent feels frustrated during book-sharing	−.44 (p=.12)	.13 (p=.65)	.28 (p=.32)	−.44 (p=.10)

and parent literacy practices such as the number of things a child does with books and parents feeling happy and close to their child during book-sharing. Furthermore, there were significant negative correlations between parent beliefs about child reading/book-sharing interest and parents feeling bored or frustrated during book-sharing with their child. There were no other significant correlations between reported beliefs about interactive books and literacy practices. However, there was a non-significant trend towards a positive correlation between parent-reported beliefs that interactive books were a source of fun for their child and parents reporting feeling bored with book-sharing with their child.

Impact of Immigration Experience on Parent Literacy Beliefs and Practices

There were no significant correlations between socio-demographic measures and parent literacy beliefs and practices (see Table 2.7). Thus, level of maternal education, monthly family income, and length of time since the mother immigrated to the U.S. were unrelated to the mother's beliefs about her child's interest in book-sharing and the importance of book-sharing for her child's development and future reading success. Similarly, socio-demographics were unrelated to mothers' beliefs that interactive books would be a source of fun or a source of education for their toddlers. There were also no significant differences between parent im-

TABLE 2.7. Impact of Socio-demographics on Beliefs about Traditional and Interactive Book-sharing

	Parent Literacy Beliefs			
	Child's interest in reading/ book-sharing Pearson's r (p-value)	Book-sharing important for future Pearson's r (p-value)	Interactive books fun for child Pearson's r (p-value)	Interactive books educational Pearson's r (p-value)
Socio-demographics				
Highest grade completed	.05 (p=.86)	.15 (p=.58)	−.28 (p=.28)	−.25 (p=.35)
Monthly Family Income	18 (p=.60)	.37 (p=.23)	.15 (p=.64)	.37 (p=.24)
Mother years in U.S.	−.13 (p=.64)	.10 (p=.71)	−.09 (p=.75)	−.04 (p=.87)

migrant groups in terms of their literacy practices, such as number of things their child did with books and parents feeling bored when book-sharing with their child (see Table 2.8).

Video-Analysis of Parent-Child Book-sharing

Videotaped parent-child book-sharing sessions were coded to capture the quantity and diversity of extra-textual language used and the participatory pat-

TABLE 2.8. Impact of Years in U.S. on Parent Literacy Practices

Immigrant Groups	Immigrant		Resident
	M (SD)	M (SD)	t-test (p-value)
Amount of Book-sharing			
Number of children's books in home	4.0 (2.4)	7.2 (6.2)	−1.11 (p=.29)
Number of things child does with books	1.6 (0.7)	1.9 (0.4)	−0.86 (p=.40)
Number of days per week spent book-sharing	1.5 (1.1)	1.4 (1.1)	0.23 (p=.82)
Parent Feelings during Book-sharing			
Parent feels happy and close	3.9 (1.1)	4.6 (0.7)	1.63 (p=.13)
Parent feels bored	1.3 (0.5)	1.6 (0.9)	0.70 (p=.50)
Parent feels frustrated	1.3 (0.8)	1.2 (0.7)	−0.10 (p=.93)

terns of parent-child interactions when sharing traditional story books and sharing the Little Touch interactive book platform after the completion of the intervention period. Video-coding and analysis explored the following questions:

1. How do parent-child book-sharing activities with traditional books compare to book-sharing activities with the interactive Little Touch book platform?

2. How do parent-child book-sharing activities with traditional and interactive story books vary for low-income Latino families who are recent immigrants compared to those who have resided in the U.S. for a longer time?

Coding of videotaped observation data was analyzed to explore these research questions.

Comparisons of Parent-Child Book-sharing with Traditional Versus Interactive Books

The first set of analyses examined the language and participation patterns of parent-child book-sharing using traditional books compared to interactive books. The first coding scheme captured the quantity and diversity of extra-textual talk as well as the time spent reading text, parent-child joint attention, and parent-child off-task. Dependent *t*-test comparisons of parent language use across book-sharing sessions with traditional versus interactive story books showed that, overall, parents and children used more language when engaged with traditional story books than with interactive story books (see Table 2.9). This finding was also consistent in terms of diversity of language, with parents not only reading text more often, but also providing more types of extra-textual talk such as labels, questions, and elaborations/descriptions when sharing the traditional book than when sharing the interactive book. There was a non-significant tendency for slightly more child talk during the traditional book-sharing than the interactive book-sharing sessions. There were not, however, any significant differences across the two book types in terms of total session duration, time spent in joint attention, or time spent off-task with roughly equal durations across the two types of activities. Finally, participants used the "talking" functions of the interactive book, including narration and object functions (e.g., labeling and activities), for roughly 40% of the total time spent book-sharing.

An interesting pattern emerges when looking at the sequence of talk and behaviors across the duration of an individual traditional book-sharing session. As Figure 2.1 shows, when the parent engaged in extra-textual talk with her toddler, she was more successful at maintaining joint attention with her child than when she read the text, which often resulted in time off-task. Looking at the sequence of talk and behaviors across the interactive book-sharing also proved interesting. Figure 2.2 shows that one parent and toddler dyad experienced sustained intervals

TABLE 2.9. t-test Comparisons of Book Type with Language Use

	Traditional Book M	Interactive Book M	p-value
Types of Language Used (Number of occurrences per session)			
Labels	17.88	5.75	0.02
Questions	30.88	3.56	0.04
Description/Elaboration	12.25	5.06	0.00
Frequency Parent Text Reading	11.69	0.94	0.00
Frequency Child Talk	5.63	1.31	0.07
Parent-Child Activity Participation			
Total Activity Duration (min.)	6.82	5.34	0.17
Duration Joint Attention (min.)	4.36	3.70	0.21
Duration Off-task (min.)	2.46	1.64	0.14

of parent-child joint attention and parent extra-textual talk during intervals that coincided with interactive functions use.

The second coding scheme was developed to contrast collaborative, synchronous, and joint parent-child endeavors from asynchronous ones in which parent and child goals do not coincide, one participant is asserting control, or one or

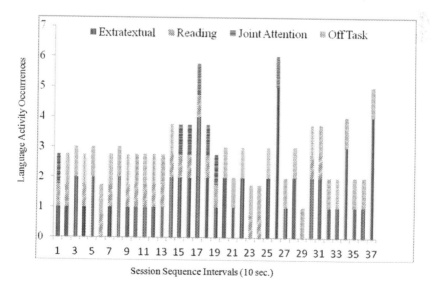

FIGURE 2.1. Occurrences of extra-textual talk, book reading, joint attention, and off-task behavior during traditional book-sharing for Family Six

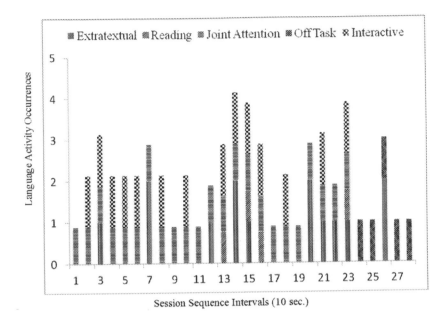

FIGURE 2.2. Occurrences of extra-textual talk, book reading, joint attention, and interactive function use during interactive book-sharing for Family 16

both participants are not engaged in the book-sharing activity. Dependent t-tests comparing participation patterns during the traditional book-sharing session with the interactive book-sharing session resulted in no significant differences in synchronous participation collaboration or negotiation participation patterns. During book-sharing with both types of books, these families spent the majority of their time (at least 60% of the total session duration) in collaborative and negotiation participation patterns. There were some non-significant tendencies toward more

TABLE 2.10   t-test Comparisons of Book Type for Interval Frequencies of Participation Patterns

Participation Patterns	Traditional Book		Interactive Book		t-test for Frequency
	Frequency	Proportion	Frequency	Proportion	p-value
Collaboration	11.87	48%	13.75	53%	0.22
Negotiation	2.87	12%	2.62	13%	0.34
Asynchronous	3.56	16%	2.187	9%	0.07
Child Distress	1.31	7%	0.87	7%	0.12
Child Off-task	0.56	2%	1.62	14%	0.06
Mother & Child Off-task	3.25	15%	1	4%	0.06

Session Intervals	Traditional Book				Interactive Book			
	Collab	Negot	Asyn	Off	Collab	Negot	Asyn	Off
1								
2								
3								
4								
5								
6								
7								
8								
9								
10								
11								
12								
13								
14								
15								
16								
17								
18								
19								
20								
21								
22								
23								
24								
25								
26								
27								
28								
29								
30								
31								
32								
33								
34								
35								
36								
37								
38								
39								
40								

FIGURE 2.3. Occurrences of participation categories (Collaborative, Negotiated, Asynchronous, Off-Task) during traditional and interaction book-sharing per 15-second interval for Family Nine

asynchronous and parent-child off-task participation patterns and fewer child off-task patterns during sessions with the traditional book compared to the interactive book. Proportion data from the two off-task participation patterns approached significance (see Table 2.10). Examinations of participation patterns over the course of individual sessions showed that during a traditional book-sharing session with her toddler, one parent spent more time in negotiation, asynchronous, and mother-child off-task participation patterns than when engaged with the interactive book in which there were more incidents of child off-task (see Figure 2.3).

Impact of Immigration Experience on Parent-Child Book-sharing Practices

Parent-child language use and participation patterns were compared across families based on their immigration experience, to determine if recently immi-

TABLE 2.11. t-test Comparisons of Language Use across Immigration Groups for Each Book Type

	Traditional Book-sharing Sessions			Interactive Book-sharing Sessions		
	Immigrant M	Resident M	p-value	Immigrant M	Resident M	p-value
Types of Language						
Labels	17.88	22.75	0.34	7.63	3.88	0.24
Questions	30.88	38.63	0.62	5.13	2.00	0.31
Description/Elaboration	12.25	15.63	0.27	7.00	3.13	0.25
Parent Text Reading	11.69	10.50	0.68	1.25	0.63	0.49
Child Talk	5.63	3.38	0.47	2.00	0.63	0.32
Activity Durations (min.)						
Total Session Duration	7.81	5.81	0.55	5.90	4.79	0.54
Duration Joint Attention	4.90	3.81	0.67	4.32	3.08	0.51
Duration Off-task	2.92	2.00	0.53	1.57	1.71	0.81
Interactive Activities Use						
Duration Narration				0.23	0.38	0.44
Duration Object				0.60	0.79	0.76
Duration Activities				1.63	0.96	0.34

TABLE 2.12. t-test Comparisons of Participation Patterns across Family Immigration Groups for Each Book Type

	Traditional Book-sharing Sessions			Interactive Book-sharing Sessions		
	Frequency (Proportion)		t-test for Frequency p-value	Frequency (Proportion)		t-test for Frequency p-value
Participation Patterns	Immigrant	Resident		Immigrant	Resident	
Collaboration	12.12 (49.54%)	11.62 (47.54%)	0.93	14.25 (55.11%)	13.25 (51.54%)	0.87
Negotiation	3.25 (14.71%)	2.5 (8.78%)	0.66	3.75 (20.78%)	1.5 (5.97%)	0.03
Asynchronous	2.75 (12.67%)	4.37 (19.44%)	0.49	1.75 (8.15%)	2.62 (10.64%)	0.61
Child Distress	0.12 (0.96%)	2.5 (12.93%)	0.10	0.00 (0%)	1.75 (13.80%)	0.14
Child Off task	0.87 (3.02%)	0.25 (1.56%)	0.50	1.50 (10.62%)	1.75 (16.42%)	0.78
M & C Off Task	3.75 (19.39%)	2.75 (9.74%)	0.71	0.75 (5.34%)	0.5 (2.03%)	0.30

grated parents approached the book-sharing activity differently than parents who were long-term residents in the U.S. Comparisons of language use across the two family groups during traditional book-sharing sessions revealed no significant differences for extra-textual talk, reading, total session duration, joint attention duration, and off-task duration (see Table 2.11). There were also no significant differences in use of different interactive functions of the Little Touch book across the two family groups (see Table 2.11).

Table 2.12 shows that, similar to the language use results, comparisons of participation patterns across immigration groups for the two types of book-sharing sessions revealed nearly no significant differences across recent and resident immigration groups for the different participation patterns. During traditional book-sharing sessions, there were no differences in participation patterns. During the interactive book-sharing session, there was one significant difference between the two family immigrant groups: parent-child dyads in recent immigrant families experienced significantly more negotiation participation patterns than did parent-child dyads in the resident families.

DISCUSSION

The Latino families that participated in this study were all low-income, consisting mostly of immigrant parents whose dominant language in the home was Spanish and many of whom did not finish high school. Given their family demographic characteristics alone, the children in these families would be characterized as "at-risk" for many different developmental and educational factors, particularly those that have to do with school achievement. Despite the strengths that these families share in terms of high degrees of family cohesion and organization and low degrees of family conflict, many of these families also experience challenges such as parental stress and child behavior problems. Add in the challenges that these families face living in a relatively affluent region of California (e.g., parents who work long hours on temporary jobs, families sharing small living quarters with one or more other families, and frequent moves to find affordable housing) and we could paint a gloomy picture of the potential futures for these children. The picture revealed by this study, however, is one of promise and potential. When provided with literacy tools like books, and a minimal amount of guidance, the parents in this study were quite capable of taking advantage of the opportunity to engage in positive, language-rich book-sharing activities with their very young children. This was true even for parents who had recently immigrated to the U.S., many of whom had not completed grade school.

The results from this study not only demonstrate the book-sharing practices afforded by technologically enhanced interactive books compared to traditional books, but also provide a window into parents' beliefs and practices regarding these two types of books as potential tools for child-centered literacy practices at home. Parent reports from interviews and questionnaires indicate that they value literacy practices such as book-sharing, they believe their children show interest in this type of activity, and they report that they enjoy sharing books with their children. Although they see both traditional and interactive books as sources of enjoyment and learning for their children, they do not report frequent book-sharing with their children and, perhaps because of limited financial resources, they have a limited library of children's books at home. Nevertheless, parents' belief that their children have interest in literacy activities corresponds to positive book-sharing experiences such as engaging in a variety of things with books and their own enjoyment levels. Overall, the parents in this study have positive orientations toward child-centered literacy activities, which may help explain why these parents seem to make the most of the opportunities afforded them by the intervention program. It is encouraging to see that this general orientation was not impacted by parents' immigration experiences, even though recent immigrant parents had significantly less formal education than parents who have been in the U.S. a longer period of time.

In this study, we asked these parents to engage in videotaped book-sharing activities with their infant or toddler with both traditional books and the interactive book. We provided the books, asked them to do what they would normally do during this type of activity, and to let us know when they were done. We then hit the record button and walked out of the room, leaving the parent and child to co-create their experience. At first glance, this might seem like a simple, straightforward type of task to ask of parents. However, even parents of three- and four-year-olds, whose children are much more verbal, have a greater attention span, and are more capable of asserting their own interests and goals into the activity, would not consider book-sharing an easy task to participate in with their child at the request of researchers, especially when placed in front a camera. This is mentioned to point out that as much as parents might want to "put on a show of social desirability," it is very challenging to maintain the show when your fellow actor, someone who might not be able to talk yet, does not have the same goal as you do and is not necessarily inclined to go along with the show. Furthermore, families experienced a sustained intervention period with opportunities to engage in book-sharing activities, so the videotaped data is close to what these parent-child dyads might typically do in our absence without a camera focused on them.

Use of extra-textual language during book-sharing is considered an effective way to introduce a quantity and complexity of language to children that extends beyond the language used when reading text. Parents engaged in more frequent and varied extra-textual talk during traditional book-sharing sessions compared to interactive book-sharing sessions. Extra-textual talk may serve an additional important function of keeping infants and toddlers engaged and on-task during traditional book-sharing sessions, especially given their capacity for focusing attention for only a limited amount of time. Despite the less frequent parent and child talk during the interactive book-sharing session, it is possible that the "talking" functions of the interactive book (including narration, object functions, and activities) not only complement parent and child talk, but also keep the child engaged in the activity. The interactive functions (language-based interactivity that provides object labels and invitations to engage in games and activities) might also serve to introduce topics for extra-textual talk. Given that the session duration and joint attention duration times for each type of book-sharing session were not significantly different, this suggests that parent-child engagement in the two types of book-sharing were varied in terms of the amount and types of language used, but both were positive and rich with potential learning opportunities.

Analyses of participation patterns provide further evidence of parents' skillful abilities to keep their very young children positively and collaboratively engaged in book-sharing activities with both types of books. The minimal occurrences of child-distress as well as dominating occurrences of collaborative and negotiation interactions demonstrate how well parents are able to understand, respond, and adjust to their child's developmental level and adopt an interactive approach to book-sharing. The one difference in participation patterns that approached significance is a tendency for toddlers to be off-task more often when engaged with the interactive book than with the traditional book. It is possible that children are more frequently off-task with the interactive book because this type of book allows the child to take on a more assertive leadership role in the book-sharing activity because they can activate different functions with the touch of a finger. Parents may need to take a greater leadership role in the traditional book-sharing, perhaps because their language (and literacy) skills are required to help keep the toddlers engaged.

The absence of significant differences in language use between recent immigrant parents and longer-term residency parents suggests that the language experiences of children from both family groups were similar when these two types of books were made available to families for an intervention period of six to seven months. This is a particularly impressive accomplishment for recent immigrant parents, as many of them had limited formal schooling. Both sets of parents have much to offer their children simply by talking with them in a sustained, one-on-one, positive engagement, and both sets of parents seem equally qualified for the job. The absence of significant differences for prevalent patterns of participation, collaboration (which, again, was the most frequent participation pattern), asynchronous, and off-task behaviors suggests that these two groups of families were not only able to successfully engage in book-sharing together in positive, mutually facilitative ways, minimizing instances of uncoordinated, discordant interactions, but also were able to do so equally well across both types of books. Both groups of parents seemed to take full advantage of the opportunities offered by the intervention, utilizing the tools provided to them to co-create with their children language-rich, socially-motivating, and engaging book-sharing sessions.

Although this study is exploratory in nature, and has a relatively small sample size, findings from this study suggest that parents of infants and toddlers are skilled facilitators of learning vis-à-vis pre-literacy activities in the home. These learning opportunities made available to them may enhance these young children's early language and literacy skills. The technological design of interactive reading books provides unique affordances for enhancing developing early literacy in the context of parent-child book-sharing, and parents and children seemed quite capable and eager to explore these affordances. These data help to identify strengths found in low-income Latino families such as family cohesion, parent education, literacy orientation, parent-child language, and participation during book-sharing. These strengths may protect children from potential negative outcomes including delayed readiness for school-based learning.

Findings from this research will inform literacy development literature and the design of technology for learning by providing insights into the processes through which low-income parents influence children's emergent literacy in the context of educationally valued artifacts such as books. This study is an important first step toward understanding how technologically enhanced interactive books might change, or even enhance, opportunities for emergent literacy skill development in the context of parent-child book-sharing, particularly for very young children. This research shifts the focus for potential redesign efforts of current educational technologies to capitalize on the social, collaborative nature of parent-child book-sharing. Overall, this research offers perspectives for addressing educational inequities by giving low-income families access to educational technologies in light of limited resources.

NOTE

This research was supported by grants from Bella Vista Family Foundation, Hellman Family Foundation, Peninsula Community Foundation, and the Stanford University Office of Technology Licensing to the first author, and from the Garcia Family Foundation and the Stanford University Vice Provost for Undergraduate Education to the second author.

Correspondence concerning this chapter should be addressed to Dr. Perez-Granados, Department of Liberal Studies, California State University Monterey Bay, 100 Campus Center, Seaside, CA 93955, Email: dperez-granados@csumb.edu, Phone: (831) 582-4322, Fax: (831) 582-3356.

REFERENCES

Abidin, R. R. (1990). *Parenting stress index—Manual* (3rd ed.). Charlottesville, VA: University of Virginia, Pediatric Psychology Press.

Armstrong, A. & Casement, C. (2000). *The child and the machine: How computers put our children's education at risk.* Beltsville, MD: Robins Lane Press.

Azmitia, M., Cooper C. R., García, E. E., & Dunbar, N. (1996). The ecology of family guidance in low-income Mexican-American and European-American families. *Social Development, 5,* 1–23.

Beals, D. E. (2001). Eating and reading: Links between family conversations with preschoolers and later language and literacy. In D. K. Dickinson & P. O. Tabors (Eds.),

Beginning literacy with language: Young children learning at home and school (pp. 75–92). Baltimore, MD: Paul H. Brookes.

Beals, D. E. & Snow, C. E. (1994). "Thunder is when the angels are upstairs bowling": Narratives and explanations at the dinner table. *Journal of Narrative & Life History, 4,* 331–352.

Bradley, R. H. & Caldwell, B. M. (1984). The HOME Inventory and family demographics. *Developmental Psychology, 20,* 315–320.

Bradley, R. H. & Caldwell, B. M. (1986). Early home environment and the development of competence: Findings from the Little Rock longitudinal study. *Children's Environments Quarterly, 3*(1), 10–22.

Bradley, R. H., Caldwell, B. M., Rock, S. L., Ramey, C. T., Barnard, K. E., Gray, C.,... Johnson, D. L. (1989). Home environment and cognitive development in the first 3 years of life: A collaborative study involving six sites and three ethnic groups in North America. *Developmental Psychology, 25*(2), 217–235.

Bransford, J. D., Sharp, D., Vye, N., Goldman, S., Hasselbring, T., Goin, L.,...the Cognition and Technology Group at Vanderbilt. (1996). MOST environments for accelerating literacy development. In S. Vosniadou, E. de Corte, R. Glaser, & H. Mandl (Eds.), *International perspectives on the design of technology-supported learning environments* (pp. 223–255). Mahwah, NJ: Lawrence Erlbaum Associates.

Briggs-Gowan, M. J., Carter, A. S., Irwin, J. R., Wachtel, K., & Cicchetti, D. V. (2004). The brief infant-toddler social and emotional assessment: Screening for socio-emotional problems and delays in competence. *Journal of Pediatric Psychology, 29,* 143–155.

Burgess, S. R. & Lonigan, C. J. (1998). Bidirectional relations of phonological sensitivity and prereading abilities: Evidence from a preschool sample. *Journal of Experimental Child Psychology, 70*(2), 117–141.

Chaney, C. (1992). Language development, metalinguistic skills, and print awareness in 3-year-old children. *Applied Psycholinguistics, 13,* 485–514.

Chomsky, C. (2001). Stages in language development and reading exposure. In S. W. Beck & L. N. Olah (Eds.), *Perspectives on language and literacy: Beyond the here and now* (pp. 51–75). Cambridge, MA: Harvard Educational Review.

Clay, M. M. (1979). *Reading: The patterning of complex behavior.* Auckland, New Zealand: Heinemann.

Dickinson, D. K., McCabe, A., Anastasopoulos, L., Peisner-Feinberg, E. S., & Poe, M. D. (2003). The comprehensive language approach to early literacy: The interrelationships among vocabulary, phonological sensitivity, and print knowledge among preschool-aged children. *Journal of Educational Psychology, 95,* 465–481.

Early Learning. (n.d.). Education: Knowledge and skills for the jobs of the future. Retrieved from http://www.whitehouse.gov/issues/education/early-childhood

George W. Bush White House Archives. (2002, January). *Fact sheet: No Child Left Behind Act.* Retrieved from: http://georgewbush-whitehouse.archives.gov/news/releases/2002/01/20020108.html

González, V. (2002). Advanced cognitive development and bilingualism: Methodological flaws and suggestions for measuring first and second-language proficiency, language dominance, and intelligence in minority children. In J. A. Castellano & E. Diaz (Eds.), *Reaching new horizons: Gifted and talented education for culturally and linguistically diverse students* (pp. 47–75). Needham Heights, MA: Allyn & Bacon.

Griffin, E. A. & Morrison, F. J. (1997). The unique contribution of home literacy environment to differences in early literacy skills. *Early Child Development and Care, 127,* 233–243.

Haden, C. A., Reese, E., & Fivish, R. (1996). Mother's extratextual comments during storybook reading: Stylistic differences over time and across texts. *Discourse Processes, 21,* 135–169.

Hammett, L. A., VanKleeck, A., & Huberty, C. J. (2003). Patterns of parents' extratextual interactions during book-sharing with preschool children: A cluster analysis study. *Reading Research Quarterly, 38,* 442–468.

Hart, B. & Risley, T. R. (1992). American parenting of language-learning children: Persisting differences in family-child interactions observed in natural home environments. *Developmental Psychology, 28,* 1096–1105.

Heath, S. B. (1983). *Ways with words: Language, life and work in communities and classrooms.* Cambridge, UK: Cambridge University Press.

Heath, S. B. (1986). Sociocultural contexts of language development. In B. E. Office (Ed.), *Beyond language: Social and cultural factors in schooling language minority students* (p. 73–142). Los Angeles, CA: California State University Evaluation, Dissemination and Assessment Center.

Huebner, C. E. (2000). Community-based support for preschool readiness among children in poverty. *Journal of Education for Students Placed at Risk, 5,* 291–314.

Hutinger, P. L., Beard, M., Bell, C., Bond, J., Robinson, L., Schneider, C., & Terry, C. (1998). *Emerging literacy and technology: Working together.* Macomb, IL: Macomb Projects.

Jordan, G., Porche, M., & Snow, C. E. (2000). Project EASE: Easing children's transition to kindergarten literacy through planned parent involvement. *Reading Research Quarterly, 35,* 524–546.

Kamil, M. L., Intrator, S. M., & Kim, H. S. (2000). The effects of other technologies on literacy and literacy learning. In M. L. Kamil, P. B. Mosenthal, P. D. Pearson, & R. Barr (Eds.), *Handbook of reading research* (vol. 3, pp. 771–788). Mahwah, NJ: Erlbaum.

Kuo, A. A., Franke, T. M., Regalado, M., & Halfon, N. (2004). Parent report of reading to young children. *Pediatrics, 113,* 1944–1951.

Labbo, L. D. & Ash, G. E. (1998). What is the role of computer-related technology in early literacy? In S. B. Neuman & K. A. Roskos (Eds.), *Children achieving: Best practices in early literacy* (pp. 180–197). Newark, DE: International Reading Association.

Laosa, L. M. & Henderson, R. W. (1991). Cognitive socialization and competence: The academic development of Chicanos. In R. R. Valencia (Ed.), *Chicano school failure and success: Research and policy agendas for the 1990s* (pp. 164–199). New York, NY: Falmer.

Latzke, M. A. (2002). *Linking individual differences in maternal mind-mindedness to social collaboration processes during mother-child pretend storytelling.* Unpublished doctoral dissertation, University of California, Santa Cruz, Santa Cruz, CA.

LeapFrog Enterprises, Inc. (n.d.). LeapFrog gaming document. Retrieved from http://www.leapfrog.com/gaming/documents/LeapFrog_Enterprises_Inc-corporate_fact_sheet.pdf

LeapFrog SchoolHouse. (n.d). Home page. Retrieved from http://www.leapfrogschoolhouse.com/home/index.asp

Leseman, P. P. M. & de Jong, P. F. (1998). Home literacy: Opportunity, instruction, cooperation, and social-emotional quality predicting early reading achievement. *Reading Research Quarterly, 33*(3), 294–318.

Leu, D. J. (2000). Literacy and technology: Deictic consequences for literacy education in an information age. In M. L. Kamil, P. Mosenthal, P. D. Peason, & R. Barr (Eds.), *Handbook of reading research* (vol. 3, pp. 743–770). Mahwah, NJ: Erlbaum.

McDonnell, S. A., Rollins, P. R., & Friel-Patti, S. (2003). Patterns of change in maternal/child discourse behaviors across repeated storybook readings. *Applied Psycholinguistics, 24*, 323–341.

McNaughton, S., Phillips, G., & MacDonald, S. (2003). Profiling teaching and learning needs in beginning literacy instruction: The case of children in "low decile" schools in New Zealand. *Journal of Literacy Research, 35*, 703–730.

Mejia-Arauz, R., Rogoff, B., Dexter, A., & Najafi, B. (2007). Cultural variation in children's social organization. *Child Development, 78*, 1001–1014.

Moos, R. H. & Moos, B. S. (1981). *Family Environment Scale manual.* Palo Alto, CA: Consulting Psychologists Press.

Moos, R. H. & Moos, B. S. (2009). *Family Environment Scale manual* (4th ed.). Menlo Park, CA: Mind Garden, Inc.

National Center for Education Statistics (NCES). (2010). *The nation's report card: Reading 2009. National assessment of education progress.* Retrieved from http://nces.ed.gov/nationsreportcard/pubs/main2009/2010458.asp

National Institute for Literacy. (2008). *Developing early literacy: Report of the National Early Literacy Panel.* Retrieved from https://www.nichd.nih.gov/publications/pubs/documents/NELPReport09.pdf

Needlman, R. (2001). Before and After Books and Reading (BABAR) study. *Reach Out and Read Newsletter.* Somerville, MA.

Office of Planning, Research, and Evaluation (OPRE). (2000). *Head Start Family and Child Experiences Survey (FACES).* Retrieved from http://www.acf.hhs.gov/programs/opre/research/project/head-start-family-and-child-experiences-survey-faces-1997-2013

Phillips, G. & McNaughton, S. (1990). The practice of storybook reading to preschool children in mainstream New Zealand families. *Reading Research Quarterly, 25*, 196–212.

Pinkard, N. (1999). *Learning to read in culturally responsive computer environments.* Ann Arbor, MI: Center for the Improvement of Early Reading Achievement.

Purcell-Gates, V. (1996). Stories, coupons, and the TV Guide: Relationships between home literacy experiences and emergent literacy knowledge. *Reading Research Quarterly, 31*, 406–428.

Purcell-Gates, V. & Dahl, K. L. (1991). Low-SES children's success and failure at early literacy learning in skills-based classrooms. *Journal of Reading Behavior, 23*, 1–34.

Sigel, I., Stinson, E. T., & Flaugher, J. (1991). Socialization of representational competence in the family: The distancing paradigm. In L. Okagaki & R. J. Sternberg (Eds.), *Directors of development: Influences on the development of children's thinking* (pp. 121–144). Hillsdale, NJ: Lawrence Erlbaum Associates, Inc.

Snow, C. E. (2001). Language and literacy: Relationships during the preschool years. In S. W. Beck & L. N. Olah (Eds.), *Language and literacy: Beyond the here and now* (pp. 161–186). Cambridge, MA: Harvard Educational Review.

Snow, C. E., Porche, M. V., Tabors, P. O., & Harris, S. R. (2007) *Is literacy enough? Pathways to academic success for adolescents.* Baltimore, MD: Brookes Publishing Company.

SRI International. (2003). *Raising A Reader™ survey: An assessment of early literacy skills and effects associated with raising a reader.* Palo Alto, CA: Author.

Valdez-Menacha, M. C. & Whitehurst, G. J. (1992). Accelerating language development through picture book reading: A systematic extension to Mexican day care. *Developmental Psychology, 28,* 1106–1114.

Wagner, R. K., Torgesen, J. K., Rashotte, C. A., Hecht, S. A., Barker, T. A., Burgess, S. R.,... Garon, T. (1997). Changing causal relations between phonological processing abilities and word-level reading as children develop from beginning to fluent readers: A five-year longitudinal study. *Developmental Psychology, 33,* 468–479.

Walker, D., Greenwood, C., Hart, B., & Carta, J. (1994). Prediction of school outcomes based on early language production and socioeconomic factors. *Child Development, 65,* 606–621.

Whitehurst, G. J. (1994). A picture book reading intervention in day care and home for children from low-income families. *Developmental Psychology, 30*(5), 679–689.

Whitehurst, G. J. & Lonigan, C. J. (1998). Child development and emergent literacy. *Child Development, 69*(3), 848–872.

CHAPTER 3

INTEGRATING AND ADAPTING AN INQUIRY TECHNOLOGY-RICH CURRICULUM IN THE CONTEXT OF A LATIN AMERICAN SCIENCE METHODS COURSE

M. Elizabeth Gonzalez and Barbara Hug

ABSTRACT

In this chapter we describe how a technology tool was used in an international context to support pre-service teachers' learning. The Galapagos Finches software, part of the Biology Guided Inquiry Learning Environment (BGuILE) project, was integrated into a pre-service science methods course in Argentina to create a context for learning and teaching science with an inquiry approach. We document how the course instructor used this tool to support pre-service teachers' learning of content, pedagogical content knowledge, and pedagogy. Suggestions on how technology can be integrated into new settings and implications for professional development in such settings are made.

Research on Technology Use in Multicultural Settings, pages 45–74.

45

INTRODUCTION

Education reforms from different countries call for inquiry teaching and learning in order to promote scientific and technology literacy (American Association for the Advancement of Science [AAAS], 1993; International Society for Technology in Education [ISTE], 2003; National Minister of Culture and Education, 1996; National Research Council [NRC], 1996). There is a growing interest in using technology, in particular computer-based tools, to promote change in classroom practices that align with the educational reforms. The use of technology tools allows students to participate in science in ways not possible in the absence of such tools. A variety of technology tools have been developed and integrated into science curricula that provide access to simulations, databases, and models for teaching different scientific concepts (e.g. Dede, 1998; Linn, 1997; Linn & Hsi, 2000; Reiser et al., 2001; Tabak & Reiser, 1997).

Teachers have a crucial role in how new technology and teaching strategies are used in the classroom. Classroom based research has shown that teachers' beliefs about technology, pedagogy, and their resulting practices, as well as the actual affordances of the tool, impact the way technology is used in the classroom (Putnam & Borko, 2000). To address these and other issues, designers of technology tools and accompanying curriculum materials carefully develop scaffolds for both teachers and students in order to engage students in a range of practices with the goal of creating opportunities for in-depth reflection at all stages of the inquiry process (Quintana et al., 2004; Reiser et al., 2001).

It is important to realize that while access to computers has become more widespread, the use of specifically designed educational technology tools has not necessarily been incorporated into the teaching practices of all teachers. In part this is due to the need for not only the development of these inquiry-based tools and curriculum materials, but also the implementation of professional development. The majority of current in-service teachers most likely did not have opportunities to experience inquiry-based technology-rich curriculum as students themselves. This lack of firsthand experience is important to remember when technology is introduced into the schools and these teachers' classrooms. As technology has become more prevalent in schools, it is critical to understand both how teachers adapt and incorporate technology into their practice as well as the conditions found within the larger school context that might impact the use of technology in inquiry teaching and learning.

Integrating technology tools as part of inquiry teaching is a challenge for teachers. The use of the tool often requires them to modify their practice as well as adopt a new curriculum for their local classrooms. When teachers adopt new curriculum, they often will modify and adapt the materials to fit their context and local needs. In doing so, tensions can be created among meeting the needs of the students, teachers, and school district and maintaining the original inquiry philosophy of the curriculum. While enactment modifications made to the intended curriculum can be moderate and maintain the inquiry philosophy, other modifications can change the original goals and intentions of the materials. These changes are in part due to the teachers' beliefs about teaching as well as the constraints of the situation that they are teaching in (Brown & Campione, 1996; Remillard, 2005). Involving teachers in professional development about the use of technology with an inquiry approach is one way to ensure that modifications happen in meaningful and appropriate ways. Identifying ways to support teachers while they learn these new skills is essential if we want teachers to use technology and inquiry methodologies as envisioned in the science education reform documents.

Aspects that lead to adoption and adaptation of materials in contexts other than where they were first developed and used has begun to be investigated (Dede, Honan, & Peters, 2005; Fishman, Marx, Blumenfeld, Krajcik, & Soloway, 2003), but few studies have focused on cross-cultural adaptations (Barab & Leuhmann, 2003; Lin, 2001). In these cases, the complexities of the adaptation can go beyond teacher support and knowledge, as characteristics related to the new context, such as differences in the educational system, must be considered as well. This chapter examines the adaptation process involved when an inquiry-based, technology-rich curriculum developed in United States was integrated into a science methods course at a community college in Argentina. The goals of this study were to:

1.   determine in what ways a technology tool was adapted to fit the local context; and
2.   begin to identify what technology integration meant to a pre-service methods course instructor and pre-service teachers.

THEORETICAL FRAMEWORK AND SELECTED LITERATURE REVIEW

Technology-Rich Curricula Integration

Educational researchers interested in understanding how curriculum innovations are adopted and adapted often focus on the challenges highlighted by tensions related to the adoption of the new materials. There has been increased documentation regarding the challenges teachers and schools face in the successful adoption and adaptation of new technology-rich curriculum (Leuhmann, 2001; Songer, Lee, & Kan, 2002; Zhao, Pugh, Sheldon, & Byers, 2002). Characteristics of the local context, availability of resources for the new curriculum implementation, teachers' knowledge and motivations about teaching and curriculum adoption, as well as flexibility in adapting the materials are key elements that lead to the use of the materials and determine the success of the adoption-adaptation. However, curriculum adoption at the school or district level seldom predicts the degree of classroom use (Honey & McMillan-Culp, 2000; Snyder, Bolin, & Zumwalt, 1996).

Availability of resources and administrative and technical support are important in the decision process that leads to curriculum adoption in the classroom

(Hoffman, 1996; Songer et al., 2002). Though, as studies have documented, investing in resources is not enough when challenging practices are embedded within the new materials (Cuban, 2001; Fishman & Pinkard, 2001). For a curriculum innovation to be successful, adequate allocation of resources needs to be accompanied with clear specifications of the intentions and goals of the innovation, professional development, and examples of successful teaching practices (Cohen & Ball, 1999).

Teachers' content knowledge and affective factors towards the new curriculum and technological tools will contribute to the successful adoption of an innovation as well (Putnam & Borko, 2000). Educational technologies and curriculum that are perceived to present teaching and learning advantages over current practices, are simple to use in the classroom, and provide teachers with successful examples of the materials used in other schools and classrooms have a greater probability of being adopted in new contexts (Songer et al., 2002). Researchers suggest that even when different models of curriculum adoption (e.g., use of highly specified innovations, top-down mandated curriculum, or case studies initiated by researchers) are used, they will lack sustainability if teachers do not overcome their concerns and anxieties about technology, believe they have ownership and flexibility to adapt the materials, and think of the innovation as relevant and compatible with their current practices (Cohen & Ball, 1999; McLaughlin, 1990; Sabelli & Dede, 2001; Songer et al., 2002).

Without room for teachers to adapt the new curriculum, the materials are more likely to be rejected and not adopted as part of an extended change. In examples of adoptions with high level of success, the curriculum materials were modified to fit local practices and contextual characteristics (Barab & Leuhmann, 2003; Squire, MaKinster, Barnett, Leuhmann, & Barab, 2003). However, this high level of modification can create tensions when examining the fidelity of the implementation between the intended and enacted curriculum (Honey & McMillan-Culp, 2000; Snyder et al., 1996). Particularly when the innovations attempt to change teachers' traditional practices to include a constructivist orientation towards the use of technology in an inquiry setting, the types of modifications made in adapting the curriculum materials can affect the success of the innovation as envisioned by the developers (Reiser et al., 2000).

Models for Curriculum Adoption and Adaptation

Researchers have begun to identify the issues teachers and schools face in adopting curriculum (Barab & Leuhmann, 2003; Dede et al., 2005; Squire et al., 2003), but little is known about the complexities and intricacies that influence teachers in adapting curricula and technology tools with an inquiry approach while meeting the everyday needs of the classroom. There have been few attempts at scaling up curriculum adoptions to engage schools and districts in integrating as well as adapting these types of reform-oriented practices in their educational systems. Successful examples involve administrators, teachers, and developers in the process of adoption-adaptation (Century & Jurist Levy, 2004; Fishman et al., 2003). Designing curriculum materials in close collaboration among software developers, curriculum designers, and teachers often ensures that the materials and tools fit the local context, so there is a high probability for curriculum adoption (Reiser et al., 2000).

Another way for the integration of inquiry-based, technology-rich curricula to occur is for teachers to participate in extended professional development efforts. These efforts focus on ways of adapting new curriculum so that the original intent of the materials is maintained within the new context (Spitulnik & Linn, 2006). However, for the adoptions to sustain through time, additional efforts are needed to ensure the materials also fit the local context and culture.

Furthermore, experienced and motivated teachers who participate in the context of researcher-teacher collaborations face different challenges than teachers who have not had these experiences or motivations (Reiser et al., 2000; Songer, Lee, & McDonald, 2003). Research suggests that adapting curriculum to acknowledge and incorporate characteristics of the local settings is a complex process (Fishman & Krajcik, 2003; Fishman et al., 2003; Fishman & Pinkard, 2001). Designers must propose ways of supporting different groups of teachers in enacting the materials and providing instances to discuss the intentions and alignment of new materials with the classroom culture (Stein, Hubbard, & Mehan, 2004). These supports can be provided through a range of partnerships, conceptual and pedagogical content knowledge supports, as well as spaces for reflecting about the teaching practices.

Technology-Rich Curriculum Integration in Pre-Service Education Programs

Numerous pre-service teacher education programs have revised their instruction to bring their programs in line with current views of teaching and learning. One area that has seen extensive change has been in how technology has become integrated in the programs to better prepare future teachers in using these tools in teaching. If using technology in new and engaging ways is a key goal of educational reform, then the preparation of new teachers will be critical for the reform success.

Of interest to us is how science methods course instructors have redesigned the courses to integrate inquiry-based technologies. The goals of using a range of technology tools in these courses are to facilitate the development of pre-service teachers' science and inquiry content knowledge, to provide a context for pre-service teachers to apply their scientific knowledge in new ways, and for pre-service teachers to become more comfortable teaching science using these tools and inquiry approach (Friedrichsen, Dana, Zembal-Saul, Munford, & Tsur, 2001). Instructors report that when technology makes the process of prediction, performing and analyzing experiments and data, and revising scientific models easier, students are able to foster a better understanding of concepts as well as the inquiry processes (Crawford, Zembal-Saul, Munford, & Friedrichsen, 2005; Otero, Johnson, & Goldberg, 1999; Zembal-Saul, Munford, Crawford, Friedrichsen, & Land, 2002).

Researchers and instructors have documented the challenges they face in integrating the technologies and structuring the methods courses around the use of these tools (Friedrichsen et al., 2001). Often instructors did not have previous experiences with technology-rich curriculum; thus they encountered challenges similar to what in-service teachers faced with a need to develop content knowledge and pedagogical content knowledge in order to use technology to support inquiry learning.

Adoption of Technology-Rich Curriculum in International Contexts

A large amount of the reported research has focused on the implementation of American innovations with groups of in-service teachers, within a school or across a school district, or in the context of methods courses taught in pre-service programs all within the United States. This focus ignores teachers in cross-cultural and international communities adapting technology tools and curricula developed in other countries for their own use. These teachers often face different types of challenges and/or a greater complexity due to differences between the culture of their educational system and the contexts for which the curriculum and technology tools were designed.

Few studies have looked at the adoption of tools and curriculum from one educational system to another. One study (Lin, 2001) described how a mathematics teacher in Hong Kong adopted and adapted a technology tool developed in the United States. Changing how the tool and curriculum were used was essential in order to fit the local context and maintain the original goal of the curriculum. The adaptation process occurred over an extended period of time and evolved based on the teacher's reflections of both her and her students' needs. Other factors that influenced the adaptation were related to the context (e.g. access to technology) and the alignment of the innovation with current practices (e.g. the need to align with specific learning objectives and teaching methods).

There have been few studies conducted in Latin American contexts that investigated the use of technology for teaching and learning science (Kozak, 2004; Valeiras & Meneses, 2005). In reviewing the literature on the adaptation of curriculum and technology tools developed in the United States for use in international contexts, no studies or reports were found that took place in Latin American educational settings. The lack of such research might be attributed to insufficient computer-based simulations compatible with local resources, language barriers, and/or cultural issues. In addition, few curriculum materials that exemplify the use of these technologies in Latin American science education contexts, as well as a shortage of professional development and workshops to help teachers integrate the technology tools in meaningful ways, might have contributed to the lack of published research reports.

More empirical work that examines how curricular innovations can be implemented across multiple classroom contexts at the international level is necessary to understand how the process of adoption and adaptation occurs. By conducting such work in a range of international settings, it will be possible to begin to understand how to promote the systematic use of a range of technologies and to identify ways to provide teachers with the necessary supports to create appropriate adaptations for their local contexts. Countries in Latin America have begun to engage in science educational reforms and could benefit from research into how these tools could be used in their local settings.

The lack of published reports about the use of technology-rich curricula in Latin American contexts and the recent push for reforms in science education led to an investigation of how one specific tool and curriculum could be used in a local South American context. It is important to understand the main features that influence the enactment of technology-rich curricula in these environments, the kind of support teachers need for developing and enacting these curricula, and how teachers adapt and integrate educational technology tools in their practices. By focusing on a specific context, an in-depth understanding of the local setting, the needs of both teachers and students, and how these characteristics might shape the curriculum goals and technology integration will be gained. In addition, the issues surrounding the adoption and adaptation of innovative curriculum materials that engage both teachers and students in learning inquiry and more meaningful science will be better understood.

PURPOSE

This chapter reports the results of an initial study looking at the issues around adopting and adapting materials developed in the United States to fit an international pre-service teacher education program in Latin America. The goals of this study were to determine in what ways a technology tool could be adapted to fit a local context, as well as to begin to identify what technology integration meant to a pre-service methods course instructor and pre-service teachers. Finally, there was interest in how the software promoted conceptual and pedagogical knowledge. It is hoped that this study will continue to be built upon as the pre-service teachers become in-service teachers. It is believed that by building from the pre-service program to the in-service classrooms, a model of how technology use within a science classroom can scale to meaningful levels of use will begin to be developed.

Differences and Similarities between U.S. and Argentina School Context

The first author used her personal experiences from growing up in Argentina and her experiences in the North American education context to develop a comparison between the Argentinean and the North American education contexts.

There exist critical differences between the two countries in the public education systems as well as the teacher education programs used to train future teachers. In the context of public education in Argentina, classes tend to be large (over 35 students), and the physical buildings in which classes are held are shared among different educational levels, such as elementary, secondary, and higher education. Teachers are not given a single classroom to teach in; rather they walk from one classroom to the other, and the students remain in the same classroom.

Education programs are organized around a set of required courses that students take in a particular order. While there are national and provincial standards that serve as a basic framework for each school, each educational program has its own curriculum, which is designed to meet the requirements. Teachers have a key role in curriculum design and implementation. Academically, Argentinean classrooms can be classified as a traditional environment, where the teacher is considered the source of knowledge and authority. In alignment with this is the belief that the purpose of courses is for students to learn content knowledge. Thus, most classes are in the format of lectures interspersed with group discussion and activities.

METHODS

Location

This study took place in a community college located in Cordoba, Argentina, during the summer of 2006. The college is one of the main community colleges that offer education programs for elementary teachers. The four-year program is organized into sets of courses covering the main subjects (sciences, mathematics, language, social sciences, and arts) and pedagogical aspects. The prospective teachers will teach in the levels EGB 1 and 2 (corresponding to American grades one through six) in elementary schools.

Course and Participants

The curriculum unit was used during a science methods course that was the first of a required two-course sequence in the area of science education. Students took this course in the first year of their education program. During the course, pre-service teachers learned science concepts as well as learning theories and science teaching strategies, developed curriculum materials, and analyzed examples of teaching practices. Students met twice a week for 80-minute class periods.

The instructor in charge of the methods course, Mrs. Mancini (pseudonym), was an experienced teacher with more than 10 years of experience and practice in a range of programs. She had degrees in chemistry and science education, taught chemistry at the secondary and tertiary levels, and had taught elementary science methods courses for several years. She had participated in a school-university partnership research project for the integration of technology in science education for the past four years. She was previously involved in the design of collaborative professional development programs for in-service teachers. This was the first time she integrated a technology tool and curriculum developed in the United States into the methods course.

Two of Mrs. Mancini's course sections, with approximately 35 pre-service science teachers each, participated in this study. Pre-service teachers ranged from 19 to 25 years of age. The majority of the pre-service teachers traveled from rural or suburban cities to attend class. Students came from lower to middle class socio-economic backgrounds, with many of them being the first in their families to attend college. The pre-service teachers did not have previous teaching or personal experience with using technology in science learning. The instructor's and pre-service teachers' participation in this project was voluntary.

Technology Resources and Software Description

The community college had a computer laboratory with 15 PC computers with Windows 2000 and CD drives. There was no Internet connection in the computer laboratory. There were no laboratory technicians in the community college to help support the instructor when she wanted to use the computers. Due to these restrictions, each course instructor had to schedule the use of the laboratory in advance, as well as prepare the necessary software, computers, and materials.

Taking these things into consideration (the school, the context of the study, and computer laboratory characteristics), we chose to focus on one particular technology tool, the BGuILE Galapagos Finches. This software and curriculum was selected for several reasons. The concepts integrated in the tool and curriculum were part of the content the teacher normally covered in the course. The software was free and available in Spanish and English (available for download: http://letus.org/bguile/). The language option was an essential feature in the selection of the software, considering that the instructor and students engaged in this research are Spanish speakers. In addition, the software can be used without connecting to the Internet, which made this tool compatible with the resources available in the school where the research was conducted.

The BGuILE Galapagos Finches software provides opportunities for students to engage in scientific inquiry investigations (Reiser et al., 2001; Tabak & Reiser, 1997). The software was used as a context for learning how populations change over time due to environmental pressures. It presented authentic data obtained by scientists from one of the Galapagos Islands (Grant, 1986; Weiner, 1994). The software has a rich data set with information about the island flora, fauna, weather, finches' characteristics for different years and seasons, habitats, food resources, and behaviors. Students propose hypotheses, select and analyze data, and construct explanations and generalizations as part of the curriculum.

Pre-service teachers worked in groups to create hypotheses that would explain why some populations of finches died and some survived during a particular time frame. In order to do this, pre-service teachers needed to apply concepts related to environmental stress, variations in individuals, and how individuals' character-

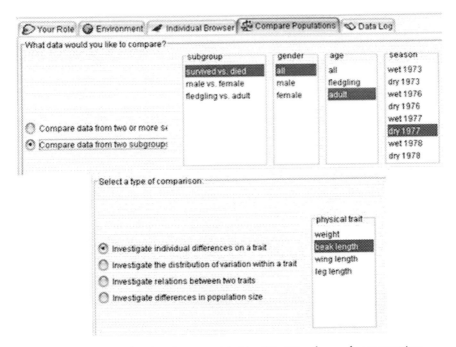

FIGURE 3.1.   Example of options provided by BGuILE software for comparing populations

istics affect population survival while creating their hypotheses. They needed to identify and analyze appropriate data to see if their hypotheses were accurate or not. Figure 3.1 shows an example of the options available in the software for data selection and analysis. The program presented results in different graphical representations important for pre-service teachers to understand (Figure 3.2).

Critical for selecting this tool for use in the classroom was the alignment of the software and the course objectives. The tool supported domain-specific use of inquiry practices, which the teacher saw as critical for her students. This was done in the context of a real-world problem, with evidence organized such that inquiry teaching and learning were supported. The software incorporated scaffolding prompts in the form of questions that allowed students to apply concept knowledge while engaged in class activities. Moreover, the amount of information in the database facilitated a flexible curriculum design, which was critical due to the background of the students. In addition, the technical requirements of the tool allowed its use in different contexts, such as the case presented here. Additional details about the software can be found in Tabak and Reiser (1997).

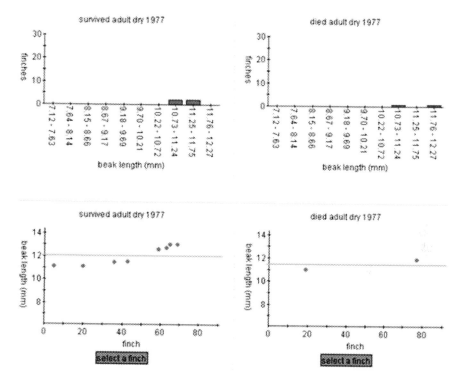

FIGURE 3.2.   Example of different types of graphics students obtained based on the hypothesis and data they decided to collect

Curriculum and Proposed Activities

The curriculum goals were to engage pre-service teachers in authentic inquiry activities, promoting reflections about the tasks and extrapolation to their future classroom environments. The unit, focusing on the use of the tool, had two main purposes. The first goal was for pre-service teachers to learn domain science content knowledge and scientific practices, such as hypotheses generation and data selection connected with scientific reasoning. The second goal was for pre-service teachers to develop pedagogical content knowledge on how to teach these concepts and how to integrate technology in their own curriculum design.

Activities were adapted from "What Will Survive," a project-based, technology-rich biology curriculum (Tzou, Bruozas, Finn, Hug, & Reiser, 2003), the LeTUS (Learning Technologies in Urban Schools) curriculum (downladed from http://letus.org/strugglesurvival.htm; Reiser et al., 2001), and the "Galapagos Investigations" activities (Benz, 2000).

We contacted Mrs. Mancini by e-mail to explain the nature of the curriculum and technology, and provided examples of how it was integrated in science methods courses in American universities and how it was used in a range of American middle schools. After discussing with her the pre-service teachers' learning experiences, the school and classroom resources, and the methods course learning goals, the first author, in collaboration with Mrs. Mancini, re-designed the proposed curricula.

During the three weeks this unit took place, three phases of instruction were used: "setting the stage," "computer-based investigation," and the "reflection stage." These phases were based on the Galapagos Finches curriculum as well as other activities designed to promote student reflections. Activities throughout these phases provided experiences and instances for the pre-service teachers to reflect on their own learning and to develop content knowledge and pedagogical content knowledge. In the "setting the stage" phase, pre-service teachers discussed their understanding about technology and technology tools, proposed examples of technology integration in the science curriculum, and discussed advantages and disadvantages of using different tools for teaching and learning science. During this phase, pre-service teachers applied their conceptual knowledge and discussed island ecosystems. In addition, pre-service teachers read materials that described the Galapagos Island ecosystem with the goal of providing concept knowledge about these islands. Next, pre-service teachers explored and brainstormed possible hypotheses to determine why some finch populations died and others survived in 1977 on the Galapagos Islands. In the "computer-based investigation" phase, pre-service teachers used the BGuILE software to collect evidence to refute or support their hypotheses. In the "reflection stage," the instructor prompted pre-service teachers to reflect on the selection of data, connections between the data and their hypotheses, and what scientific concepts were necessary to explain the data and hypotheses. In addition to thinking about the science, pre-service teachers were asked to reflect on how this experience aligned with their prior understanding and expectations of teaching with technology.

Data Sources

Data from this exploratory case study was analyzed using a qualitative methodology (Yin & Campbell, 2002). Data included classroom observations, videotapes and audiotapes of classroom activities, field notes, teacher materials and notes, and interviews with the course instructor and pre-service teachers. Classroom observations focused on pre-service teachers' roles and discourses during class instruction. Pre-service teachers were videotaped and audiotaped while they engaged in the curriculum activities and while using the software. Field notes, videotapes, and audiotapes were used to identify classroom dynamics and pre-service teachers' understanding of science content, technology, and pedagogy as reflected in pre-service teachers/pre-service teachers' and instructor/pre-service teachers' dialogues. Field notes and the recorded materials helped identify events to include in the follow-up interviews and the emerging codes of analysis.

Field notes, interviews, and classroom videotapes were used for understanding the local context as well as pre-service teachers' and instructor's knowledge about technology and science integration. Findings on science technology-rich enactments and suggestions for teaching strategies and uses of technology for inquiry teaching (Otero et al., 1999; Otero et al., 2005; Squire et al., 2003; Tabak & Reiser, 1997; Wisnudel Spitulnik & Krajcik, 1998) were used to guide the elaboration of the semi-structured pre-interviews. Results from classroom enactments helped identify emergent codes focusing on the instructor/pre-service teachers' and pre-service teachers/pre-service teachers' interactions. Codes and examples of classroom events guided the development of the semi-structured post-interview protocol. Interviews were done pre- and post-enactment of the unit. Pre-service teachers were randomly selected for interviews that were audio-taped and subsequently transcribed. In the semi-structured interviews, questions related to their expectations and beliefs about technology integration in the science curricula and their reflections about this practice were asked.

Prior to the start of the enactment, Mrs. Mancini engaged in the curriculum activities and learned to use the technology tool. The first author and Mrs. Mancini met two times before the curriculum enactment and engaged in a reflective work cycle in order to become familiar with the software. The goals were for the instructor to become familiarized with the tool, recognize areas where she might have difficulties in teaching and enacting the curriculum, and identify instances where the pre-service teachers might have conceptual and technical difficulties.

Mrs. Mancini worked with the tool on her own, participating in the same type of activities she would use in the classroom. She proposed hypotheses about why some finches in the Galapagos Islands died and others survived during the 1977 dry season, and then she discussed with the researcher her hypotheses and possible issues she envisioned as challenging for the pre-service teachers. Then, she used the software to select data to support or refute her hypotheses and proposed explanations. Next, she discussed with the first author the steps she followed and the challenges and problems she encountered. The instructor used these opportunities to decide how the technology would be used and integrated into the curriculum and what technology learning goals would be emphasized. Throughout this process she reflected on her ideas of how to integrate and adapt technology in the methods course curriculum, her concerns about pre-service teachers' conceptual knowledge, uses of technology, and what she thought needed to be integrated as part of pedagogical concept knowledge. Questions asked by the researcher that prompted these reflections included: How is this curriculum innovation different from current practices in the science methods course? What do you think pre-service teachers' conceptual and technological difficulties will be? How do you think you can address these difficulties? How do you think the classroom and school context will influence the enactment?

Examples were provided to the instructor on how the curriculum was used in middle school classrooms, as well as examples of research that integrated the BGuILE software in methods courses in United States universities. Conversations were carried out by the instructor and researcher focusing on the instructors' ideas and conceptions about technology integration in the science curriculum, how different policies and incoherencies between policies and allocation of resources influenced technology adoption, and different ways of integrating technology.

TABLE 3.1. Issues that Contributed to the Curriculum Adaptation

Sub-questions	Examples of Categories (Issues that promote curriculum adaptation)	Examples of Codes (How the curriculum was adapted)
How does the instructor's knowledge and motivations influence on the curriculum adaptation?	Instructors' pedagogical content knowledge • Knowledge and beliefs about students' difficulties with specific science and inquiry skills content • Knowledge and instructional strategies for teaching Instructors' experiences with the technology tool and innovative curriculum	The instructor identified areas pre-service teachers did not have experience with (e.g. data analysis) and proposed strategies to scaffold pre-service teachers. Instructor identified aspects in the use of the technology tool that were challenging; she decided to include modeling strategies and whole class data collection to overcome these issues.
How do pre-service teachers' experiences influence on the instructor's decisions to adapt the curriculum?	Conceptual knowledge Inquiry skills	Based on pre-service teachers' problems applying scientific knowledge in analyzing data, the instructor focused on one possible explanation (lack of food sources) for why finches die. Based on pre-service teachers' problems during different stages of the inquiry process, the instructor focused on the process of data analysis.
How does the science methods course determine changes in the innovative curriculum?	Course contents and goals	Instructor included whole class discussions about issues related to the "Nature of Science," which pre-service teachers had learned about previously in the course.
How does the context determine curriculum adaptations?	Classroom context • Time • Number of pre-service teachers School context • Number of computer • Location of resources	Number of participants and amount of computers determined teaching strategies. Pre-service teachers worked in small groups at the computer laboratory. The amount of time the groups were able to work in the laboratory prompted the instructor to cut the amount of material covered.

Data Analysis

Data analysis was conducted in several phases. The three phases of instruction proposed in the curriculum were used to determine the main episodes of analysis and comparison between the initial curriculum and classroom practices. Then the researcher watched videotapes of classroom activities and all instances of instructor/pre-service teachers' and pre-service teachers/pre-service teachers' dialogues, and notes from classroom observations were transcribed. The curriculum enactment was compared with the proposed curriculum. This comparison and general information about the classroom and school context were used to determine what issues influenced curriculum adoption and adaptation.

During the second phase, the categories of analysis were refined. Emphasis was placed on teaching strategies used by the instructor, pre-service teachers' use of the software, strategies for data selection, and conceptual knowledge application. The research questions and other sub-questions emerging from this analysis were used during the interviews. Analysis of the interview transcripts and the notes of instructor/researcher meetings focused on understanding participants' engagement with the software and the curriculum adaptation process. Once all interviews and notes from the instructor/researcher meetings were transcribed, the final categories were defined and the codes for how the curriculum was adapted were determined. Examples of sub-questions, codes, and categories used to determine how the curriculum was adapted are provided in Table 3.1.

FINDINGS AND DISCUSSION

The initial goals of this study were to determine how the use of a novel technology-rich curriculum changed and was changed by the classroom context, instructor, and pre-service teachers' previous experiences and content knowledge. The instructor had the freedom to adopt and adapt the curriculum as she felt necessary in order to integrate it into the current practices. She had the option to alter the curriculum materials to incorporate them in the course as she had always taught it, or use them in new ways to fit the local environment while maintaining the key inquiry elements proposed in the innovation. Analysis of the data revealed that two main factors contributed to the instructor's decisions in adopting the materials: the ways the instructor engaged with the tool and curriculum materials, and her perceptions about the technology tool complexity and compatibility with the local context. We found four issues that contributed to the curriculum adaptation: the classroom and school context, pre-service teachers' conceptual knowledge and inquiry skills, aspects related to the science methods course curriculum, and the instructor's experiences with the software. The use of the software and these changes served to reveal pre-service teachers' domain-specific knowledge and supported the development of the instructor's pedagogical content knowledge. We observed changes in the instructor's ideas on how to integrate and use technology in the science classroom.

This section is structured around the adoption and adaptation themes. Evidence from both the instructor's and pre-service teachers' engagement with the tool is used to illustrate major points.

Factors Affecting the Instructor's Decisions on Curriculum Adoption

Before considering how the technology was adapted to the context of the science method course, we need to determine what prompted the course instructor to adopt the curriculum. Two things were conducive to the adoption of the innovative curriculum materials. One aspect was related to the instructor's perception of the technology tool's complexity and compatibility with the classroom and school resources. The possibility to work in close relationship with the researcher was the second issue that had a positive influence on the instructor's decision to adopt the curriculum.

Although the instructor's personal motivations and previous experiences with technology influenced her motivation and decision to adopt this technology rich-curriculum in her methods course, one main aspect Mrs. Mancini considered in her decision to adopt the curriculum was the characteristics of the technology (e.g. the software was in Spanish, it didn't need an Internet connection for using it, and it was easy to install). Knowing the tool had these features and was compatible with the resources available in the school context helped the instructor to form an attitude conducive to curriculum adoption. Moreover, this provided the instructor the opportunity to overcome her anxieties about the tool, the confidence necessary to install the software herself, and the opportunity to think of managing any technical problems she might encounter during the curriculum enactment.

The contact with the researcher was also of importance for the instructor to decide to adopt the curriculum. During the first interview, Mrs. Mancini discussed with the researcher how the tool and curriculum was integrated in the schools and methods courses in the United States. This provided her with a better understanding of the curriculum goals and possible changes to adapt the materials to her classroom context. The period of practice-reflection cycles, which the instructor spent engaging with the curriculum and software, became essential for her decision to adopt the curriculum innovation and to adapt it to her classroom while maintaining the inquiry elements integrated in the materials. In the first interview, the instructor mentioned the following about what she expected would happen with pre-service teachers when they first used the tool:

Instructor: I think that the teacher's guidance role is essential.

Researcher: What would you expect students will do when they engage with the software?

Instructor: Probably some students might not know what to do, how to select and compare data. Other people will try to look for ways of doing it themselves and don't ask for help, while others will engage in the activity, analyze, and think about it, in a similar way I did.

Reflective instances that occurred during the engagement with the tool helped the instructor identify possible challenging contexts for her students and helped her select teaching strategies to be used in the course. Planning ways to guide pre-service teachers in technology use and thinking of problem-solving situations that might occur during the practice sessions helped the instructor to overcome anxieties related to the use of a novel tool and prepared her for making decisions to adapt the curriculum to the classroom context. As this case study shows and other authors agree (Songer et al., 2002), a learning-focused, sustained, and reflective professional development approach is crucial for successful curriculum adoption and adaptation. This study found that the type of professional development approach used is important independent of the context, international or local.

The emphasis the instructor put on understanding the initial context the curriculum and technology tool was developed for and how that influenced her interpretation and reflections on her own practice have important implications for curriculum and software designers and professional development models. We consider it necessary to include with the innovative materials examples of intended practices as well as strategies that scaffold teachers in ways of integrating the tools in their own practices.

Factors Affecting the Curriculum Adaptation

The instructor adopted the curriculum and how the technology was used based on: school and classroom allocation of resources, pre-service teachers' conceptual knowledge and inquiry skills, the methods course goals and curriculum, and the instructor's teaching experiences and motivations. We present examples of how each of these aspects shaped how the new curriculum was enacted in the following sections.

Instructor's Pedagogical Content Knowledge and Experiences with the Technology Tool

Initial analysis and changes of the curriculum innovation were based on the instructor's perception and understanding of the local context. Her reflections on how to integrate the curriculum and BGuILE software in the science methods course helped her decide how to adapt the curriculum to the local context. Other authors considered similar stages in the adaptation of innovations (Leuhmann, 2002; Lin, 2001); however, in this case study, these reflections occurred after the instructor was able to compare and understand some of the differences between the American and Argentinean educational systems and possible approaches in using the curriculum. Actual instances of curriculum adaptations occurred during the classroom enactments. Comparisons and explanations of how a curriculum is enacted in different contexts seem to be important in providing instructors strategies for their own curriculum adaptations.

As Mrs. Mancini expressed in the second interview, she used her own experience with the tool and the researcher's scaffolding process as a model for enacting the curriculum and scaffolding her own students (pre-service teachers):

Researcher: How do you think you can guide different groups of students?

Instructor: I'd probably do what you did with me. I think it was important to look at the software together, so I'll be able to guide them [students] in a similar way.

Researcher: What did you find more useful in the prompts I used to guide you?

Instructor: You have a better understanding of the software, the data available, and an idea of what to expect from the data. You can ask questions to guide the process without giving the answer. I'm afraid I will not be able to do the same, but I don't have problems in asking you for help.

The types of teaching strategies proposed in the new curriculum and the integration of technologies must be taken into consideration because they might influence how the curriculum is adapted. It is believed that adaptations related to teaching and learning strategies are connected to the teacher's pedagogical content knowledge and teaching beliefs. The adaptations usually reflect teachers' concerns in these areas as well as the characteristics of the context. For example, during the reflective work cycle the instructor started to think about her practice and the inquiry teaching approach included in the innovation. Mrs. Mancini expressed:

I think it is important to think about the teacher as guidance. But where is the limit between that teacher who guides in a reflective way, and a teacher who directs students. I think we need to wait and see what happens…[in the practice]. To whom are we guiding? To those students who ask more, to those who have more problems? What do we do when there are 45 students in a class? Or what happens when we have five or 10 student groups we need to guide? The risk might be that we don't guide some of the groups, or don't guide enough some of the students' groups…

Scaffolding and keeping track of the progress in each student group was a concern for Mrs. Mancini. In this case, she combined the proposed strategy, small group activities, with the usual teaching strategy used in her classroom, whole class discussions. During the class period she alternated several times between these strategies. These changes allowed her a better way of guiding all her students. Also, the use of the new strategy provided pre-service teachers a way of experiencing a new learning context, while the whole class discussions help them ease the tensions the new situation provoked. The instructor's concerns are similar to those expressed by other teachers about inquiry teaching (Hammer, 2000). In this case, it is believed that the instructor's teaching experiences and knowledge of the pre-service students helped her to keep the main inquiry features of the curriculum innovation while changing it to fit the local context. However, this might not be the case when comparing experienced and novice teachers' changes made during curriculum adaptations. Other research found that the type of changes and proposed strategies are different in these groups (Reiser et al., 2000), thus leading to different types of adaptations. More research in this area is necessary to provide different groups of teachers the support needed for successful adaptations that fit their classroom context and maintain the goals of the innovations.

Science Methods Course Curriculum and Goals

During the science methods course pre-service teachers discussed scientific concepts related to the nature of science. For example pre-service teachers read about science induction-deduction methods, what constitutes data, and objectivism, among other topics. The instructor actively looked for opportunities and instances to connect the content in the curriculum innovation with the content taught in the course. During the curriculum enactment the instructor used whole class discussions as a teaching strategy and a space for emphasizing and reflecting about possible connections between the innovative curriculum unit and the concepts pre-service teachers learned previously in the course.

After the classroom enactment, the instructor began to think about possible changes in the science methods course curriculum that would integrate the new curriculum. Several authors have emphasized that connections between current classroom practices and new innovations are essential for adoption of new materials (Barab & Leuhmann, 2003; Squire et al., 2003). This case study corroborated the importance of these relationships and the key role the instructors have in doing these comparisons. It is believed that having a positive experience during curriculum adoption is essential to motivating the instructor in the adoption of the innovation. It is unknown if the personal characteristics of the instructor in this study and her motivations were a main factor in the thought process and decisions she made in adapting the materials. Moreover, it is not known what would have happen if the innovative materials were not related to the course curriculum or if the curriculum enactment had a different outcome. More research that considers these factors is necessary.

Pre-Service Teachers' Conceptual Knowledge and Inquiry Skills

The pre-service teachers recognized their own lack of understanding and experiences in learning with a scientific inquiry approach. For example, they mentioned they did not have prior experiences in creating hypotheses. Also, several groups of pre-service teachers had limited views of what constituted data and the different types of evidences collected by scientists.

Alternative conceptions related to the nature of science and what constituted valid data collection were observed in pre-service teachers. They thought that experiments were essential for obtaining data and that this usually occurred in the laboratory. These beliefs conflicted with the types of data presented as evidence in the software (graphics, field notes, charts, and tables). Pre-service teachers' misconceptions and their lack of inquiry skills used to analyze graphs, tables, and scientific journal notes constrained their use and analysis of data. In this case, several groups preferred analyzing scientists' journal notes about individual finches' behaviors instead of graphics about different finch populations.

Some pre-service teachers perceived the software as less valuable because it did not present data as text. For example, one of the pre-service teachers, Anna, mentioned that the software did not give her all the required information necessary to support their proposed hypothesis. Some pre-service teachers, rather than searching the data provided by the software to support their hypotheses, explored other resources they were more familiar with, such as the Internet, as sources of knowledge to try to explain why finches died or survived during 1977 in the Galapagos Islands. Pre-service teachers understood the goal of science to present "the truth." This belief led them to look for one correct explanation to the questions that they were asking. The software did not provide the pre-service teachers with a single "true" answer, and some groups of pre-service teachers started to review their understanding of the nature of science.

The group of pre-service teachers that was interviewed valued the experience of using the software and mentioned how the technology challenged their idea of the methods used by scientists to collect data and how different groups of scientists have different explanations for the same data. Implications of how the software can be used to foster and enhance a better understanding of the nature of scientific inquiry must be considered.

On the other hand, the instructor viewed the technology and new curriculum as a space where different aspects of the nature of science could be experienced and practiced. These opportunities enhanced the instructor's motivation in integrating the curriculum and were valued as one reason for future classroom adaptations. In one of the whole class discussions that occurred during the second day of the curriculum enactment, Mrs. Mancini asked pre-service teachers: "What is a scientific explanation?" Reflections upon this question lead students to think about secondary hypotheses and how hypotheses connected to data collection. In another instance, at the end of this class period, Mrs. Mancini concluded the class by reflecting on the processes of data collection and analysis. She said to her students: "These activities [referring to the processes of writing hypotheses, selecting and analyzing data] might help us think about science and the process of science in another way. Scientists might have different explanations for the same type of data." The statement generated several discussions among students related to their ideas on scientific data and when and how scientists collected data. During this discussion questions such as "How do you think scientists explain the data collected?" and "Are there parameters that allow me to think some data are better than others?" were asked.

During the pre-service teachers' group discussions on data analysis, a commonly Lamarkian conception was present. In several of the groups, pre-service teachers tried to explain changes in the finch populations as "need-driven adaptations." Pre-service teachers used this alternative framework to explain individual as well as population changes. For example, Alejandra believed that finches learned new diet behaviors in order to survive. Maria explained the changes in beak length for the finches that survived the dry season of 1977 as growth that occurred during the finches' life span. These pre-service teachers held the idea that change involves individual transformations that occur during the organisms' life span, are driven by necessity, and are usually determined by environmental factors. These findings were consistent with other studies of pre-service teachers in similar contexts within the United States (Crawford et al., 2005).

Usually, pre-service teachers did not recognize or acknowledge their misconceptions about natural selection and evolution. However, the instructor valued the use of the technology as a resource that made explicit pre-service teachers' alternative conceptions. In this case, the instructor recognized pre-service teachers' misconceptions and promoted class discussions about these issues. Mrs. Mancini is currently considering future curriculum enactment where she provides evidence of pre-service teachers' alternative explanations through the use of technology.

School and Classroom Resources

Decisions on what to change and how to integrate the technology into the curriculum were influenced by the local context characteristics. Activities proposed in the curriculum required students to work in small groups for generating hypotheses, to discuss with other groups and the whole class the selected hypotheses, and to use the computers for selecting and analyzing data for supporting the revised hypotheses. The location and availability of resources, as well as the number of pre-service teachers enrolled in each course section, constrained the use of technology and the curriculum enactment. For example, because the computer laboratory was shared by other grade levels and groups in the school, careful planning was needed on how often and when the instructor used the computers. In this case, with one of the pre-service teacher groups, the instructor decided to change the order and type of activities proposed in the original curriculum unit due to constraints in time and resources. Pre-service teachers were introduced to the software first, and then they generated hypotheses. This change in the order of activities narrowed the type of hypotheses pre-service teachers proposed. Also, because students did not have previous experiences on how to generate hypotheses, these changes promoted the application of appropriate conceptual knowledge in writing hypotheses. Thus, the changes helped pre-service teachers understand the process of generating hypotheses and its relation to previous conceptual knowledge.

The following are examples of hypotheses explaining "Why many finches died during 1977" proposed by one group of pre-service science teachers previous to the introduction of the technology, and a second group where the technology was introduced first and then pre-service teachers elaborated their hypotheses:

Group 1 (hypotheses elaboration, and technology introduction):

Carlos: Many finches died because of the phenomenon El Niño that produced changes in Islands' weather.

Maria: A disease affected the finches' population. (Second class period, group 1).

Group 2 (technology introduction, and hypotheses elaboration):

Juan: The finches died because the lack of rain affected the amount of food available.

Elena (elaborating from Juan hypothesis): It was hard for the finches to find food because the lack of rain affected the food available. (Second class period, group 2).

Other decisions and changes in the curriculum enactment and teaching strategies used were related to the availability of resources at the school. The number of computers and pre-service teachers who participated in the course required the instructor to constitute and manage large (six to eight students) groups of students when working with the computers. The course instructor mentioned that this situation added to her challenges of learning new skills and using a new technology for teaching science.

Technology Integration in the Science Curriculum: Instructor and Pre-Service Teachers' Perceptions

In the initial stage of the curriculum enactment, pre-service teachers discussed what technology resources they were familiar with and how they would integrate them in their teaching practices. Pre-service teachers mainly mentioned the use of the Internet as the only technology resource they were familiar with and that they might have considered for integrating in their own teaching practices. Even though pre-service teachers were aware of some problems different schools have, such as the lack of an Internet connection and computers, they believed that their students would be able to engage in computer-based activities. It seemed that this group of pre-service teachers related the use of the Internet to finding "updated information and scientific content knowledge." The idea that the most updated information is posted on the Web meant that pre-service teachers preferred to use web resources for teaching and learning instead of other print materials. A common misconception pre-service teachers had was that information found on the web was reliable and that it was only a matter of selecting the correct keywords to find it.

Equating technology tools with media for communication or Internet resources seemed to be particular to this learning community. Current research and projects funded by the Argentinean government proposed the use of the web and different communication technologies as primary resources for teaching. This might have limited pre-service teachers' examples of available technology resources that they can integrate in their own curriculum proposals. Also, when pre-service teachers were prompted to consider their experiences in different school contexts and the possibilities of using the Internet as a teaching strategy, none of them considered the lack of an Internet connection as a barrier to using this resource. Supporting teachers to evaluate what possible technology tools might be integrated in the science curriculum based on the characteristics of the school context might help teachers in integrating technology. After the enactment of this curriculum material, pre-service teachers have begun to consider the availability of other technology resources, although most of them are not sure how they can actually integrate these tools in their practices.

On the other hand, Mrs. Mancini focused on more general aspects about teaching beliefs and the use of technology. She had similar perceptions about technology and its uses for teaching science as her students; however she related her first impression of the BGuILE software with her understanding of science and common science teaching and learning practices. For her the use of the tool pointed out evident differences between teaching and learning in the Argentinean and American educational systems. She mentioned:

> My first impression when I open the program was, "There is nothing here." I was expecting mostly high amount of text-based information about the finches, what they eat, what they do, how they behave. I have the sensation that the content was missing. Something that it connects with our encyclopedic way of learning... Then, I realized that the software provide mainly with inquiry process, that it was ok I couldn't find a lot of content knowledge information. And I started to think about the difficulties of integrating those inquiry processes to the curricula, and how we related them to everyday activities.

In the final interview Mrs. Mancini elaborated on the advantages the software provided to experience inquiry and how that challenged the current teaching and learning practices in the context of Argentinean education:

> It doesn't matter some students have problems with the content, with their previous conceptions; the software put them in a context where they need to think about hypotheses, collect and analyze data. That was a very important advantage of the technology, and a new way of thinking [about] the use of technology tools in science teaching. Something that was an innovation for the students was that they are not collecting data. In general, when teaching about inquiry the stress is put on data collection. That takes time and usually there is not enough time to analyze those data. Here, the data collection was done, the emphasis was on selecting and analyzing data. The most important learning skills were to "read" data, compare and analyze them, decide what data to select, and what to discard. This is not usually done as part of the learning process, and I believe it is very important.

CONCLUSION

Data gathering through classroom observations and interviews helped identify aspects that contributed to curriculum adaptation and how the materials were changed to fit the local context. Overall, it was found that the instructor's experiences, pedagogical content knowledge, and understanding of her students influenced what aspects of the curriculum the instructor decided to adapt. Mrs. Mancini's reflections and analysis of the innovation in light of the local context were essential to the decisions made on what to change and what to preserve from the curriculum innovation. Leuhman (2002) found that teachers identified and used similar stages in curriculum customization: (a) teachers analyze and critique the innovation based on their perceptions of local needs and characteristics, (b) teachers visualize changes to address those challenges, and (c) teachers plan the implementation of those adaptations. In this case study we found this process of reflective adaptation occurred in several stages and in two contexts. Initial changes in the innovations occurred when the instructor engaged with the curriculum and technology tool. Possible adaptations were revised and verified during the classroom enactment. These reflective processes and instances are shown in Figure 3.3.

When promoting technology and curriculum adaptation it is imperative to reflect on gaps between the new proposal and current practices. Approaching changes in a gradual way (from traditional lecture-based teaching strategies to a combination of traditional and structured inquiry strategies, to the use of more open inquiry approaches) might ensure successful adoption of new practices. It is believed that during these adaptations experienced teachers use their in-depth pedagogical knowledge to determine the modifications that best fit the local context, thus promoting successful curriculum adaptations. Technology and curriculum integration is a process that must consider the current practices and local context to succeed. The challenge for the instructor is to support the integrity of the innovation, while at the same time interconnecting the traditional practices

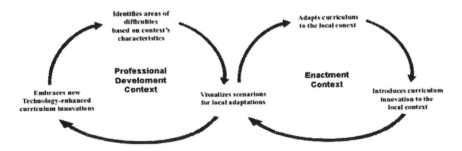

FIGURE 3.3.   Processes of reflective adaptation that occurred when implementing an inquiry technology rich curriculum

with the new proposed enactments. In this case study this challenge generated tensions between the inquiry-based teaching strategies integrated in the new curricula and technology used and current classroom practices. To solve these tensions the instructor felt it necessary to use a guided inquiry approach instead of open inquiry teaching. Moreover, the pre-service teachers' lack of experiences in learning with inquiry influenced how they performed in the activities and consequently prompted changes in the new curriculum enactment.

Experiences during initial engagement with the innovations were important for successful curriculum adaptation. The work cycle Mrs. Mancini and the first author used for her to experience the curriculum activities and technological tool provided the instructor modeling strategies and the opportunity to reflect about possible changes necessary for the curriculum adaptation. This should be taken into account when designing professional development activities, which should include spaces for teachers' reflections about possible instances of curriculum adaptation. It is suggested that curriculum and technology developers consider in the design of materials instances conducive to these reflections, for example integrating educative features in the curriculum proposals (Schneider & Krajcik, 2002).

The instructor's decisions in regard to pedagogical and pedagogical content knowledge become even more important when the context does not provide all the support or necessary resources. For example, when adopting a technology-rich curriculum not only new resources such as computers, but also a context different from the traditional classroom (e.g. the computer laboratory) is used. These prompt changes in how the enactment occurs. In the context analyzed, the amount of resources available prompted major changes in the curriculum integration. In this case the instructor used the proposed strategies combined with the strategies she used every day in her practices. Reflections on the characteristics of the local context and curriculum enactment provided the instructor with opportunities to enhance her practices while promoting the search for alternative teaching and learning strategies. The instructor mentioned possible strategies to consider in the future might be to divide the whole class into groups who will conduct technology-based activities and other tasks at alternate times.

Researchers consider the characteristics of the context one of the barriers for technology integration (Songer et al., 2002). In this case, the new curriculum and technology altered the traditional ways the instructor taught and the social arrangements where the enactment occurred. The curriculum prompted the instructor to make changes in her practice. The instructor's ongoing reflections of her practice were imperative for turning these contextual constraints into an opportunity for enhancing her practice.

The use of the software and these changes provided a positive context for engaging in inquiry teaching and learning. It is felt that additional modifications need to be made to how the tool was used in the methods course in order to try and develop the content understanding of pre-service teachers. This was a useful tool for the methods instructor to uncover misconceptions about the biology content that the pre-service teachers held. These misconceptions were not anticipated and additional instruction needs to occur in order to teach the necessary content.

The project has begun to pilot a new approach for in-service and pre-service professional development that will have implications for future teachers in Argentina. The results showing that pre-service teachers were willing to engage and reflect on the use of technology in their own teaching and learning were encouraging. Much more needs to be done before complex and dynamic relations among technological tools, curricular innovations, and integration in cross-cultural environments can be conceptualized. Similar studies will provide important insights into the factors to be considered when designing and developing technologies and instructional materials that can be adapted into different cultural contexts.

IMPLICATIONS AND IMPORTANCE OF THE RESEARCH

There are few research studies focusing on the design, development, and enactment of technology-rich science curricula in Latin American contexts. This study contributes to research concerning science curriculum development and the integration of technology tools for teaching and learning science in the context of Argentina. The purpose of this study was to examine the modifications a teacher made to a technology-rich curriculum, developed in one context, in order to adopt and enact it in her own classroom. The goals were to gain insight into the reasons of her choices. Mrs. Mancini provided an opportunity to analyze how a teacher, who by her own initiative decides to adopt an innovation, accomplished this activity. Hers is an exemplar for other teachers who might seek to engage in the adoption of technology-rich curriculum innovations developed for other contexts.

This exploratory study has identified a series of pre-service teachers' challenges that might impact their future adaptations and implementation of technology-rich science curricula in their local settings. There is interest in examining if these challenges can be generalized to other pre-service and in-service teachers in Argentina and Latin America. Additional studies to explore these issues are currently being planned.

ACKNOWLEDGMENT

This research was partially funded by the Tinker Field Research Grant Competition, Summer 2005, Center for Latin American and Caribbean Studies, International Studies Bldg. University of Illinois at Urbana-Champaign. We thank Marina Masullo and Nora Valeiras, colleagues from the University of Córdoba, the school teacher, and principal. Without them this research would not have been possible.

REFERENCES

American Association for the Advancement of Science [AAAS]. (1993). *Benchmarks for science literacy*. New York, NY: Oxford University Press.

Barab, S. A. & Leuhmann, A. L. (2003). Building sustainable science curriculum: Acknowledging and accommodating local adaptation. *Science Education, 87*(4), 454–467.

Benz, R. (2000). *Ecology and evolution: Islands of change.* Arlington, VA: NSTA Press.

Brown, A. L. & Campione, J. C. (1996). Psychological theory and the design of innovative learning environments: On procedures, principles and systems. In L. Schauble & R. Glaser (Eds.), *Innovations in learning: New environments for education* (pp. 289–325). Hillsdale, NJ: Erlbaum.

Century, J. R. & Jurist Levy, A. (2004, April). *Sustaining change: A study of nine school districts with enduring programs.* Paper presented at the meeting of the National Association for Research on Science Teaching, Vancouver, B. C.

Cohen, D. K. & Ball, D. L. (1999). *Instruction, capacity, and improvement* (CPRE Research Report Series No. RR–43). Retrieved from http://cpre.org/Publications/rr43.pdf

Crawford, B. A., Zembal-Saul, C., Munford, D., & Friedrichsen, P. (2005). Confronting prospective teachers' ideas of evolution and scientific inquiry using technology and inquiry-based tasks. *Journal of Research in Science Teaching, 42*(6), 613–637.

Cuban, L. (2001). *Oversold and underused: Computers in the classroom.* Cambridge, MA: Harvard University Press.

Dede, C. (Ed.). (1998). *Learning with technology, ASCD yearbook.* Alexandria, VA: Association for Supervision and Curriculum Development.

Dede, C., Honan, J. P., & Peters, L. C. (2005). *Scaling up success. Lessons learned from technology-based educational improvement.* San Francisco, CA: Jossey-Bass.

Fishman, B., Honey, M., Hug, B., Light, D., Marx, R. W., & Carrigg, F. (2003, April). *Exploring the portability of reform: One district's approach to adaptation.* Paper presented at the Annual Meeting of the American Educational Research Association, Chicago, IL.

Fishman, B. & Krajcik, J. S. (2003). What does it mean to create sustainable science curriculum innovations? A commentary. *Science Education, 87*(4), 564–573.

Fishman, B., Marx, R. W., Blumenfeld, P., Krajcik, J. S., & Soloway, E. (2003). *Creating a framework for research on systemic technology innovations.* Evanston, IL: LeTUS Report Series.

Fishman, B. & Pinkard, N. (2001). Bringing urban schools into the information age: Planning for technology vs. technology planning. *Journal of Educational Computing Research, 25*(1), 63–80.

Friedrichsen, P. M., Dana, T. M., Zembal-Saul, C., Munford, D., & Tsur, C. (2001). Learning to teach with technology model: Implementation in secondary science teacher education. *Journal of Computers in Mathematics and Science Teaching, 20*(4), 377–394.

Grant, P. R. (1986). *Ecology and evolution of Darwin's finches.* Princeton, NJ: Princeton University Press.

Hammer, D. (2000). Teacher inquiry. In J. Minstrell & E. H. van Zee (Eds.), *Inquiring into inquiry learning and teaching in science* (pp. 184–215). Washington, DC: American Association for the Advancement of Science.

Hoffman, R. (1996). School technology integration: An automated needs assessment and planning tool. In J. Willis, B. Robin, & D. A. Willis (Eds.), *Technology and teacher education annual* (pp. 1012–1016). Charlottesville, VA: Association for the Advancement of Computing in Education.

Honey, M. & McMillan-Culp, K. (2000, October). *Scale and localization: The challenge of implementing what works.* Paper presented at the Wingspread Conference on Technology's Role in Urban School Reform: Achieving Equity and Quality, Racine, WI.

International Society for Technology in Education [ISTE]. (2003). *National educational technology standards for students (NETS*S).* Retrieved from http://www.iste.org/standards/nets-for-students

Kozak, D. (2004). Las TICs en el aula: El proyecto aulas en red de la ciudad de Buenos Aires. *Revista Iberoamericana de Educación.* Retrieved from http://www.rieoei.org/deloslectores/610Kozak.pdf

Leuhmann, A. L. (2001). *Factors affecting secondary science teachers' appraisal and adoption of technology-rich project-based learning environments.* Unpublished doctoral dissertation, University of Michigan, Ann Arbor, MI.

Leuhmann, A. L. (2002, April). *Understanding the appraisal and customization process of secondary science teachers.* Paper presented at the annual meeting of the American Educational Research Association, New Orleans, LA.

Lin, X. (2001). Reflective adaptation of a technology artifact: A case study of classroom change. *Cognition and Instruction, 19*(4), 395–440.

Linn, M. C. (1997). Learning and instruction in science education: Taking advantage of technology. In D. Tobin & B. J. Fraser (Eds.), *International handbook of science education* (pp. 372–396). Dordrecht, the Netherlands: Kluwer.

Linn, M. C. & Hsi, S. (2000). *Computers, teachers, peers: Science learning partners.* Mahwah, NJ: Lawrence Erlbaum.

McLaughlin, M. W. (1990). The Rand change agent study revisited. *Educational Researcher, 19*(9), 11–16.

National Minister of Culture and Education. (1996). *Los CBC en la escuela de 1er ciclo.* Buenos Aires, Argentina: Ministerio de Cultura y Educacion Press.

National Research Council [NRC]. (1996). *National science education standards.* Washington, DC: National Academic Press.

Otero, V., Johnson, A., & Goldberg, F. (1999). How does the computer facilitate the development of physics knowledge by prospective elementary teachers? *Journal of Education, 181*(2), 57–89.

Otero, V., Peressini, D., Meymaris, K. A., Ford, P., Garvin, T., Harlow, D.,…Mears, C. (2005). Integrating technology into teacher education: A critical framework for implementing reform. *Journal of Teacher Education, 56*(1), 8–23.

Putnam, R. & Borko, H. (2000). What do new views of knowledge and thinking have to say about research on teacher learning? *Educational Researcher, 29*(1), 4–15.

Quintana, C., Reiser, B. J., Davis, E. A., Krajcik, J. S., Fretz, E., Duncan, R. G.,…Soloway, E. (2004). A scaffolding design framework for software to support science inquiry. *The Journal of Learning Sciences, 13*(3), 337–386.

Reiser, B. J., Spillane, J. P., Steinmuller, F., Sorsa, D., Carney, K., & Kyza, E. (2000). Investigating the mutual adaptation process in teachers' design of technology-infused curricula. In B. Fishman & S. O'Connor-Divelbiss (Eds.), *Proceedings of the Fourth International Conference of the Learning Sciences* (pp. 342–349). Mahwah, NJ: Erlbaum.

Reiser, B. J., Tabak, I., Sandoval, W. A., Smith, B. K., Steinmuller, F., & Leone, A. J. (2001). BGuILE: Strategic and conceptual scaffolds for scientific inquiry in biology classrooms. In S. M. Carver & D. Klahr (Eds.), *Cognition and instruction: Twenty -five years of progress* (pp. 263–305). Mahwah, NJ: Lawrence Erlbaum.

Remillard, J. T. (2005). Examining key concepts in research on teachers' use of mathematics curricula. *Review of Educational Research, 75*(2), 211–246.

Sabelli, N. & Dede, C. (2001). *Integrating educational research and practice: Reconceptualizing the goals and process of research to improve educational practice.* Retrieved from http://www.virtual.gmu.edu/SS_research/cdpapers/integrating.htm

Schneider, R. & Krajcik, J. S. (2002). Supporting science teacher learning: The role of educative curriculum materials. *Journal of Science Teacher Education, 13*(2), 167–217.

Snyder, J., Bolin, F., & Zumwalt, K. (1996). Curriculum implementation. In P. W. Jackson (Ed.), *Handbook of research on curriculum* (pp. 402–435). New York, NY: Macmillan.

Songer, N. B., Lee, H.-S., & Kan, R. (2002). Technology-rich inquiry science in urban classrooms: What are the barriers to inquiry pedagogy? *Journal of Research in Science Teaching, 39*(2), 128–150.

Songer, N. B., Lee, H.-S., & McDonald, S. (2003). Research towards an expanded understanding of inquiry science beyond one idealized standard. *Science Education, 87*(4), 490–516.

Spitulnik, M. W. & Linn, M. C. (2006, April). *Professional development and teachers' curriculum customizations: Supporting science in diverse middle schools.* Paper presented at the Meeting of the National Association for Research in Science Teaching, San Francisco, CA.

Squire, K. D., MaKinster, J. G., Barnett, M., Leuhmann, A. L., & Barab, S. A. (2003). Designed curriculum and local culture: Acknowledging the primacy of classroom culture. *Science Education, 87*(4), 468–489.

Stein, M. K., Hubbard, L., & Mehan, H. (2004). Reform ideas that travel far afield: Two cultures of reform in District #2 and San Diego. *Journal of Educational Change, 5*(2), 161–194.

Tabak, I. & Reiser, B. J. (1997, December). *Complementary roles of software-based scaffolding and teacher-student interactions in inquiry learning.* Paper presented at the Conference on Computer Support for Collaborative Learning (CSCL), Toronto, Canada.

Tzou, C., Bruozas, M., Finn, L., Hug, B., & Reiser, B. J. (2003). *Struggle in natural environment: What will survive?* (Unpublished manuscript). Northwestern University, Evanston, IL.

Valeiras, N. & Meneses, J. (September 2005). *Modelo constructivista para la enseñanza de las ciencias en línea.* Paper presented at the VII International Conference of Research in Didactics of Science Education, Granada, Spain.

Weiner, J. (1994). *The beak of the finch: A story of evolution in our time.* New York, NY: Vintage Books.

Wisnudel Spitulnik, M. & Krajcik, J. (1998). Technological tools to support inquiry in a science methods course. *The Journal of Computers in Mathematics and Science Teaching, 17*(1), 63–74.

Yin, R. K. & Campbell, D. T. (2002). *Case study research: Design and methods.* Thousand Oaks, CA: SAGE Publications.

Zembal-Saul, C., Munford, D., Crawford, B. A., Friedrichsen, P., & Land, S. (2002). Scaffolding preservice science teachers' evidence-based arguments during an investigation of natural selection. *Research in Science Education, 32,* 437–463.

Zhao, Y., Pugh, K., Sheldon, S., & Byers, J. L. (2002). Conditions for classroom technology innovations. *Teachers College Record, 104*(3), 482–515.

CHAPTER 4

INTEGRATING FLEXIBLE LANGUAGE SUPPORTS WITHIN ONLINE SCIENCE LEARNING ENVIRONMENTS

Douglas Clark, Brian Nelson, Robert Atkinson, Frank Ramirez-Marin, and William Medina-Jerez

ABSTRACT

Students learn best when instruction builds upon the resources and knowledge that they bring to the classroom. We have developed multilingual scaffolding for English language learners within an online science project. The scaffolding allows students to freely switch the "paragraph" and "support" languages in terms of both written and spoken text. Students can therefore harness their proficiencies with written and spoken English and Spanish as they switch back and forth to make sense of the science concepts and the critical academic English. This chapter presents preliminary analysis of student usage of these supports.

Research on Technology Use in Multicultural Settings, pages 75–105.

INTRODUCTION

While some English language learners (ELLs) have had extensive schooling in their native tongue prior to arriving in the United States, others may have had minimal formal instruction. Despite this fact, it has been argued that all students bring valuable linguistic, social, and scientific resources from their home experiences and cultures to the classroom (Fradd & Lee, 1999; Lee & Fradd, 1998, 2001). Our research group, Technology Opening Diverse Opportunities for Science (TODOS), has worked to develop and test language supports in online learning environments that draw upon these resources to help students learn science while simultaneously building academic English language proficiency. Considerable research suggests that cutting off students entirely from their primary language in the classroom may have negative effects on academic achievement and a variety of affective measures (August & Hakuta, 1997; Ovando, Collier, & Combs, 2003; Valdes, 2001). Instead, research demonstrates the efficacy of allowing students to use their primary languages to support their progress in gaining mastery of their second language as well as critical subject matter competence (Echevarria, Vogt, & Short, 2000; Rosebery, Warren, & Conant, 1992; Rosebery, Warren, Conant, & Hudicourt-Barnes, 1992; Snow, Met, & Genessee, 1989; Warren & Rosebery, 1995). We are therefore working to develop language supports that harness students' meta-linguistic knowledge as the students switch between Spanish and English to support scientific conceptual development and academic language proficiency. Online learning environments provide a promising medium for these supports in terms of potential versatility and wide dissemination of benefits. Our initial work focuses on Spanish-speaking students in Arizona, but our eventual goal focuses on implementing these supports to serve multiple groups of students simultaneously in the highly diverse classrooms across the country and around the world.

BACKGROUND

The United States continues to diversify ethnically and racially. This diversification is especially pronounced among school-age children (García, 2001a). With this growing diversity, promoting educational equity in our classrooms has become a critical challenge and goal for teachers, administrators, and policymakers, as demonstrated in multiple reports by the National Research Council (e.g., Smelser, Wilson, & Mitchell, 2001; Tienda & Mitchell, 2006; Welch-Ross, 2012). Many linguistically diverse students have unsuccessful schooling experiences in which their strengths and needs are not adequately addressed (García, 2001b). Science classes, which are traditionally considered "culture-free," actually often foster inhospitable and intractable environments for diverse learners (Banks, 1993; Lee & Fradd, 1998; Peterson & Barnes, 1996; Warren, Ballenger, Ogonowski, Rosebery, & Hudicourt-Barnes, 2001).

Language learners cannot afford to postpone learning science and other subject areas while they learn English. Not only must students pursue appropriate grade-level science inquiry for its own sake, but supporting language learning through content, such as science, has also been shown to be the most effective means of building academic language proficiency (Chamot & O'Malley, 1994; Mohan, 1979; Short, 1999). With its multiple opportunities for hands-on and visual interaction with academic concepts, science provides rich contexts to support academic language development (Chamot & O'Malley, 1986, 1994; De Avila & Duncan, 1984). Although it requires substantial time and support to develop (Collier, 1987, 1989; Hakuta, Butler & Witt, 2000), academic language proficiency is critical to students' future success in science and throughout school.

Our goal is to explore the integration of students' home language into an online science learning environment to support the students' understanding of science and the surrounding academic English discourse. Our language-support development efforts are grounded in research on: (a) language as a resource in learning and teaching in the content areas, (b) native language (Spanish in the current study) as a resource in learning a second language (English in the current study), (c) scaffolding for reading in a second language, and (d) computer-supported collaborative science learning environments.

Language as a Resource in Learning and Teaching in the Content Areas

Peal and Lambert (1962) suggest that the intellectual experience of acquiring two languages contributes to advantageous mental flexibility, superior concept formation, and a generally diversified set of mental abilities. U.S.-related research with Chicano bilingual children reported by Kessler and Quinn (1985, 1987) supplies empirical support for the emerging understanding that, all things being equal, bilingual children outperform monolingual children on specific measures of cognitive and meta-linguistic awareness. Kessler and Quinn (1987) engaged bilingual and monolingual children in a variety of symbolic categorization tasks that required their attention to abstract, verbal features of concrete objects. Spanish/English, Chicano bilingual children from low socioeconomic status (SES) backgrounds outperformed both low and high SES English monolingual children on these tasks. Such findings are particularly significant given the criticism by MacNab (1979) that many bilingual "cognitive advantage" studies have used only high SES subjects of non-U.S. minority backgrounds. Meta-linguistic advantages have also been reported for low SES Puerto Rican students (Galambos & Hakuta, 1988). Goncz and Kodzepeljic (1991) and Swain and Lapkin (1991) provide overviews of international work in this area. A common finding of these "cognitive flexibility" studies is that bilingual children have mastered the ability to strategically use their understandings of multiple languages to acquire new academic material (García, 2001a). This metalinguistic ability could prove highly advantageous in a technology-driven learning environment that facilitates the access to both languages during the teaching event.

Learning, from a constructivist perspective, involves students building upon and reorganizing prior knowledge in interaction with new ideas and experiences. A student's first language represents a critical component of the student's prior understanding (Cole & Cole, 2001; García, 2001a, 2002; Tharp & Gallimore, 1988). Traditional academic culture in U.S. schools, however, tends to: (a) exclude systematically the histories, languages, and experiences of diverse students from the curriculum, (b) impose a "tracking system" that restricts access to higher-order curricula, and (c) limit access to developmentally appropriate learning configurations (García, 2001b; García & Lee, 2008). While traditional curricular configurations tend to ignore the linguistic resources of diverse students, studies indicate that there are important advantages associated with using students' home language in the curriculum. Curricula incorporating students' home language provide important cognitive and social foundations for students' success in the second language (García, Bravo, Dickey, Chun, & Sun-Iminger, 2002), have a positive effect on measures of academic achievement in school (August & Hakuta, 1997), and promote participation and positive relationships in the classroom (Au & Kawakimi, 1994; Trueba & Wright, 1992).

The National Research Council (August & Hakuta, 1997) reviewed optimal learning conditions for linguistically diverse students and made several recommendations relevant to the design of the learning environment, including: (a) provision of a customized learning environment, (b) use of native language in instruction, (c) a balanced curriculum focusing on both higher order and basic skills, (d) opportunities for practice, (e) systematic student assessment, and (f) staff and parent involvement. Other studies support these findings regarding the importance of incorporating students' linguistic resources into the curriculum (Berman, 1992) and of the use of inquiry and cognitively complex learning (Thomas & Collier, 1995). Rosebery, Warren, and Conant (1992) also support these conclusions and place strong emphasis on the importance of authentic activities to induct students into the discourse of science. García and Lee (2008) similarly suggest focusing on: (a) bilingual/bicultural skills and awareness, (b) high expectations for diverse students, (c) treatment of diversity as an asset, (d) attention to and integration of home cultures/practices, (e) maximizing student interactions across categories of English proficiency, (f) student and teacher input in lesson planning and design, (g) a thematic approach to learning activities with the integration of various skills, and (h) language development though meaningful interactions and communications.

Native Language as a Resource in Learning a Second Language

A number of studies have found that instructional time spent in a student's native language is positively related to academic achievement measures in their adopted second language. For example, using a large national sample, Ramirez,

Pasta, Yuen, Billings, and Ramey (1991) studied children in English-only, late exit, and early exit bilingual programs and found that children could receive substantial amounts of primary language instruction without diminishing their acquisition of English language and reading skills and that doing so allowed them to catch up to their English-speaking peers in English language arts, reading, and math. Meta-analyses (Greene, 1998; Willig, 1985) and two research reviews conducted by the National Research Council (August & Hakuta, 1998; Meyer & Fienberg, 1992) reach similar conclusions.

A limitation of using academic achievement measures to evaluate programs for ELLs, as is commonly done in the program comparison literature, is that such measures are generally not constructed in relation to a theory of language ability (Thompson, DiCerbo, Mahoney, & MacSwan, 2002), leaving us with limited understanding of the independent impact of bilingual instructional programs on the separate constructs of academic achievement and English language development. For instance, learners' test scores may increase due to improved language ability but reflect little actual growth in the academic content areas. Conversely, increases in test scores may reflect greater mastery of content but only minimal second language proficiency, sufficient enough to improve comprehension of test items but not reflective of substantive gains in English language proficiency. Furthermore, while program evaluation research is helpful in setting initial hypotheses, it does not in itself help us understand the specific mechanisms responsible for the observed outcomes. For that, a specific learning theory must be constructed and evaluated.

A well-known, though somewhat controversial, hypothesis that predicts gains in second language ability for children in native language instructional environments is known as the comprehensible input hypothesis (Krashen, 1985, 1996). The central component of a theory of second language learning, the comprehensible input hypothesis proposes that second language learners acquire a new language by understanding messages. Hence, Krashen's model proposes that native language instruction provides a conceptual framework for ELLs, which in turn gives them a conceptual and analytical framework to make English-medium messages comprehensible. Creating second language messages that are comprehensible to learners, in turn, results in acquisition of both vocabulary and grammatical structure because learners' knowledge of the underlying semantic message permits them to analyze the grammatical structure at a subconscious level. Although this suggestion has not previously been tested empirically, theoretical work in first language acquisition, similarly aimed at explaining gaps between language input and learner output, has also proposed that children use "semantic bootstrapping" to decode messages and make complex inferences about underlying linguistic structure. For instance, Grimshaw (1981) and Pinker (1984) provide evidence suggesting that children use their knowledge of word meaning to infer syntactic properties of lexical items.

Scaffolding for Reading in a Second Language

Much of current research into second-language reading centers on the cognitive processes students employ when reading in a second language. A cognitive-processing inspired model of reading comprehension in a second language posits that learners make use of a combination of bottom-up (symbol decoding) and top-down (prediction-making, inference) skills in an effort to construct a mental model representing the meaning of the text as viewed through the filter of an individual's prior knowledge (Mayer, 1997; Plass, 1998; Plass, Chun, & Mayer, 1998). For students who have already mastered the mechanical processes of reading and who have a vast and ever-growing repertoire of their native-language vocabulary, a relatively large proportion of their reading effort in that first language is spent on top-down skills and mental model making. For students reading in their second language, particularly those students with low to moderate proficiency levels in their new language, much of the reading effort is expended on vocabulary acquisition and syntactic decoding (Chun & Plass, 1996). Consequently, these students have less cognitive processing capacity to develop a working mental model and are less likely to comprehend second-language texts in an efficient manner.

To scaffold these low-level processes, learning aids have long been employed in the form of vocabulary supports accompanying second-language texts, in either the native or second language of the readers (Lomicka, 1998; Nation, 1990). The design of vocabulary instructional supports for second-language reading comprehension can be broadly divided into two categories, direct and incidental. Direct vocabulary instruction has the longest history. In fact, for most of history, learning a new language meant learning to translate that language into one's own. Now labeled as the grammar translation method, this type of learning was used as a form of mental exercise. Vocabulary study usually involved memorizing bilingual vocabulary lists (Zimmerman, 1997). The use of bilingual vocabulary lists is alive and well today. This method is tried and true, and researchers still tout its effectiveness (Hatch & Brown, 1995; Laufer, 1997; Nation, 1990).

Direct vocabulary instruction received a blow with the introduction of the communicative approach. This learning method supported the idea that language is meant to be used for communication and that fluency is more important than accuracy. With its focus on communicative competency, the communicative approach saw a swing away from attention to form and, consequently, direct attention to vocabulary. Instead, communicative method supporters promoted the idea that new vocabulary should be learned incidentally, through natural exposure to the language via spoken or written communication (Zimmerman, 1997). The idea of incidental vocabulary learning was taken a step further by Steven Krashen, in his natural approach (Krashen, 1989; Krashen & Terrell, 1983). By getting comprehensible input in the form of large amounts of text, Krashen believed students would naturally pick up new vocabulary through reading.

For second-language learners, the only support they receive under the natural approach while reading a new passage comes from the context of the second-language text itself. The context supposedly enables them to guess the meaning of new words by gathering clues from the text or dialog in which they occur. Students are directly instructed to employ a series of active strategies to guess the meaning of unfamiliar words. While evidence exists for the efficacy of the approach (Nation, 1990), some dispute the usefulness of this "guessing method" (Haynes, 1993; Kelly, 1990; Laufer, 1997). It has been found that students need to know at least 95% of the words in a passage before they can comprehend the text (Hirsh & Nation, 1992; Laufer, 2003). Since basic comprehension of a passage seems to be a prerequisite for contextual guessing, the end result is that second-language learners need to have native-like language proficiency to make use of guessing techniques. Another criticism is that picking up vocabulary by reading or speaking is not very efficient (Groot, 2000).

Consequently, some researchers now advocate a direct focus in vocabulary instruction but within the context of the reading "act." In addition to teaching students guessing strategies, instructional designers/teachers provide glosses with definitions or translations of target words and/or phrases in the margins of a second-language reading text. As the students read, they can look to the margins to get the meaning of new words. There has been much debate over the efficacy of glosses in increasing second-language reading skills and comprehension. Opponents of glosses believe that such aids deprive students of the opportunity to construct an understanding of new vocabulary through contextual guessing and make it too easy for them to get the information they need in their first language without actually having to do the work of learning second-language vocabulary and grammatical structures. In addition, glosses may reduce fluency in second-language reading by leading students to focus on individual word-level decoding (Koren, 1999). Proponents of glosses state that the native-language word or phrase-level translations serve as "just-in-time" scaffolds allowing students to focus on top-down skills without getting bogged down by deficiencies in the second-language vocabulary (Chun & Plass, 1996; Gettys, Imhof, & Kautz, 2001; Lomicka, 1998).

While traditionally, such glosses have consisted of native-language or second-language definitions and grammatical information, more recently they have included pictures, sample sentences, and in computer-based glosses, animations and sound recordings (Roby, 1999). Numerous studies have found that computer-based glossing does help both reading comprehension and vocabulary retention (Cobb, 1997; Laufer & Hill, 2000; Lomicka, 1998; Roby, 1999).

In addition, researchers have investigated what, if any, effect the modality of computer-based vocabulary scaffolds has on reading comprehension. One benefit of text-based glossing delivered by computer is that the definitions can be invisible unless needed, allowing the reader to focus more fully on the main text (Davis, 1989). Also, because computer-based learning environments support multimedia capabilities, vocabulary scaffolds can be designed to incorporate text, audio (spoken translations), images (example photos or figures), and video to aid in learner comprehension (Chun & Plass, 1996, 1997).

The literature is divided on the advisability of so-called "multi-modal" approaches to scaffolding. On one hand, supporters cite the need to account for different learning styles and preferences among learners. The inclusion of scaffolds in multiple formats allows learners to gather information in the form most beneficial to them (Martinez-Lage, 1997). In addition, they cite the benefits of dual-coding in short-term memory through simultaneous presentation of graphical and textual supports (Plass et al., 1998). On the other hand, others have written that multiple modalities presented at once can lead to cognitive overload and a problem of split-attention. For example, Mayer describes how presenting information in two modes that are perceived in the same mental "channel" can tax the cognitive resources of learners (Mayer, 1997; Mayer & Moreno, 1998).

A number of researchers have investigated the intersection between learner selection of language support modalities in a multi-modal learning environment and learning outcomes. Laufer and Hill (2000) studied the relationship between learner selection of support modalities and vocabulary acquisition. ELLs in Hong Kong and Israel participated in a computer-based reading program called "Words in Your Ear" that allowed them to select vocabulary support in a variety of modalities while reading a text passage. Students could choose to read native-language (Chinese) or second-language (English) translations, listen to words pronounced in English, see a word's root, or view "extra information" about the word in English (levels of formality, phonemic transcription, related meanings, etc.). In addition, they could choose to hear the entire passage read aloud in English. Overall, the researchers found that the use of the glosses had a positive effect on vocabulary learning, albeit they found no conclusive evidence that use of any given form of gloss was more effective than any other. For the Israel-based students, mixed use of native-language and second-language text-based glosses led to the greatest word retention, whereas for the Hong Kong students, use of second-language definitions was most effective. In addition, learner choices between the Israel- and Hong Kong-based students differed. Those in Hong Kong chose second-language definitions most often, and those in Israel chose native-language translations most often. Both groups rarely selected word roots, "extra information," or audio recordings of definitions or of the entire passage (Laufer & Hill, 2000).

A similar study that investigated student preference for learning support modalities also found that the majority of the English-speaking students in a French language class chose to view native-language (English) translations of single words and expressions versus other types (Davis & Lyman-Hager, 1997). On the other hand, other researchers have found that ELLs prefer video-based glosses over text or audio glosses (Al-Seghayer, 2001; Sakar & Ercetin, 2005). In addition, low-proficiency second-language readers have been found to make use of multiple-modality supports (text, graphics, and sound), while higher-proficiency readers are more likely to stick with a single form of support (native-language or second-language text-based glosses) (Gasigitamrong, 2003; Hegelheimer & Tower, 2004). For example, Gasigitamong (2003) conducted an extensive study of how second-language readers used multi-modal glosses. A group of American students studying the Thai language completed a computer-based reading program featuring glosses with text-based native-language translations and second-language definitions, images, and audio. Gasigitamong found that low- and high-proficiency students both used native-language text-based translations most often. Low-proficiency readers used second-language audio glosses twice as much as high-proficiency students, while high-proficiency students used second-language text-based glosses twice as much as low-proficiency students (Gasigitamong, 2003). In our current study, we further investigate the patterns of interaction students undertake with multimedia glosses in the context of second-language reading passages.

Research on Computer-Supported Collaborative Learning Environments to Support Science Learning

Online science learning environments provide potentially powerful vehicles for this pedagogy because of the versatility of technology. In theory, we should be able to incorporate meta-linguistic supports for multiple groups of diverse learners within a single environment to allow multiple groups of learners to access linguistically-appropriate supports in the same classroom simultaneously. While our initial work focuses on Spanish-speaking students in Arizona, our eventual goal focuses on implementing these supports for multiple groups to better serve students in the highly diverse classrooms across the country and around the world.

Technology has already been harnessed to create structured environments to support science inquiry learning (e.g., Edelson, Gordin, & Pea, 1999; Linn & Hsi, 2000). Within the realm of science learning environments, collaborative online learning environments reflect the emerging computer-supported collaborative learning (CSCL) paradigm (Koschmann 1996) and offer great potential for language learners. CSCL reflects social constructivism (Bauersfeld, 1995; Cobb, 1994), Soviet socio-cultural theory (Cole & Engestrom, 1993; Leont'ev, 1974; Vygotsky, 1978), and situated cognition (Brown, Collins, & Duguid, 1989; Greeno, 1989; Lave, 1988). CSCL-based collaborative online learning environments typically involve content resources or materials, activities or assignments, assessments, collaboration tools (e.g., e-mail, discussion board, calendar, chat room, videoconferencing), information about participants (e.g., bios, webpages), representation tools (e.g., simulation tools, modeling tools, shared whiteboards, shared virtual workspace), help features (e.g., systems-based or human tutor/instructor), and search tools (Spitulnick, Bouillion, Rummel, Clark, & Fischer, 2003). Examples of these collaborative online learning environments include Munic Net-based learning in Computer Science (MUNICS) (Troendle, Mandl, Fischer, Koch, Schlichter, & Teege, 1999), Knowledge Forum (Scardamalia & Bereiter, 1996), Knowledge Master (Erlach, Hausmann, Mandl, & Trillitzsch, 2000; Erlach, Reinmann-Rothmeier, Neubauer, & Mandl, 2001; Winkler & Mandl, 2002), and the Web-Based Inquiry Science Environment (WISE) (Linn, Clark, & Slotta, 2003). These environments not only provide rich visualizations and contexts but also provide powerful opportunities for the social supports and discourse that sheltered instruction researchers consider critical in scaffolding academic language development (Chamot & O'Malley, 1994; Johnson, Johnson, Holubec, & Roy, 1984; Kagan, 1986).

THE WOLVES PROJECT: INTEGRATING LANGUAGE SUPPORTS INTO AN ONLINE SCIENCE LEARNING ENVIRONMENT

This chapter discusses our early work on developing language supports within a week-long project about wolf ecology and management. For purposes of brevity, we refer to this project simply as "Wolves." The work represents the integration of our participation in two different grants funded by the National Science Foundation. The first is a Center for Learning and Teaching grant named Technology Enhanced Learning in Science (TELS). The second is a Mathematics Science Partnership grant named Project Pathways. Much of the technology for the Wolves project draws on the work of the TELS grant and its predecessors, including the modeling components and some of the original source material. Our participation in the Pathways grant focuses more specifically on the language supports.

The Core Online Learning Environment

The Web-based Inquiry Science Environment (WISE) engages students in the intentional process of diagnosing problems, critiquing experiments, distinguishing alternatives, planning investigations, researching conjectures, searching for information, constructing models, debating with peers, and forming coherent arguments about science (see http://wise.berkeley.edu). The TELS grant, and its predecessor grants, conducted the research and development of WISE. Students work collaboratively in WISE projects, actively using materials and software from the World Wide Web. This environment allows researchers and teachers to organize Internet resources into pedagogically useful and appropriate inquiry projects for students. To promote knowledge integration, WISE projects help students engage in sustained reasoning, monitor their own progress, and identify new questions and opportunities to apply their knowledge. WISE partnerships have created projects on a broad range of topics, including the causes of declining amphibian populations, responses to the worldwide threat of malaria, decisions concerning genetic modification of foods, design of houses for desert climates, design of rainforest investigations, critique of environmental plans, analysis of water quality, and interpretation of conflicting claims about life on Mars. Approximately 1,000 teachers have run WISE projects with approximately 90,000 students. The WISE library includes over 50 projects that have undergone classroom testing and demonstrated an impact on knowledge integration.

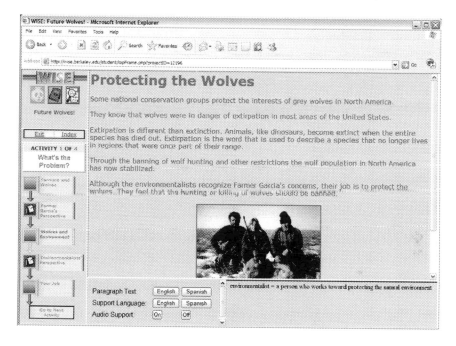

FIGURE 4.1. Screenshot of the WISE environment software. Note. The navigation bar that the students use to move between steps and activities is shown on the left. A content page with language supports is shown in the main window.

WISE incorporates many tools and features, including reflection notes, cognitive hints, online discussions, causal maps, data visualizations, and the Sense-Maker argument editor. Teachers select from a library of projects that includes lesson plans, assessments, scoring rubrics, connections to standards, and opportunities to customize the projects. Teachers can monitor and grade student work, provide formative feedback during a project run, and manage their student accounts. WISE (see Figure 4.1) incorporates an inquiry map to communicate the patterns that students follow to investigate a topic. The map enables students to work individually and independently on their projects, rather than constantly asking the teacher for guidance on what to do next (Edelson et al., 1999; Feldman, Konold, & Coulter, 2000; Linn & Hsi, 2000). WISE incorporates prompts to help students reflect as well as monitor their progress. WISE also includes hints and evidence pages designed to add ideas about the topic the student is investigating.

Specialized Scaffolding with the Wolves Project

The TODOS research group has developed software incorporating specialized language supports. We developed this software to operate in conjunction with

WISE. As discussed, our research focuses on supporting science and language learning by giving students meta-linguistic choices in terms of the language of materials and allowing them to shift back and forth as they study science in an online learning environment. There is significant debate in the bilingual education community about the optimal format for primary language delivery with respect to the advantages of previewing in one language and reviewing in another, alternating languages, or using both languages concurrently (August & Hakuta, 1997; Ovando et al., 2003). To investigate this question, our future research will be able to control when and how language-switching between the first and second language is made available. The current study, however, focuses on the default condition, which allows students to switch whenever they choose. We outline the initial language supports under investigation below:

- Students choose and freely switch the language in which the paragraph text is displayed, which we refer to as the "paragraph language."
- When students move the mouse cursor over a word or phrase in the paragraph text, a small textbox "pops up" immediately above it with that same word or phrase in the "support language" that the student has chosen. In addition, an audio file of that same text is played in the support language. Students choose and freely switch the support language. Note that the support language can be different from, or the same as, the paragraph language. This allows students to hear the pronunciations of the paragraph text or translations of it.
- When students click the mouse on a word or short phrase in the paragraph text, they receive a short definition with examples in the support language at the bottom of the screen.

Our goal involves allowing students to harness their understanding of both spoken and written Spanish and English and bootstrap their understanding of both the content and the languages while minimizing cognitive load. We hope to show that providing students with these nuanced language switching capabilities, rather than students defaulting only to Spanish, will encourage students to freely switch between Spanish and English to build stronger understanding in science while producing more sophisticated academic English in their project artifacts.

Logging Capabilities

At the core of this research is a logging tool that we have developed as part of the specialized supports described above. The logging tool tracks the time and occurrence of: (a) the opening and closing of each page that includes our language supports, (b) all switches made by the student between English and Spanish for either the paragraph or support languages, (c) each word or phrase that the student "mouses over" to get the audio files and text pop-ups in the support language, and

(d) each word or phrase that the student "clicks" to get the extended definitions in the support language.

The Curriculum

The Wolves project requires four to six hours of class time. The project is intended for middle school. The students in the current analysis investigated wolves for a total of six hours spread over four class periods. The project involves four major activities: (1) an introduction to the nature of the challenges involved in balancing the needs of humans, wolves, and the ecosystem; (2) an investigation of wolves' role within the ecosystem; (3) an investigation of current management plans; and (4) the development of a new management plan to better balance the needs of wolves, humans, and ecosystems in the form of a letter to the governor.

The first activity of the project presents the perspectives of various participants in the wolf management controversy. Students focus particularly on the perspectives of farmers and environmentalists regarding the problem of wolf attacks on domestic animals. The second activity introduces students to the basic biology of wolves, food chains, and predator-prey relationships. The third activity investigates wolf management options and strategies that have been implemented by different states. The fourth and final activity focuses on a culminating project that engages students in writing a letter to the governor outlining a management plan that they believe best serves the needs of wolves, humans, and the environment.

Students in the Current Study

The data for this study were collected in an eighth-grade classroom in an inner city school in Arizona. Eleven students of varying levels of English proficiency completed the Wolves project under the supervision of their science teacher and one of the authors of this chapter. Ninety-eight percent of the population at the school qualifies for free or reduced lunch, and 75% of the students at this school are Hispanic. The students' English proficiency was benchmarked using their scores on the Stanford English Language Proficiency test (SELP).

Out of the eleven students, nine were bilingual (English-Spanish) of varying levels of English proficiency, one was a monolingual native English speaker, and one was a monolingual native Spanish speaker who had arrived in the U.S. just two months before the study was conducted. According to the official school designations, five students were classified as ELLs and six were classified as English-proficient students. Ten of the eleven students were Hispanic and one student was Caucasian. Eight out of the eleven students were eighth graders and three were seventh graders, all of them ranging from twelve to fourteen years of age. Four of the students were female and seven were male. All of the students were participants of the fall inter-session 2005.

PRELIMINARY FINDINGS

Our investigation focuses on three potential concerns:

1. Do students actually use the language supports?
2. How do they use the supports?
3. Do bilingual students engage with the material solely in their native language?

The first and second issues are common in research and development for scaffolding and supports in learning environments. Will students actually use the supports? Or will they activate the supports out of curiosity a few times at the beginning of the project and then ignore them for the rest of the project?

The third issue focuses on the students' choices of languages. The ongoing debate between proponents of English-only and dual-language instruction accentuates the importance of this issue. Opponents of dual-language instruction often suggest that providing students access to their native language will result in the

TABLE 4.1. Data from the Logging Tool about Student Usage Patterns in Each Activity and Step

Curriculum Segment			Event Occurrence Frequency				Total Time in Each Language			
Activity	Step	Number of Pages	Mouse Over	Short Definition	Support Language	Paragraph Language	Paragraph Language English	Spanish	Support Language English	Spanish
1	Step 1	1	37	9	6	5	1:00:18	0:33:48	1:00:18	0:43:34
	Step 2	1	29	3	3	7	0:14:53	0:01:02	0:14:53	0:04:05
	Step 3	1	44	1	4	1	0:16:55	0:00:38	0:16:55	0:00:38
	Step 4	1	5			1	0:00:03	0:00:09	0:00:03	0:00:28
2	Step 1	3	290	29	8	26	1:30:09	0:12:13	1:30:09	0:28:16
	Step 2	4	372	32	6	12	2:47:58	0:11:30	2:47:58	0:34:09
	Step 3	3	696	47	6	16	4:22:39	0:34:38	4:22:39	1:01:18
	Step 4	4	533	58	7	18	4:50:29	0:06:02	4:50:29	0:47:12
3	Step 1	3	741	81	8	9	7:59:49	0:02:49	7:59:49	0:09:37
	Step 2	3	534	134	19	23	6:03:17	0:01:10	6:03:17	0:01:21
	Step 3	2	111	21	1	3	1:34:50	0:01:20	1:34:50	0:12:19
	Step 4	3	41	2			0:20:35		0:20:35	
Totals			3433	417	68	121	31:01:55	1:45:19	31:01:55	4:02:57

Note. Activity 4 is not included because Activity 4 focuses on writing the letter to the governor and therefore doesn't include the language supports (although the students returned to the first three activities during this activity to gather further information).

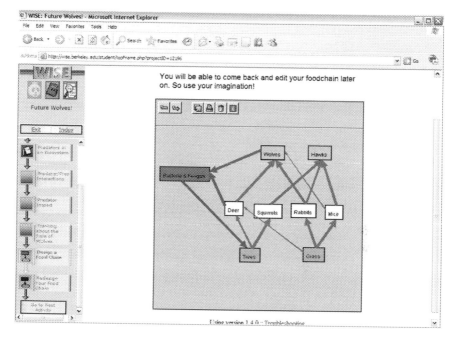

FIGURE 4.2. The Food Chain tool is one of the many tools native to the WISE environment. Note. Students use it to create food chains or other causal maps.

students engaging solely in their native language, rather than in English, resulting in the students making little progress in developing proficiency with English. Our investigation therefore contributes to the resolution, or at least clarification, of this debate.

General Usage Patterns

To give a sense of the overall usage of the different functionalities, Table 4.1 presents the frequency of each event category during each step of the first three activities. The fourth activity is not included in Table 4.1 because that activity focused on writing the letter rather than introducing new content. Our language supports therefore do not play a prominent role in the fourth activity itself. Students went back to the first three activities during the fourth to gather information, but the logging tool would count those actions as occurring within those respective activities. In reading Table 4.1, each row represents an activity step that incorporates our language supports. Other types of steps native to the WISE environment, such as note-taking steps or food chain creation steps (see Figures 4.2 and 4.3), do not incorporate our language supports and are therefore not included in Table 4.1. In analyzing Table 4.1, it is important to note the number of pages of content

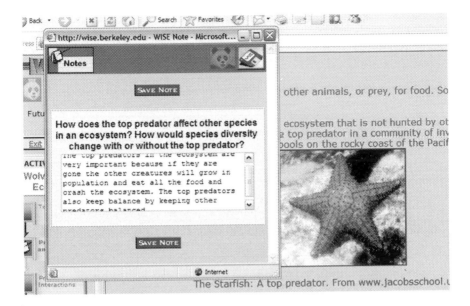

FIGURE 4.3. Students synthesize their thoughts about the concepts in the project using note taking windows.

associated with each step. Each page of content involves approximately 10 lines of text with a total of 100–150 words (see Figure 4.1 for a sample page).

Table 4.1 demonstrates that the answer to our first question is that students clearly use the supports. Overall, the "mouse-over" was the most frequent event, while clicking for a short definition was the second most frequent event, switching the paragraph language was the third most frequent event, and switching the support language was the fourth most frequent event (see Table 4.1). Mouse-over event frequencies include the mouse-over events necessary to trigger the short definitions. More detail about each of these functionalities is discussed in the paragraphs below.

Short Definition Functionality

The short definition functionality was used heavily by students in both Spanish and English. The short definition functionality requires intentionality to the extent that the students must click on words in the text in order to receive the definitions. When interviewed, several students reported that it was "useful to get the meaning of the words I didn't know...if you don't know the meaning of a word it [the content] won't make sense to you." During the course of the project many concepts related to the biology and management of the wolves in North America were introduced to the participants, which potentially resulted in students' frequent use of the short definition functionality in the second and third activities.

Paragraph Language Functionality

The paragraph language functionality allows students to actively switch the language of the default text (English) to Spanish in the paragraphs. Students appear to have multiple reasons for switching languages. Curiosity about the tool or the languages most likely drove some of these events, but based on the interviews, data analysis, and observations, it seems clear that the participants used the tool not only out of curiosity but in a purposeful manner. Sometimes this involved "making sense" of the content of a particular activity. The utility for new English learners is clear; "Usé español porque no hablo inglés" (I used Spanish because I don't speak English). Other students explained, "Fue útil cambiar el idioma... pude entender más" (It was helpful to switch the language... I could understand more). Students chose Spanish for the paragraph text for 15.1% of the total time on the project. This fact might suggest that the paragraph text tool might have provided students with support for understanding or clarification during the activities; nonetheless, most students did not rely on Spanish-only to complete the project.

Support Language Functionality

The support language functionality includes both audio as well as text "pop ups." The audio component of the support language functionality was useful for students. One student explained, "It was useful to learn how to pronounce a word I didn't know." Another student stated that "It was useful only for the words that I couldn't read or pronounce." When asked about this functionality, another student mentioned, "Me gusto que podía escuchar en español y leer en ingles...si escuchaba una palabra [en Espanol] yo la leía en inglés" (I liked [the fact that] I could listen to it [the word/text] in Spanish and read it in English...if I listened to a word [in Spanish] I read it in English). Another student explained, "Si, porque si no quería leer pues solo escuchaba" (Yes [the tool was useful], because if I didn't want to read I just listened to it [the text/word]).

In contrast to the audio component of the support language functionality, the "pop-up text" component was not considered as useful. In fact, none of the students recalled using the tool two months later; "No me acuerdo de eso" (I don't remember that). Ideally, the "pop-up text" tool would provide students with visual assistance in the form of a written translation of the text when the support language differs from the paragraph language. Low recall by the students about the pop-ups may spring from technology limitations. Ideally the audio and the pop-ups would be triggered simultaneously upon a mouse-over event. In the current version, however, older computers don't necessarily provide the two simultaneously. It is possible that the students moused over the text fast enough for the audio files to be triggered but not long enough for the pop-ups to show up on the screen because once the cursor moves away the pop-ups are programmed to disappear. These issues will have to be further analyzed to see if modifications to the tool can be implemented to improve its functioning.

Need for Language Supports in the Instructions for the Non-Content Steps

Finally, some of the participants expressed various degrees of difficulty in terms of understanding the navigation and instructions within the project. The "navigation bar" (shown in Figure 4.1) allows students to browse through the different activities and steps of the project. While the navigation bar is relatively straightforward for native English-speakers familiar with computers, it is part of the parent environment and therefore does not include our translation capabilities. Therefore, the instructions (if any) and the title of the activities portrayed in the navigation bar of a given activity remain in English for the duration of the project. As a result, students who are ELLs rely heavily on teachers and/or assistants to become acquainted with the project's environment. Clearly we need to develop supports for students with lower technology and/or English familiarities.

Increasing Frequency of Usage Over Time

Encouragingly, use of the mouse-over and short definition functionalities increased in the second and third activities even when accounting for the increased number of pages per step (the steps in the second and third activities involve more pages of content as described in Table 4.1). If the students were merely activating the functionalities due to novelty, we would expect higher usage in the first activity followed by a decline in usage over the course of the project. Instead we see consistent and increasing usage over time. One explanation of the increased usage is that students encountered increasing amounts of unknown terminology as the difficulty of the content in activities two and three increased in comparison to activity one. Another interpretation is that the students began to understand the affordances of the functionalities and so increased their usage as the project progressed.

Switching between English and Spanish

Students used Spanish functionality most heavily during the first two days of the project (Table 4.2). Spanish usage on day one accounted for 26.7% of the total time for paragraph language and 8.5% for support language. Spanish usage on day two accounted for 8.6% of the total time for paragraph language and 10.3% for support language. Their most heavy usage of Spanish coincided with activities one ("What's the problem?") and two ("Wolves and the Ecosystem"). The higher usage of Spanish at the beginning of the project (activity one) might simply indicate curiosity in hearing the Spanish. As one student explained, "I used Spanish to see how it [the tool] worked…whenever you guys [the teacher, aids, and investigator] reminded us about it [the availability of the tool]." It is also possible that the students used Spanish heavily during day one and day two in order to make sense of the content to which they were being exposed. As another student explained, "Fue útil cambiar el idioma…pude entender más" (It was helpful to switch the language… I could understand more). Another student explained, "Usé

TABLE 4.2. Percentage of Time in Spanish and English by Day and Student

	Student	Paragraph Text		Support Language	
Day	Name	English	Spanish	English	Spanish
Day 1	Julio	82.3%	17.7%	99.5%	0.5%
	Pedro	90.9%	9.1%	77.9%	22.1%
	Graciela	50.6%	49.4%	79.9%	20.1%
	Maria	62.2%	37.8%	79.5%	20.5%
	Enrique	73.3%	26.7%	78.4%	21.6%
	Jose	81.8%	18.2%	98.7%	1.3%
	Ezra	80.3%	19.7%	99.2%	0.8%
	Pepe	75.1%	24.9%	99.9%	0.1%
	Chuy	81.7%	18.3%	100.0%	0.0%
	Maria	49.2%	50.8%	99.1%	0.9%
	Isabel	83.5%	16.5%	99.7%	0.3%
Subtotal		73.3%	26.7%	91.5%	8.5%
Day 2	Julio	93.0%	7.0%	90.5%	9.5%
	Pedro	88.6%	11.4%	87.9%	12.1%
	Graciela	84.9%	15.1%	84.8%	15.2%
	Maria	88.0%	12.0%	85.6%	14.4%
	Enrique	91.9%	8.1%	91.1%	8.9%
	Jose	91.7%	8.3%	91.6%	8.4%
	Ezra	91.7%	8.3%	87.6%	12.4%
	Pepe	96.0%	4.0%	89.9%	10.1%
	Chuy	89.3%	10.7%	87.9%	12.1%
	Maria	90.4%	9.6%	90.1%	9.9%
	Isabel	100.0%	0.0%	100.0%	0.0%
Subtotal		91.4%	8.6%	89.7%	10.3%
Day 4	Julio	92.6%	7.4%	100.0%	0.0%
	Pedro	84.3%	15.7%	100.0%	0.0%
	Graciela	87.4%	12.6%	100.0%	0.0%
	Maria	93.7%	6.3%	100.0%	0.0%
	Enrique	82.6%	17.4%	100.0%	0.0%
	Jose	85.3%	14.7%	99.5%	0.5%
	Ezra	97.3%	2.7%	100.0%	0.0%
	Pepe	96.4%	3.6%	100.0%	0.0%
	Chuy	82.7%	17.3%	100.0%	0.0%
	Maria	88.4%	11.6%	100.0%	0.0%
	Isabel	100.0%	0.0%	100.0%	0.0%
Subtotal		89.9%	10.1%	100.0%	0.0%
Total		84.9%	15.1%	93.7%	6.3%

Note. Day 3 is not included due to a technical issue with the logging tool.

Español porque no hablo Inglés" (I used Spanish because I don't speak English). During day four, students worked to complete activity four, which focused on writing the letter rather than introducing new content. Instead they were working to synthesize what they had learned in activities one through three. Activity four therefore does not include any content language supports (because there is no content in activity four per se). Students were free to go back and review information that they considered necessary in order to write their letter. Table 4.2 suggests that students did return to the first three activities and review information about the project in order to write the letter because almost all of the students used the paragraph text tool in Spanish (10.1% of total time in day four). On the whole, interactions using Spanish accounted for the 15.1% of the total time for the paragraph language and 6.3% of the time for the support language.

Interestingly, all students, including the presumably monolingual native English student, showed interactions with the Spanish versions. This raises the interesting question of influences that Spanish-speaking peers and communities may have on monolingual English speakers in terms of their curiosity. Another interesting question focuses on the relatively low overall usage of the Spanish functionalities in terms of whether the English-only instruction influences or intimidates non-native English speakers to hide or limit the use of their native language.

Portraits of Individual Students

Table 4.2 presents the amounts of time spent in Spanish and English each day by each student (data on day three is not included due to a technical issue with the logging tool). To provide more insight into these numbers, we now present three of the students in a bit more detail. These students were chosen to represent a range of English language proficiency according to the SELP. All of the students described in the paragraphs below were eighth graders. It should also be noted that this was the first time participating in Web-based science instruction for all of the students.

Maria

Maria is fourteen. Both of her parents are Mexican immigrants. She was born in the U.S., where she has spent most of her life, except for two years that she lived in Mexico. Although her first language is Spanish, she is proficient in both English and Spanish. She uses English at home when interacting with family members (her stepfather is a non-Hispanic English-monolingual) and Spanish when interacting with close friends and school friends. She mentioned that she often gets assistance from her stepfather when doing homework. She owns a computer, which she uses when doing school work.

Maria is therefore proficient in English, uses primarily English at home, and receives formal instruction in English. In spite of her English proficiency, Maria took advantage of the Spanish functionality within the project, particularly in terms of the short definitions. On the first day, Maria's usage of Spanish functionalities totaled 50.8% of the time for paragraph language and 0.9% for support language. On the second day, Maria's usage of Spanish functionalities totaled 9.6% for paragraph language and 9.9% for support language. On the fourth day, Maria's usage of Spanish functionalities totaled 11.6% for paragraph language and 0.0% for support language. She appeared to use her first language in order to make sense or clarify vocabulary, concepts, and terminology included in the content of the project. When interviewed about the language tool, she stated "The language tool was useful to understand words I didn't know … [by] clicking on the word and getting its definition and learn what it meant." In addition she stated that "it [the language tool] was useful to learn how to pronounce a word I didn't know."

Pepe

Pepe is a 13-year-old Mexican immigrant who arrived in Arizona about two months prior to the implementation of the study. He is native speaker of Spanish. Spanish is spoken at home. Neither of his parents speaks English and therefore cannot assist him with his school work although, according to Pepe, one of his brothers assists him occasionally. Pepe was categorized by the SELP test at a "pre-emergent" English proficiency level.

During an interview, Pepe was asked whether or not it had been difficult for him to understand the instructions that were part of the project. Pepe stated "Si, poco por que estaban en inglès y no en español" (Yes, a little bit because they [the instructions] were in English and not in Spanish). The Web-based technology was difficult for this student as well. When asked whether Pepe had a computer at home, Pepe stated "No, no tengo computadora en casa" (No, I don't have a computer at home). Similarly, when asked the question "Can you type?" he affirmed "No, no escribo rápido…escribo despacio" (No, I don't. I don't type fast…I type slowly). When asked, he explained that he does not consider himself "good at using computers."

Pepe showed low Spanish usage for the paragraph and support language functionalities considering his low English proficiency. On the first day, Pepe's usage of Spanish functionalities totaled 24.9% for paragraph language and 0.1% for support language. On the second day, Pepe's usage of Spanish functionalities totaled 4.0% for paragraph language and 10.1% for support language. On the fourth day, Pepe's usage of Spanish functionalities totaled 3.6% for paragraph language and 0.0% for support language. When using the English text and Spanish support tool, Pepe showed a lower level of Spanish usage than that of his classmates with advanced and/or intermediate English proficiency levels. This suggests that Pepe's lower familiarity with computers may have diminished the utility that he might have derived from the supports considering his low English proficiency. We expected him to make much higher use of the language tools in Spanish.

Pedro

Pedro is thirteen and was born in Arizona. His parents are Mexican immigrants. He has lived his whole life in Arizona. His first language is Spanish, which is also the language spoken at home. His English proficiency is intermediate as indicated by the SELP test. Presumably due to the home/school language difference, Pedro mentioned that he does not receive any assistance from his parents when doing school work. When asked about his use of computers, Pedro stated that he has one at home, which he usually uses to look up information to do his homework. He also mentioned that he feels comfortable using computers.

Pedro used the Spanish versions of the paragraph language and support language functionalities for a small percentage of days one and two. On the first day, Pedro's usage of Spanish functionalities totaled 9.1% for paragraph language and 22.1% for support language. On the second day, Pedro's usage of Spanish functionalities totaled 11.4% for paragraph language and 12.1% for support language. On the fourth day, Pedro's usage of Spanish functionalities totaled 15.7% for paragraph language and 0.0% for support language. English appeared to be the preferred language to complete the project even though he is bilingual (Spanish-English) and has an intermediate proficiency level. When asked about the usefulness of switching languages to obtain relevant information for the project, Pedro stated the following: "It (switching languages) wasn't helpful because I didn't use much Spanish. I preferred using English to do the project…I do my school stuff in English." Pedro appeared to take pride in his English proficiency.

Students' Reactions to the Environment

Interviews revealed that most of the participants liked having access to language supports in the Wolves project. Most of the participants stated that they encountered little difficulty accessing and completing the project. A few students, however, stated that even though they enjoyed working on the project, they did not like computers very much. Most of these students said that they did not have a computer at home.

The interviews highlighted a number of specific needs served by the language tool. At one end of the spectrum, when students whose English language proficiency was limited or intermediate were asked if it was useful to be able switch between Spanish and English, the students often explained that "Fue útil cambiar el idioma… pude entender más" (It was useful to switch languages…I could understand more) and "Si, porque yo hablo español y entiendo mejor en Español" (Yes, because I speak Spanish and I understand better in Spanish).

At the other end of the spectrum, when English-proficient students were asked whether or not it was helpful to be able to switch between Spanish and English, they responded by stating "it wasn't helpful because I didn't use much Spanish" or "No, I hardly ever used it [the tool]… I used the language tool just out of curiosity to see how it worked and when you guys reminded students about it." However, when the same students were asked whether it was useful to listen to the information in English, the students often responded with explanations such as: "It was useful to learn how to pronounce a word I didn't know"; "Yes [it was useful] a couple of times when I didn't know how to pronounce the word"; and "It was useful only for the words I couldn't read or say...pronounce."

When interviewed about the activities, many of the students acknowledged that "constructing the food chain on the computer" had been the activity they liked the most, even though some perceived it as challenging and somewhat difficult. Similarly, many of the students acknowledged enjoying writing the letter to the governor even though many of them found it very challenging. As one student explained, "The letter was the hardest part of the project because you had to know what to put in it...it was difficult to think...organize the ideas." As another student stated, "Writing the letter was the most difficult part of the project because it was difficult to come up with ideas... but that was fun." The students' expression of enjoyment for the most conceptually challenging aspects of the project reinforces calls for ELLs to receive challenging age-appropriate conceptual content regardless of their English proficiency (e.g., August & Hakuta, 1997; García, 2001b, 2002; García & Lee, 2008; Thomas & Collier, 1995).

The largest difficulty mentioned by a few students related to difficulties understanding instructions during the activities of the project. When asked in an interview if it was "difficult to understand what you had to do," one of the students stated that "[the instructions were] somewhat difficult to understand...it wasn't clear what I had to do." Another student mirrored this sentiment, "Sí, poco por que estaban en Inglés y no en Español" (Yes, a little since they were in English and not in Spanish). In the current version of the project, only the Wolves-specific content steps include translation functionality. Other steps native to the parent WISE software, such as note-taking steps and food chain creation steps (Figures 5.2 and 5.3), do not include these translation capabilities. Understandably, language issues are not limited solely to content. We will address these issues in future research.

CONCLUSIONS

Based on the analysis described in the previous sections, the language support tools appear to provide positive pedagogical value as outlined in the following paragraphs.

Students evidenced purposeful interactions with the language support tools. The data analysis of usage in terms of "short definition" clicks, "mouse-overs" for audio and text pop-ups, and language switches (switches between Spanish and English for the support and paragraph languages) suggest that students interacted with the language tool in a purposeful manner. The increased frequency of usage in the second and third activities further suggests that student usage was not driven solely by curiosity.

ELLs do not default solely to Spanish. None of the participants identified as bilingual interacted with the tools using only one of the languages that they speak

(English or Spanish). Interestingly, the cumulative time (15.1% for paragraph language and 6.3% for support language) that the participants spent interacting with the tool in Spanish in this particular study suggests that providing students access to their native language does not necessarily result in the students engaging with the content material solely in their native language. Instead it appears that in this case the functionalities provided useful access to the content and second language for the students.

The language supports helped English-proficient and English-monolingual students. The data analysis and interviews suggest that English-proficient speakers, including the monolingual speaker of English, may have used the tool in order to make sense of the content and, in some cases, listen to the pronunciation of English words with which they were not familiar. This finding suggests the utility of language supports for a range of students extending beyond the ELL classification.

The project's technology and environment appear appealing for the students. Most of the participants stated during interviews that they enjoyed the experience of interacting with the Wolves project and the language supports through a computer. During interviews, the participants referred to images, interactive tools, language supports, the learning environment, and the content itself as attractive components of the project. This may be because this project involved conceptually richer content than is often provided to ELLs. This finding supports the importance of providing age-appropriate conceptually-rich content as opposed to the unfortunate practice of providing content that lowers the conceptual grade-level along with the English proficiency grade-level (e.g., August & Hakuta, 1997; García, 2001b; García & Lee, 2008; Thomas & Collier, 1995).

There is a need to integrate language and computer-use supports for all aspects of the project. Understanding instructions was difficult for some students. These language issues with instructions were further complicated in some cases by a lack of familiarity with computers. As a result, students heavily relied on teachers and/or assistants to become acquainted with the project's environment in terms of the use of the navigation bar and language tools. It is clearly important to provide more universal supports both in terms of language and technology.

FINAL THOUGHTS

As our schools diversify ethnically and linguistically, instructional approaches must undergo a concomitant metamorphosis to better serve the changing demographics. The efficacy of approaches that allow second language learners to use their native tongue in educational settings shows great promise. Internet-based learning environments, such as WISE, also show promise for diverse students. Our preliminary findings suggest the potential affordances of combining the two.

Our tentative findings support claims that first- and second-language supports provide valuable resources for learning in content areas such as science. The language supports allowed students to marshal their understanding, both spoken and written, in English and Spanish, to engage with unfamiliar concepts and terminology. Researchers contend that this approach is successful because enhanced conceptualization results when students are given the chance to use both their native and second languages (e.g., August & Hakuta, 1997, 1998, 2005). These types of supports also potentially provide affective supports that promote positive social and cognitive outcomes that are necessary to support effective relationships in the classrooms, especially for newcomers from linguistically and culturally diverse communities. This corresponds with research indicating that incorporating students' home language into curricula provides important cognitive and social supports for students' success in the second language (García, 2002). These supports can also have a positive effect on measures of academic achievement in school (August & Hakuta, 1997) and promote participation and positive relationships in the classroom (Au & Kawakimi, 1994; Trueba & Wright, 1992).

Our preliminary findings also support research indicating that providing students with significant portions of instruction in their native language can improve rather than harm the growth of their skills and performance in English (Ramirez et al., 1991). In the interviews, students explained various ways that access to Spanish language helped them make sense of the English terminology. Using Spanish was relevant when students were confronted with content that appeared confusing due to novel tasks and terminology. Students with basic emergent English proficiency skills often made more frequent use of Spanish to complete the various assignments in the project but still engaged heavily with English. These findings prompt further discussion related to the idea that children can receive substantive native language instruction without diminishing their acquisition of English language and reading skills and that doing so allows them to catch up to their English-speaking peers in English language arts, reading, and math as found in other studies (August & Hakuta, 1998; Greene, 1998; Meyer & Fienberg, 1992; Willig, 1985).

Finally, our preliminary findings support claims that a significant aspect of successful reading involves comprehension of vocabulary. The Wolves project provided different forms of language supports to allow students with different levels of English proficiency to make sense of the overall ideas, and thus helped students bootstrap their understandings of both languages. The language supports available to the students in the form of different modalities of text and audio build on the suggestions of other research: (a) native-language word or phrase-level translations serve as "just-in-time" scaffolds (Chun & Plass, 1996; Gettys et al., 2001; Lomicka, 1998); (b) computer-based glossing substantially supports reading comprehension (Cobb, 1997; Laufer & Hill, 2000; Lomicka, 1998; Roby, 1999); and (c) provision of scaffolding in multiple formats allows learners to gather information in the formats most beneficial to them (Martinez-Lage, 1997).

In conclusion, computer-supported learning environments provide potentially powerful opportunities to support students from culturally and linguistically diverse communities. While the current project only provides supports in Spanish and English, the model could easily be expanded to simultaneously support speakers of multiple languages in the same classroom. The supports in the Wolves project are certainly only the beginning of what could be possible in terms of a more comprehensive structure of supports. For example, outcomes could be dramatically improved by unifying supports across all aspects of the project rather than providing supports only in the content activity steps. Furthermore, software might be developed to conduct a rudimentary analysis of a student's usage profile and language proficiency scores and then adjust the supports that the student receives to optimize the student's experience. Environments incorporating advanced supports of these types will potentially help increase ELLs' access to conceptually-rich curricular activities while simultaneously helping them make sense of the surrounding academic language that is so crucial to their success in school and beyond.

REFERENCES

Al-Seghayer, K. (2001). The effect of multimedia annotation modes on L2 vocabulary acquisition: A comparative study. *Language Learning & Technology, 5*(1), 202–232.

Au, K. H. & Kawakimi, A. J. (1994). Cultural congruence in instruction. In E. R. Hollins, J. E. King, & W. C. Hayman (Eds.), *Teaching diverse populations: Formulating a knowledge base* (pp. 5–24). Albany, NY: State University of New York Press.

August, D. & Hakuta, K. (1997). *Improving schooling for language minority children: A research agenda.* Washington, DC: National Academy Press.

August, D. & Hakuta, K. (Eds.). (1998). *Educating language minority children.* Washington, DC: National Academy Press.

August, D. & Hakuta, K. (2005). Bilingualism and second-language learning. In M. Suarez-Orozco, C. Suarez-Orozco, & D. B. Qin (Eds.), *The new immigration: An interdisciplinary reader* (pp. 233–248). New York, NY: Routledge.

Banks, J. (1993). The canon debate, knowledge construction, and multicultural education. *Educational Researcher, 22*(5), 4–14.

Bauersfeld, H. (1995). The structuring of structures: Development and function of mathematizing as a social practice. In P. Steffe & J. Gale (Eds.), *Constructivism in education* (pp. 137–158). Hillsdale, NJ: Lawrence Erlbaum Associates.

Berman, P. (1992, April). *Meeting the challenge of language diversity: An evaluation of California programs for pupils with limited proficiency in English.* Paper presented at the Annual Meeting of the American Educational Research Association, San Francisco, CA.

Brown, J. S., Collins, A., &, Duguid, P. (1989). Situated cognition and the culture of learning. *Educational Researcher, 18,* 32–42.

Chamot, A. U. & O'Malley, J. M. (1986). *A cognitive academic language learning approach: An ESL content-based curriculum.* Washington, DC: National Clearinghouse for Bilingual Education.

Chamot, A. U. & O'Malley, J. M. (1994). *The CALLA handbook.* Reading, MA: Addison-Wesley.

Chun, D. M. & Plass, J. L. (1996). Effects of multimedia annotations on vocabulary acquisition: Using CyberBuch. *Modern Language Journal, 80*(2), 183–198.

Chun, D. M. & Plass, J. L. (1997). Research on text comprehension in multimedia environments. *Language Learning & Technology, 1*, 60–81.

Cobb, P. (1994). Where is the mind? Constructivist and sociocultural perspectives on mathematical development. *Educational Researcher, 23*(7), 13–20.

Cobb, T. (1997). Is there any measurable learning from hands-on concordancing? *System, 25*(3), 301–315.

Cole, M. & Cole, S. R. (2001). *The development of children.* New York, NY: Worth Publishers.

Cole, M. & Engestrom, Y. (1993). A cultural-historical approach to distributed cognition. In G. Salomon (Ed.), *Distributed cognitions: Psychological and educational considerations* (pp. 1–46). New York, NY: Cambridge University Press.

Collier, V. P. (1987). Age and rate of acquisition of secondary language for academic achievement in a second language. *TESOL Quarterly, 23*, 509–531.

Collier, V. P. (1989). How long? A synthesis of research on academic achievement in second language. *TESOL Quarterly, 23*, 509–531.

Davis, J. N. (1989). Facilitating effects of marginal glosses on foreign language reading. *Modern Language Journal, 73*, 41–48.

Davis, J. N. & Lyman-Hager, M. A. (1997). Computers and L2 reading: Student performance, student attitudes. *Foreign Language Annals, 30*(1), 58–72.

De Avila, E. & Duncan, S. (1984). *Finding out and descubrimiento: Teacher's guide.* San Rafael, CA: Linguametrics Group.

Echevarria, J., Vogt, M., & Short, D. (2000). *Making content comprehensible to English language learners: The SIOP model.* Needham Heights, MA: Allyn & Bacon.

Edelson, D. C., Gordin, D. N., & Pea, R. D. (1999). Addressing the challenges of inquiry-based learning through technology and curriculum design. *The Journal of the Learning Sciences, 8*(3 & 4), 391–450.

Erlach, C., Hausmann, I., Mandl, H., & Trillitzsch, U. (2000). Knowledge master—A collaborative learning program for knowledge management. In T. Davenport & G. Probst (Eds.), *Knowledge management case book* (pp. 179–197). Erlangen, Germany: Publicis MCD Verlag.

Erlach, C., Reinmann-Rothmeier, G., Neubauer, A., & Mandl, H. (2001). Ein virtuelles weiterbildungsseminar zur ausbildung zum knowledge Master. In G. Reinmann-Rothmeier & H. Mandl (Eds.), *Virtuelle seminare in hoschule und weiterbildung* (pp. 69–105). Bern, Switzerland: Huber.

Feldman, A., Konold, C., & Coulter, B. (2000). *Network Science, a decade later: The Internet and classroom learning.* Mahwah, NJ: Lawrence Erlbaum Associates.

Fradd, S. H. & Lee, O. (1999). Teachers' roles in promoting science inquiry with students from diverse language backgrounds. *Educational Researcher, 28*(6), 14–20.

Galambos, S. & Hakuta, K. (1988). Subject-specific and task-specific characteristics of metalinguistic awareness in bilingual children. *Applied Psycholinguistics, 9*, 141–162.

García, E. (2001a). *Student cultural diversity: Understanding and meeting the challenge.* Boston, MA: Houghton Mifflin.

García, E. (2001b). *Understanding and meeting the challenge of student diversity* (3rd ed.). Boston, MA: Houghton Mifflin.

García, E. (2002). Bilingualism and schooling in the United States. *International Journal of the Sociology of Language, 155–156*, 1–92.

García, E., Bravo, M. A., Dickey, L. M., Chun, K., & Sun-Iminger, X. (2002). Rethinking school reform in the context of cultural and linguistic diversity: Creating a responsive learning community: A case study. In L. Minaya-Rowe (Ed.), *Teacher training and effective pedagogy in the context of student diversity* (pp. 147–210). Greenwich, CT: Information Age Publishing.

García, E. & Lee, O. (2008). Creating culturally responsive learning communities. In A. Rosebery & B. Warren (Eds.), *Teaching science to English language learners* (pp. 147–150). Arlington, VA: NSTA Press.

Gasigitamrong, J. (2003). *An analysis of the vocabulary gloss selections of college-level L2 readers when reading a narrative hypermedia text in Thai.* Unpublished doctoral dissertation, Northern Illinois University, DeKalb, IL.

Gettys, S., Imhof, L. A., & Kautz, J. O. (2001). Computer-assisted reading: The effects of glossing format on comprehension and vocabulary retention. *Foreign Language Annals, 34*(2), 91–106.

Goncz, B. & Kodzepeljic, D. (1991). Cognition and bilingualism revisited. *Journal of Multicultural Development, 12,* 137–163.

Greene, J. (1998). *A meta-analysis of the effectiveness of bilingual education.* Claremont, CA: Tomas Rivera Policy Institute.

Greeno, J. G. (1989). Situations, mental models, and generative knowledge. In D. Klahrand & K. Kotovsky (Eds.), *Complex information processing* (pp. 285–318). Hillsdale, NJ: Lawrence Erlbaum Associates.

Grimshaw, J. (1981). Form, function, and the language acquisition device. In C. L. Baker & J. McCarthy (Eds.), *The logical problem of language acquisition* (pp. 165–182). Cambridge, MA: MIT Press.

Groot, P. J. M. (2000). Computer assisted second language vocabulary acquisition. *Language Learning & Technology, 4*(1), 60–81.

Hakuta, K., Butler, Y. G., & Witt, D. (2000). *How long does it take English learners to attain proficiency?* (Policy Report No. 2000-1). Santa Barbara, CA: University of California, Linguistic Minority Research Institute.

Hatch, E. M. & Brown, C. (1995). *Vocabulary, semantics, and language education.* New York, NY: Cambridge University Press.

Haynes, M. (1993). Patterns and perils of guessing in second language reading. In T. N. Huckin, M. Haynes, & J. Coady (Eds.), *Second language reading and vocabulary learning* (pp. 46–64). Norwood, NJ: Ablex Publishing Corp.

Hegelheimer, V. & Tower, D. (2004). Using CALL in the classroom: Analyzing student interactions in an authentic classroom. *System, 32*(2), 185–205.

Hirsh, D. & Nation, P. (1992). What vocabulary size is needed to read unsimplified texts for pleasure? *Reading in a Foreign Language, 8*(2), 689–696.

Johnson, D., Johnson, R. T., Holubec, E. J., & Roy, P. (1984). *Circles of learning: Cooperation in the classroom.* Alexandria, VA: Association for Supervision and Curriculum Development.

Kagan, S. (1986). Cooperative learning and sociocultural factors in schooling. In California State Department of Education, *Beyond language: Social and cultural factors in schooling language minority students* (pp. 231–298). Los Angeles, CA: Evaluation, Dissemination, and Assessment Center, California State University.

Kelly, P. (1990). Guessing: No substitute for systematic learning of lexis. *System, 18*(2), 199–208.

Kessler, C. & Quinn, M. E. (1985). Positive effects of bilingualism on science problem solving abilities. In *Perspectives on Bilingual Education* (pp. 289–296.). Washington, D.C.: Georgetown University Press.

Kessler, C. & Quinn, M. E. (1987). ESL and science learning. In J. Crandall (Ed.), *ESL through content-area instruction* (pp. 55–87). Englewood Cliffs, NJ: Prentice Hall Regents.

Koren, S. (1999). Vocabulary instruction through hypertext: Are there advantages over conventional methods of teaching? *Tesl-Ej, 4*(1), 1–18.

Koschmann, T. (1996). Paradigm shifts and instructional technology. In T. Koschmann (Ed.), *CSCL: Theory and practice of an emerging paradigm* (pp. 1–23). Mahwah, NJ: Lawrence Erlbaum.

Krashen, S. (1985). *The input hypothesis: Issues and implications.* London: Longman.

Krashen, S. (1989). We acquire vocabulary and spelling by reading: Additional evidence for the input hypothesis. *The modern language journal, 73*(4), 440–464.

Krashen, S. (1996). *Under attack: The case against bilingual education.* Culver City, CA: Language Education Associates.

Krashen, S. D. & Terrell, T. D. (1983). *The natural approach: Language acquisition in the classroom.* Retrieved from http://www.eric.ed.gov/ERICWebPortal/recordDetail?accno=ED230069

Laufer, B. (1997). The lexical plight in second language reading: Words you don't know, words you think you know, and words you can't guess. In J. Coady & T. N. Huckin (Eds.), *Second language vocabulary acquisition: A rationale for pedagogy* (pp. 20–34). New York, NY: Cambridge University Press.

Laufer, B. (2003). Vocabulary acquisition in a second language: Do learners really acquire most vocabulary by reading? Some empirical evidence. *Canadian Modern Language Review, 59*(4), 565–585.

Laufer, B. & Hill, M. (2000). What lexical information do L2 learners select in a CALL dictionary and how does it affect word retention? *Language Learning and Technology, 3,* 58–76.

Lave, J. (1988). *Cognition in practice: Mind, mathematics, and culture in everyday life.* New York, NY: Cambridge University Press.

Lee, O. & Fradd, S. H. (1998). Science for all, including students from non-English language backgrounds. *Educational Researcher, 27*(3), 12–21.

Lee, O. & Fradd, S. H. (2001). Instructional congruence to promote science learning and literacy development for linguistically diverse students. In D. R. Lavoie (Ed.), *Models for science teacher preparation: Bridging the gap between research and practice* (pp. 109–126). Dordrecht, the Netherlands: Kluwer Academic Publishers.

Leont'ev, A. N. (1974). The problem of activity in psychology. *Journal of Russian and East European Psychology, 13*(2), 4–33.

Linn, M. C., Clark, D. B., & Slotta, J. D. (2003). WISE design for knowledge integration. *Science Education, 84*(4), 517–538.

Linn, M. C. & Hsi, S. (2000). *Computers, teachers, peers: Science learning partners.* Mahwah, NJ: Erlbaum.

Lomicka, L. (1998). To gloss or not to gloss: An investigation of reading comprehension online. *Language Learning & Technology, 1*(2), 41–50.

MacNab, B. L. (1979). Cognition and bilingualism: A reanalysis of studies. *Linguistics, 17,* 231–255.

Martinez-Lage, A. (1997). Hypermedia technology for teaching reading. In M. D. Bush & R. M. Terry (Eds.), *Technology-enhanced language learning* (pp. 121–163). Lincolnwood, IL: National Textbook Co.

Mayer, R. E. (1997). Multimedia learning: Are we asking the right questions? *Educational Psychologist, 32*(1), 1–19.

Mayer, R. E. & Moreno, R. (1998). A split-attention effect in multimedia learning: Evidence for dual processing systems in working memory. *Journal of Educational Psychology, 90*(2), 312–320.

Meyer, M. M. & Fienberg, S. E. (1992). *Assessing evaluation studies: The case of bilingual education strategies.* Washington, DC: National Academy of Sciences.

Mohan, B. (1979). Relating language teaching and content teaching. *TESOL Quarterly, 13*, 171–182.

Nation, I. S. P. (1990). *Teaching and learning vocabulary.* Boston, MA: Heinle and Heinle.

Ovando, C. J., Collier, V. P., & Combs, M. C. (2003). *Bilingual and ESL classrooms: Teaching in multicultural contexts.* New York, NY: McGraw-Hill Higher Education.

Peal, E. & Lambert, W. E. (1962). The relation of bilingualism to intelligence. *Psychological Monographs: General and Applied, 76*(546), 1–23.

Peterson, P. L. & Barnes, C. (1996). Learning together: The challenge of mathematics, equity, and leadership. *Phi Delta Kappa, 77*(7), 485–491.

Pinker, S. (1984). Visual cognition: An introduction. *Cognition, 18*(1), 1–63.

Plass, J. L. (1998). Design and evaluation of the user interface of foreign language multimedia software: A cognitive approach. *Language Learning & Technology, 2*, 35–45.

Plass, J. L., Chun, D. M., & Mayer, R. E. (1998). Supporting visual and verbal learning preferences in a second-language multimedia learning environment. *Journal of Educational Psychology, 90*, 25–36.

Ramirez, J., Pasta, D., Yuen, S., Billings, D., & Ramey, D. (1991). *Final report: Longitudinal study of structured English immersion strategy, early-exit and late-exit transitional bilingual educational programs for language minority children.* San Mateo, CA: Aguirre International.

Roby, W. B. (1999). "What's in a gloss?" A response to Lara L. Lomicka's "To gloss or not to gloss: An investigation of reading comprehension online." *Language Learning & Technology, 2*(2), 94–101.

Rosebery, A. S., Warren, B., & Conant, F. R. (1992). Appropriating scientific discourse: Findings from language minority classrooms. *The Journal of the Learning Sciences, 2*(1), 61–94.

Rosebery, A. S., Warren, B., Conant, F. R., & Hudicourt-Barnes, J. (1992). Chèche Konnen: Scientific sense-making in bilingual education. *Hands On! 15*(1), 1–19.

Sakar, A. & Ercetin, G. (2005). Effectiveness of hypermedia annotations for foreign language reading. *Journal of Computer Assisted Learning, 21*(1), 28–38.

Scardamalia, M. & Bereiter, C. (1996). Computer support for knowledge-building communities. In T. Koschmann (Ed.), *CSCL: Theory and practice of an emerging paradigm* (pp. 249–268). Mahwah, NJ: Lawrence Erlbaum.

Short, D. (Ed.). (1999). *Integrating language and content for effective sheltered instruction programs.* New York, NY: Teachers College Press.

Smelser, N. J., Wilson, W. J., & Mitchell, F. (2001). *America becoming: Racial trends and their consequences* (vol. 2). Washington, DC: National Academies Press.

Snow, M. A., Met, M., & Genessee, F. (1989). A conceptual framework for the integration of language and content in second/foreign language instruction. *TESOL Quarterly, 23*, 201–217.

Spitulnik, M., Bouillion, E., Rummel, N., Clark, D. B., & Fischer, F. (2003). Collaborative online environments for lifelong learning: design issues from a situated learning perspective. *The International Journal of Educational Policy, Research and Practice, IV*(1), 83–116.

Swain, M. & Lapkin, S. (1991). Heritage language children in an English-French bilingual program. *Canadian Modern Language Review, 47*(4), 635–641.

Tharp, R. & Gallimore, R. (1988). *Rousing minds to life: Teaching, learning and schooling in social context.* Cambridge, MA: Cambridge University Press.

Thomas, W. P. & Collier, V. P. (1995). *A longitudinal analysis of programs serving language minority students.* Washington, DC: National Clearinghouse on Bilingual Education.

Thompson, M. S., DiCerbo, K. E., Mahoney, K., & MacSwan, J. (2002). Exito en California? A Critique of Language Program Evaluations. *Education Policy Analysis Archives,* 10(7). doi:10.14507/epaa.v10n7.2002

Tienda, M. & Mitchell, F. (2006). *Multiple origins, uncertain destinies: Hispanics and the American future.* Washington, DC: National Academies Press.

Troendle, P., Mandl, H., Fischer, F., Koch, J. H., Schlichter, J., & Teege, G. (1999). MUNICS: Multimedia for problem-based learning in computer science. In S. D. Franklin & E. Strenski (Eds.), *Electronic educational environments* (pp. 38–50). London, UK: Kluwer Academic Publishers.

Trueba, H. T. & Wright, P. G. (1992). On ethnographic studies and multicultural education. In M. Saravia-Shore & S. Arvizu (Eds.), *Cross-cultural literacy: Ethnographies of communication in multiethnic classrooms* (pp. 299–338). New York, NY: Garland.

Valdes, G. (2001). *Learning and not learning English: Latino students in American schools.* New York, NY: Teachers College Press.

Vygotsky, L. S. (1978). *Mind in society: The development of the higher psychological processes.* Cambridge, MA: Harvard University Press.

Warren, B., Ballenger, C., Ogonowski, M., Rosebery, A., & Hudicourt-Barnes, J. (2001). Rethinking diversity in learning science: The logic of everyday language. *Journal of Research in Science Teaching, 38*, 529–552.

Warren, B. & Rosebery, A. (1995). *"This question is just too, too easy!" Perspectives from the classroom on accountability in science.* Santa Cruz, CA: National Center for Research on Culture and Language.

Welch-Ross, M. (2012). *Language diversity, school learning, and closing achievement gaps: A workshop summary.* Washington, DC: National Academies Press.

Willig, A. (1985). A meta-analysis of selected studies on the effectiveness of bilingual education. *Review of Educational Research, 55*, 269–317.

Winkler, K. & Mandl, H. (2002). Knowledge Master: Wissensmanagement—weiterbildung mit WBT. In U. Dittler (Ed.), *E-Learning-Erfolgsfaktoren und einsatzkonzepte mit interaktiven medien,* (pp. 205–215). München, Germany: Oldenburg.

Zimmerman, C. B. (1997). Historical trends in second language vocabulary instruction. In T. N. Huckin (Ed.), *Second language vocabulary acquisition: A rationale for pedagogy* (pp. 5–20). New York, NY: Cambridge University Press.

CHAPTER 5

CASE STUDIES OF ONLINE TESTING IN MULTICULTURAL SCHOOL DISTRICTS

**Brooke Kandel-Cisco, Jacqueline R. Stillisano,
Trina J. Davis, and Hersh C. Waxman**

ABSTRACT

In this chapter, the authors use excerpts from in-depth case studies to explore the implementation of computer-based testing in diverse contexts. The case studies describe the online testing experiences of six Texas school districts and several individual campuses within each district. The challenges that district personnel reported experiencing in planning and implementing online assessments are highlighted, and the issues that may differentially affect students in multicultural contexts based on variables such as setting (i.e., urban or rural), student age (i.e., elementary or secondary), district financial resources, and student language status (English learner or native English-speaking) are described in detail.

INTRODUCTION

Recent reforms emphasize the use of testing in public schools, and nearly every state uses large-scale exams to quantify district and student level performance.

Research on Technology Use in Multicultural Settings, pages 107–119.

The results of these exams are commonly utilized to make critical educational determinations about issues such as student retention and graduation, teacher and administrator pay, and school effectiveness. Policy-makers' desire to improve the convenience and efficiency of these state testing programs has catalyzed interest in developing alternatives to paper and pencil tests (PPT). As the quantity and quality of technology available in schools expands rapidly, computer-based testing (CBT) is increasingly recognized as a possible vehicle for streamlining large-scale exam administrations.

CBT is a term used generally to refer to testing that utilizes computers for administration and includes online testing as well as exams that have been loaded onto a computer. CBT is primarily executed through one of two designs. Fixed or linear tests are similar to PPT in that exams consist of a set number of questions that test takers receive. Adaptive CBT, in contrast, tailors exams to the test taker's performance, meaning that items are individually selected for each examinee based on previous question responses (Parshall, Spray, Kalohn, & Davey, 2002). It has been hypothesized that CBT, whether fixed or adaptive, offers several advantages to test administrators over PPT including the potential convenience of immediate scoring and reporting, reduced handling of bulky materials, and improvements in test security (Way, Davis, & Fitzpatrick, 2006). The advantages to students have also been noted. CBT has the potential to offer a wider variety of item types, including interactive questions, and accommodations, such as large print tests, can provide better access to some student populations (Bennett, 2001, 2002; Thompson, Thurlow, Quenemoen, & Lehr, 2002).

A primary area of research focusing on the use of technology for testing has examined CBT and PPT comparability. This line of research has sought to understand the influence of administration mode (i.e., computer or paper) on examinee performance. Examining the comparability of CBT and PPT is important because if the mode of test administration influences outcomes, valid conclusions cannot be drawn across students or time. Recent meta-analyses have synthesized administration mode effects on student mathematics and reading assessments and, overall, indicate that administration mode does not have a statistically significant effect on achievement test scores (Wang, Jiao, Young, Brooks, & Olson, 2007, 2008). These meta-analyses examined mode effects at the test level; however, it has been hypothesized that comparability likely depends more on the type of item than the administration mode (Parshall et al., 2002). In a comparative study examining mode comparability at the item level, for example, Keng, McClarty, and Davis (2008) found advantages favoring PPT examinees. Specifically, students who took PPT were more successful than students who took CBT on longer test items that required scrolling and mathematics items requiring graphing or geometric manipulations.

While test- and item-level comparability is an important consideration in CBT, another issue that must be addressed is the variant settings in which CBT is administered (i.e., urban or rural, presence of English language learners [ELLs], etc.) and the extent to which school districts and school personnel in those settings are ready and willing to use CBT. The implementation of CBT is seemingly complex in that a host of factors such as space and security for testing, student familiarity with technology, and availability of hardware must be considered, and these factors are certainly influenced by the context in which CBT is implemented. While CBT may be seamlessly integrated into a technology-rich district, for example, another district may not even have adequate Internet access. These issues of context are important because no matter how great the potential of technology to facilitate testing, if the resources are not available or personnel are not prepared, the advantages are unlikely to be realized.

In this chapter, we explore some of the complexities of implementing CBT in diverse contexts. We use excerpts from in-depth case studies to describe the online testing experiences of six Texas school districts and several individual campuses within each district. While the full case studies include information on both the perceived benefits of and challenges to large-scale online testing, this chapter specifically highlights the challenges that district personnel reported experiencing in planning and implementing online assessments. In examining the issues faced by the districts, we pay special attention to the challenges that may differentially affect students in multicultural contexts based on variables such as setting (i.e., urban or rural), student age (i.e., elementary or secondary), district financial resources, and student language status (ELL or native English-speaking).

METHODS

Participants

The school districts that comprised our study were purposefully chosen to represent the diverse school districts located in the state. A list of school districts was developed using criteria that balanced the following demographic factors: (a) geographic area within the state, (b) student enrollment count for the 2007–2008 academic year, (c) count of online tests delivered to an individual district during the 2007–2008 academic year, (d) number of ELLs, (e) number of students identified as economically disadvantaged, (f) district's 2006–2007 registered wealth-per-average-daily-attendance, and (g) district's intention to participate in the summer online administration of the state's standardized exit level exam. Using this list of potential participants, school districts were offered the opportunity to participate in the study on a voluntary basis. A total of six districts participated in the study, and Table 5.1 notes key demographic information for the districts.

Data Collection

The study utilized multiple cases (i.e., districts) to describe the online testing experiences of the participating school districts. A set of interview questions was developed for both district and campus visits, based on similar instruments recently used in evaluations using case study methods (Houston, Eugeni, & Wax-

TABLE 5.1.   Demographic Information for Participating Districts

District	Total student population	Percent of students who are economically disadvantaged students	Percent of students who are ELLs	Student ethnicity as percent of total student population				
				African-American	Hispanic	Asian	White	Other
A	160,000	84	31	30	65	<1	5	<1
B	37,000	73	50	<1	97	<1	2	<1
C	200,000	80	30	29	59	3	8	<1
D	1,200	97	50	<1	98	<1	<1	<1
E	45,000	32	11	7	25	3	65	<1
F	30,000	60	10	11	40	3	46	<1

man, 2006; Waxman, Houston, & Cortina, 2001; Waxman, Houston, Profilet, & Sanchez, 2005). The interview questions asked participants about experiences with online testing, perceptions of student and teacher responses to online testing, and the challenges and benefits of online testing for students, teachers, and administrators. Through structured prompts, the researchers explored, reflected back, encouraged the participants to expand their expositions, and requested stories from the participants. Careful notes were taken of the participants' responses during the interviews; and the researchers observed, and later interpreted and recorded, participants' body language and facial expressions as further data to be examined. In total, 35 district-level and 42 campus-level personnel volunteered to participate in the study, and data from approximately 1,925 hours of interviews were collected. Additionally, ethnographic notes recorded during informal observations at the schools in which personnel were interviewed were used as a second source of information.

Data Analysis

Data analysis for this study occurred in three distinct, but overlapping, phases. In the first step, the researchers became intimate with the data by reading and re-reading each interview multiple times, and marking any passages deemed interesting or important. In the second phase of the data analysis, the research team developed case study narratives of each district, delineating the districts' and campuses' experiences with online testing and participants' perceptions of the challenges of online testing for their organization and their students.

In the final step, the researchers developed a cross-case analysis of the data. Researchers began by reducing the text in order to identify what was of most interest and importance, utilizing a constant comparison method of coding passages. The team performed this process of reducing the data inductively, allowing the themes to emerge from the participants' words rather than beginning with a hypothesis or theory to substantiate. During the process of reading and identifying passages of interest, the team began to look for words or phrases to identify categories into which the marked passages might fit. Names for the categories were tentative at first, emerging from the identified passages rather than from some pre-conceived idea of the researcher. Data were sorted into categories and coded as a process for developing an organizational framework for the case studies addressing the question of the districts' readiness for online testing and any costs or challenges associated with attaining a complete readiness for administration of online assessments.

RESULTS

As we conducted an inductive analysis of the data, several themes prevalent across the six school districts began to emerge. The 11 themes initially identified are detailed in Table 5.2. For the purposes of this chapter, we then conducted a secondary analysis with a focus on the specific challenges within and across the 11 original themes that may exert specific influence on the implementation of online testing in multicultural settings. Four themes emerged from this secondary analysis: (1) inequitable access to technology, (2) lack of district resources, (3) balancing instruction with testing, and (4) effects on schools with high numbers of ELLs.

TABLE 5.2.   Challenges to Implementing Online Testing

Themes	District A	District B	District C	District D	District E	District F
Lack of computers and equipment	√	√	√	√	√	√
Lack of space	√	√	√	√	√	√
Scheduling problems	√	√	√	√	√	√
Need for training	√	√	√	√	√	√
Infrastructure/System Set-up/Connectivity	√	√	√	√	√	√
Personnel	√	√	√	√	√	√
Need to balance instruction & testing	√	√	√		√	√
Cost	√	√	√		√	√
Unequal access to computers and technology skills	√	√	√	√		√
Security	√	√		√		
Inability to accommodate students with special needs		√	√	√		

Inequitable Access to Technology

The term "digital divide" has been widely used to refer to asymmetrical access to technology among disadvantaged groups, and it has been demonstrated that diverse students, especially those from high-poverty communities, frequently experience minimal access to and use of technology (Mouza, 2008; Muñoz, 2002). A majority of the district personnel interviewed for our study confirmed the presence of digital gaps in their districts. They decried students' lack of access—or lack of equitable access—to the computers and technology skills necessary for online testing. Most of these differences were attributed to the socio-economic status of the students; many district and school administrators told us, for example, that students from low-socio-economic families have limited access to computers outside of school and consequently experience anxiety about online testing.

Several school administrators from a district located along the U.S. border, for example, voiced concerns that much of their largely immigrant student population lives in very poor communities where some do not have electricity or running water and, as such, are not exposed to technology outside of the classroom. One of the most powerful anecdotes shared by a school administrator relates to the poverty that affects many of these students: a young girl came to school each day with wet hair, which she dried under the school restroom hand dryer, because her house had no electricity. The point of the story the school administrator shared is that her students do not have the luxury of making technology a major priority in their lives.

While in some settings, such as the district mentioned above, lack of access to technology is pervasive among most of the student population, other districts experienced highly variant levels of technology access among their students. An elementary principal in an urban school reflected on variation in access within her school noting, "Some kids are more comfortable with paper and pencil testing while others would be just fine with the computer, but we're trying here to level the playing field for *all* students." Similarly, a district technology coordinator noted variation in technology access across the district:

> My perception is…we've been doing some surveys of technology in schools. We're seeing a pattern: On campuses where students tend to have more access to computers *out* of school, we're seeing more computers *in* the school. My hunch is that if students are coming into school and they're already tech savvy, there's more pressure on the school to have technology. The concern is, we don't want online testing to widen the gap between affluent and less affluent students.

These examples illustrate how online testing may benefit some students in a school or district, yet put other students, especially those from higher poverty homes, at a disadvantage.

In addition to noting the role of poverty in students' level of access to technology, several district personnel mentioned digital differences by grade levels. Some district personnel argued, for example, that younger students (i.e., elementary school students) were more technology "savvy" than middle school or secondary school students. More often, however, participants argued that younger students would have more difficulties with the eye-and-hand coordination required to manipulate a mouse or type on a keyboard. One technology coordinator, for example, related that for an online third grade reading exam, test administrators had to log in each student because the students would have taken too much time typing in their names. Another district addressed this problem by providing keyboard tutoring for students who did not use keyboards often. These situations present several issues, however, that should be considered in relation to the appropriateness of online testing:

- Should students who cannot efficiently type their name be asked to demonstrate knowledge via online tests, especially in high stakes situations?
- Should instructional time be spent teaching keyboarding skills in order to prepare for online testing?
- To what extent are students from economically disadvantaged homes who do not have access to technology outside of school differentially provided basic computer skills instruction (i.e., keyboard tutoring) at the cost of content instruction?

Lack of District Resources

A lack of district resources to implement online testing was another critical issue referenced by nearly every district. Districts reported that in addition to the start-up costs related to purchasing computers and equipment, new monies would need to be set aside each year to purchase replacement computers and maintain adequate connectivity. Personnel from one district pointed out that even electricity costs would be dramatically higher if all the schools in the district used online testing.

Access to computers for online testing is a problem for many schools. An elementary school technology specialist in a large, urban district, for example, stated:

> We just need the proper infrastructure. Right now, we don't have enough computers. We're a learning center, a Title I school...we need computers. I've gotten in the last couple of years, maybe 30 [computers] donated, and had that not happened, some classrooms wouldn't even have teacher computers.

Other participants noted that even if they had the resources to buy more computers, they would not have the classroom space and, in the case of districts with a large number of portable classrooms, electricity sufficient to power more than a few computers.

Infrastructure and connectivity problems were also referenced by all the districts as a major challenge in implementing online testing. Each district provided several examples of the problems schools experienced related to connectivity and infrastructure problems. These problems included issues related to electrical power, telephone connections, bandwidth, servers, caching, and web-based testing. Several districts told us they would have to rewire many of their schools with computer ports and electricity in order to accommodate large-scale online testing. Additionally, many school administrators revealed that the Internet connections in their schools are not robust enough to support large numbers of students testing online at the same time. An elementary principal in an urban school noted:

> Getting us facilities that worked would be the main thing, because the system is really slow and it breaks down sometimes. We tap into the district server. We would need for that to be strengthened and upgraded. It slows way down or it stops when we get on it. We don't have an infrastructure strong enough. We need to be sure we have enough working computers that can get into the system and stay there, so children have time to do what they need to do.

The challenges related to connectivity and infrastructure are different for rural school districts who rely on small-scale service providers for Internet access during online testing. One superintendent from a rural district shared his district's experiences with Internet access during online testing:

> For us in these rural towns, one of the things a lot of folks do not understand about online, they tend to gravitate toward the district, how many computers, network, etc. I would be a poster child in District D in why some people would be against this thinking. We had 10 gigs for the desktop and many people did not know what that was. We can run a lot of traffic and a lot of machines. However, our phone service is not what I would call good and reliable. During rainstorms, the phones will go down, and the phone company stuff will go down, or if a drunk runs off the road, you are down for quite a while. Big towns are running on a major company system, but in the rural areas, small little places, they have big problems. They cannot repair the equipment as easily.

Although the districts and schools reported varying needs in terms of computers and Internet access, all the districts expressed concern regarding where to find the funding to address the issues of initial start up and long-term maintenance of technology, and participants were concerned with the large amounts of money that would be diverted from other areas and go into upgrading technology. This issue of limited resources is most pronounced in districts with high numbers of students from economically disadvantaged communities that require many layers of support services.

Balancing and Aligning Instruction and Testing

Nearly all the districts discussed the need to balance instruction and testing, and participants focused primarily on three specific concerns related to online testing: (1) extensive restriction of computer lab use due to testing, (2) reduction in sophisticated and authentic integration of technology, and (3) alignment between the format of classroom-based instruction and assessments with large-scale online tests.

Although many schools had computer labs that could be utilized for testing, large-scale online testing forced the computer and technology applications classes that would normally use the computer labs to be re-located to classrooms where no computers were available, sometimes for weeks at a time. One participant recalled:

> Last year we had to kick seven teachers out of their labs for three days. Even if we were aggressive about our testing schedule, in 2014 it would take two weeks to do all the testing online. We can't kick people out of their classrooms for two weeks. It's just a huge problem. I cannot imagine how we could get even just the third grade kids tested. It would take days, which means the library would be shut down totally—there's just no place else. Can't use the cafeteria because lunch starts at 10:30, plus the wiring isn't right.

In addition to the loss of instructional time for computer classes, participants noted that the classroom changes made to accommodate online testing communicate that technology is not important. A district technology coordinator shared, "The teachers are flexible, but they don't think it's fair. They think it's the wrong message to send their classes about the importance of technology." Technology classes are not the only subject area to lose instructional time due to online testing. Participants shared that information media and physical education courses also were interrupted as one or more classes had to be moved into the library or gym for several weeks so that the students' regular classrooms could be used as a testing site.

In addition to the concern for lost instructional time, participants suggested that shuffling students around and testing students in unfamiliar settings would put students at a disadvantage in terms of test performance. In a limited testing window, schedules that are designed to accommodate computer availability may trump the desire to maintain normalcy for students. One district had to move students out of their regular school building for online testing. An IT specialist in that district described busing students to a different campus, noting some of the challenges he encountered, "Busing was difficult. We didn't have teachers going with us [on the buses], just technology specialist people, and we didn't really know the students. Not knowing the students made it difficult to proctor [the test]." An IT coordinator from another district that had to bus high school students to computer labs at area elementary schools shared that busing presented "many unique challenges...the dynamic of bringing high school students into elementary schools and the security for the elementary students."

Authentic technology integration was a second issue for which participants purported a balance between instruction and testing must be struck. While some district personnel suggested that online testing raised the status of technology in education, others offered that online testing inhibited authentic integration of technology into instruction. A district superintendent, for example, stated "It would seem to me, online testing forces schools to be lab happy, where you can march in and test," and several IT specialists as well as a district curriculum coordinator noted that online testing encouraged a greater emphasis on basic technology skills (i.e., keyboarding) and drill and kill applications at the expense of real integration of technology skills and more creative uses of technology. Participants not only suggested that large-scale online testing reorients the use of technology away from authentic integration, but also that the actual process of online testing prevents teachers from using computer applications. One teacher at a small, rural intermediate school, for example, noted that two years ago teachers had to give up one of their classroom laptops for online testing, and the laptops have not yet been returned for classroom use, while a high school technology coordinator shared that due to limited Internet connectivity, teachers could not use the Internet for instructional purposes during online testing.

The lack of alignment between classroom instruction and assessment and online state-wide standardized exams was also offered as a concern surrounding online testing. Several participants suggested the strategies that students are currently taught for paper testing, such as highlighting or circling key points, may not work as well on the computer and that teachers may not know how to help students develop useful strategies for taking online content area tests. One principal reported, for example, that "some of the math teachers were telling the kids not to take the e-test because of not being able to use the strategies." Not only does this suggest that teachers may need more training in terms of online strategies, but also that teachers should consider using online assessments during class so that students are familiar with online formats. Conversely, however, if the online tests after which teachers fashion classroom assessments are linear and focus only on basic skills, the result could be an increase in so-called "kill and drill" instruction in the classroom.

Effects on Schools with High Numbers of English Language Learners (ELLs)

While our interviews with district and school personnel revealed that inequitable technology access, limited district resources, and a lack of alignment between classroom assessments and online exams affected students taking online tests in many different contexts, these issues are amplified in Texas schools with high numbers of ELLs. In Texas, the English language proficiency of every ELL in grades K–12 is assessed using the Texas English Language Proficiency Assessment System (TELPAS). Beginning in grade two, the reading portion of the TELPAS is in a multiple choice format and, recently, large numbers of ELLs have begun to take the TELPAS reading test online. This means that in addition to administering state achievement tests in content areas to every student, districts with a large percentage of ELLs, such as District D, must also administer the TELPAS reading test to many students. Additionally, because ELLs tend to be concentrated in communities that experience high levels of poverty, the contexts in which districts administer these tests are likely characterized by relatively fewer resources (i.e., computers) and more accommodations (i.e., extended time for testing, small group administration) that are implemented to support ELLs in testing situations, which further exacerbates issues such as computer shortages and balancing instruction and assessment. One district level administrator noted, for example, how the TELPAS administration limited access to computers for students:

> Some campuses were frustrated about having to displace some of their classrooms. TELPAS wasn't given to everyone, but they had to commandeer computers for small groups of kids and they couldn't be used for anyone else. Untimed assessment takes up a whole computer for an entire day for one child.

Despite the increased space constraints that stem from testing large numbers of ELLs, district and school personnel acknowledged the importance of providing accommodations to these students, especially in light of the fact that TELPAS results are an important factor in determining the services provided to ELLs. A principal at a high school along the border shared, "It takes longer for them [ELLs] to process. It is a longer process. We have 700-plus TELPAS kids here." A teacher who works specifically with ELLs at the high school also highlighted the large number of ELLs on her campus and mentioned administering exams in small groups as required for some ELLs. She noted, "Small grouping is one of the biggest issues." Yet other participants noted a less positive attitude toward the adjustments necessary to administer the TELPAS reading test. A district level coordinator stated that online testing "eats up bandwidth" to the extent that no one else can access the Internet during online testing and continued, "Classroom teachers hate the TELPAS [reading test] because we reserve 70% of the district bandwidth for Pearson. They know during that window, there will be no technology in the classroom."

CONCLUSION

The information we collected through interviews with over 75 district and school personnel highlighted the challenges of implementing online testing in multicultural contexts that must be considered before large-scale testing, and especially that which is high stakes in nature, is mandated. Inequitable access to technology, lack of district resources, and a lack of alignment between what happens in the classroom and online tests were serious obstacles that districts felt had to be addressed before expanded online testing could be implemented. Although all districts involved in our case study recognized a value to online testing, they acknowledged that full-scale online testing is something that cannot happen overnight. Specifically, the districts believed a phase-in process of several years is essential in order for them to be ready for online testing.

In addition to a phase-in period for implementing large-scale online testing, the results indicate that flexibility may be an important component in successful online testing in multicultural contexts. While the diverse districts in our study reported relatively similar concerns surrounding online testing, the framework through which the large, urban districts view these concerns is very different in some cases than the framework through which the small, rural districts view the same concerns. For example, in discussing technology infrastructure challenges, District D revealed problems in even accessing the Internet. Conversely, in discussing technology infrastructure concerns, District E was concerned with how many hits their "barracuda" (their network) can handle. This example seems to suggest that a "one size fits all" mandate from the state will leave some districts, and more importantly, some students, at a disadvantage, and that the amount of financial and expert assistance each district will need in order to fully implement online testing may very well need to be considered on a case-by-case basis.

We hope that the online testing lessons learned in school districts across Texas and documented in this study can be a starting point for policy-makers and administrators considering mandating and/or implementing large-scale exams in multicultural settings. The contexts in which exams are administered, the resources available, and the experiences and characteristics of the students are factors that must be considered when implementing an online testing system that is efficient, but most importantly, that is equitable in providing all students the opportunity to demonstrate knowledge.

REFERENCES

Bennett, R. E. (2001). How the Internet will help large-scale assessment reinvent itself. *Educational Policy Analysis Archives, 9*(5). Retrieved from http://epaa.asu.edu/ojs/article/view/334/460

Bennett, R. E. (2002). Inexorable and inevitable: The continuing story of technology and assessment. *Journal of Technology, Learning, and Assessment, 1*(1). Retrieved from http://ejournals.bc.edu/ojs/index.php/jtla/article/view/1667/

Houston, W. R., Eugeni, M. L., & Waxman, H. C. (2006). *Successful initiatives in the recruitment and retention of community college students: Making a difference in the lives of students.* Houston, TX: Institute for Urban Education.

Keng, L., McClarty, K. L., & Davis, L. L. (2008). Item-level comparative analysis of online and paper administrations of the Texas Assessment of Knowledge and Skills. *Applied Measurement in Education, 21,* 207–226.

Mouza, C. (2008). Learning with laptops: Implementation and outcomes in an urban, underprivileged school. *Journal of Research on Technology in Education, 40,* 447–472.

Muñoz, J. S. (2002). Disintegrating multiculturalism with technology. *Multicultural Education, 10*(2), 2–48.

Parshall, C. G., Spray, J. A., Kalohn, J. C., & Davey, T. (2002). *Practical considerations in computer-based testing.* New York, NY: Springer.

Thompson, S. J., Thurlow, M. L., Quenemoen, R. F., & Lehr, C. A. (2002). *Access to computer-based testing for students with disabilities* (Synthesis Report 45). Retrieved from http://www.cehd.umn.edu/NCEO/onlinepubs/synthesis45.html

Wang, S., Jiao, H., Young, M. J., Brooks, T., & Olson, J. (2007). A meta-analysis of testing mode effects in grade K–12 mathematics tests. *Educational and Psychological Measurement, 67,* 219–238.

Wang, S., Jiao, H., Young, M. J., Brooks, T., & Olson, J. (2008). Comparability of computer-based and paper-and-pencil testing in K–12 reading assessments. *Educational and Psychological Measurement, 68,* 5–24.

Waxman, H. C., Houston, W. R., & Cortina, L. (2001). Determining program quality of a social service collaborative using case study methods and moving towards participatory evaluation. In D. M. Hinn, A. P. Benson, & C. Lloyd (Eds.), *Visions of quality: How evaluators define, understand, and represent program quality* (pp. 135–151). Amsterdam, the Netherlands: Elsevier.

Waxman, H. C., Houston, W. R., Profilet, S. M., & Sanchez, B. (2005). *Making a difference in the lives of abused and neglected children: Research on the effectiveness of a court appointed advocate program.* Houston, TX: Child Advocates Inc.

Way, W., Davis, L., & Fitzpatrick, S. (2006, April). *Score comparability of online and paper administrations of Texas Assessment of Knowledge and Skills.* Paper presented at the annual meeting of the National Council on Measurement in Education, San Francisco, CA.

CHAPTER 6

DECONSTRUCTING THE DIGITAL DIVIDE IN RESEARCH

Moving From a View of the Poor as "Other" to the Poor as "Us"

Cecelia Merkel

ABSTRACT

While the digital divide metaphor is useful in identifying groups lacking access to technology, this approach does not adequately contextualize the experience of "have-nots" as they attempt to integrate technology into their lives. This chapter describes the experience of participants taking part in a computer distribution and training program designed to address the digital divide. This study used a situated approach to explore how participants used computer and Internet technology when given the chance and the real barriers that they experienced in trying to adopt new literacy practices.

INTRODUCTION

The digital divide is a metaphor used by scholars and policy makers to refer to the problem of a lack of access to technology and the consequences associated with a

Research on Technology Use in Multicultural Settings, pages 121–138.

lack of access for "have-not" groups. Underlying this metaphor is a classification system that creates categories of advantage or disadvantage relative to people's access to technology. Sometimes the most interesting thing about classification systems is what is left out when a person is placed into one category or another. The digital divide metaphor leaves out the lived experience of members of marginalized groups, the unique ways that they bring technology into their lives when given the chance, and the way that a lack of resources (technical, human, economic, etc.) can impinge on people's ability to adopt new literacy practices.

This chapter reports on a study that explored technology use among low-income families taking part in a computer training and distribution program, the Community Networking Initiative (CNI). The starting assumption was that program participants were successful technology users who could use technology to make a difference in their own lives, the lives of their families, and their communities. The focus of this study was on showing the many diverse ways that people brought technology into their lives, the ways that they addressed technical problems that they encountered, and the barriers that they faced in making technology a part of their daily lives. This experience is used to reflect on some of the research issues involved in studying marginalized technology users and the challenges involved in evaluating programs such as the CNI program.

DECONSTRUCTING THE DIGITAL DIVIDE

Research on home computing suggests that computers and the Internet are becoming embedded in daily life. People blend online habits with more traditional methods to accomplish a variety of goals such as communicating with friends, family, or colleagues; finding information relevant to their daily lives; participating in games and other entertainment pursuits; and completing transactions online (Rainie & Horrigan, 2005; UCLA Center for Communication Policy, 2004). People use technology to support and maintain existing social relationships in their homes, in the workplace, in their neighborhoods, and in community organizations (Horrigan, 2001; Wellman & Hampton, 1999; Wellman, Quan Haase, Witte, & Hampton, 2001).

Given that technology has become a part of everyday life, concerns have been raised about marginalized groups who may not have access to computer and Internet technology. A series of studies generated by the U.S. Department of Commerce is used most often to describe the characteristics of people who are classified as technology "have-nots"—those with a lower income, less education, single parent households, minorities (especially Hispanics and African-Americans), and those from rural areas (U.S. Department of Commerce, 1995, 1998, 1999, 2002, 2004). Technology "have-nots" are less likely to have access to computers and the Internet and as a consequence are less likely to have access to the presumed benefits associated with technology use such as increased educational opportunities, better job prospects, and information needed to address everyday life challenges. The solutions offered from the digital divide perspective are usually stated in terms of increasing access to technology for people who belong to the "have-not" group and presumably working to increase their technology literacy skills.

The Department of Commerce reports have raised debate about whether education, socio-economic status, or race is the most important variable in explaining variations in access to technology (Hoffman, Novak, & Schlosser, 2000; Martin, 2003; Robinson, DiMaggio, & Hargittai, 2003). More recently, discussions about the digital divide have involved concern about people's access to broadband Internet connections, especially for people living in rural areas (Fox, 2005; Parker, 2000; U.S. Department of Commerce, 2004). Others point to additional divides that should be considered such as age (Millward, 2003) and online skills (Hargittai, 2002).

The digital divide metaphor is based on a classification system that creates categories of advantage or disadvantage relative to people's access to technology. Classification systems are not neutral; they do some kind of work such as instantiating a bureaucracy or assisting in knowledge production (Bowker & Star, 1999). The great danger when we apply classification systems to people is that we are simultaneously creating profiles about the types of people that are at an advantage or disadvantage in life. For those in the advantaged group, their knowledge and experience seem natural and the infrastructure tends to support their identity. For those in the disadvantaged group, their knowledge and experience is not valued and the infrastructure torques their identities to fit the categories that have been imposed. The assumption is made that if only the poor (and other marginalized groups) will get some training or if we can provide them with a computer, then they will automatically have access to all the benefits associated with technology use.

The arguments underlying the digital divide metaphor are not new, and they need to be placed within the larger context of policy initiatives geared towards addressing the poverty problem in this county. Public policy and research concerning the poor tends to take a "supply side" view of poverty, in which the cause of poverty is attributed to a deficiency in the individual (Katz, 1989, 1995; O'Conner, 2001). Katz (1989, 1995) has traced the way that the poor have been defined in American society since the 1800s. He found that one consistent feature of definitions of the poor is that they are treated as a group that is in need of improvement in some way. In taking a supply side view of poverty, researchers and policy makers foreground the need for the poor to transform their lives by overcoming perceived deficits in literacy and life management skills. Other significant issues such as politics, power, resource distribution, and equality are often put in the background or ignored completely.

When it comes to participation in literacy programs, many have documented the ways that people and their experiences do not neatly fit into the categories of advantaged and disadvantaged (Connell, 1994; Horsman, 1990; Rockhill, 1987; Stuckey, 1991; Taylor & Dorsey-Gaines, 1988). The work of Taylor and Dorsey-Gaines (1988) is useful because they argue that you cannot treat a family's "low-income" status as a simple contextual variable that can be accounted for and then dismissed. Taylor and Dorsey-Gaines carried out their research by describing the reading and writing activities that occurred in people's homes in a low-income neighborhood. The value of their approach is that they started from the premise that the "poor" people that they were studying were worthy and interesting and successful readers and writers. Based on this approach, they caught literacy activities that might be missed because those who are poor are often not perceived as being successful and because their experience is often not directly studied.

There is a growing list of researchers that argue that the digital divide may not be the most productive way to address disparities in technology use among marginalized groups (Clark, Demont-Heinrich, & Webber, 2004; DiMaggio & Hargittai, 2001; Gurstein, 2003; Mehra, Merkel, & Bishop, 2004; Merkel, 2004; Warschauer, 2003). Much of the criticism of the digital divide metaphor concerns its overemphasis on providing *access* to hardware and software, while ignoring the social infrastructure needed to support technology *use*. This recognizes that there is a difference between providing people with access to technology and supporting people as they make technology use a part of their practice—a much more difficult problem to address.

There are a few studies that point to a research agenda in which low-income users are viewed as active technology users capable of solving local community problems and using technology to achieve their own purposes. Pinkett (2003), for example, studied technology use in Camfield Estates, a low-to-moderate-income housing development in Boston. One of the unique features of this research project is that the residents generated local community information that was made available to other residents. In a similar vein, the Afya Project is a participatory action research project geared towards removing the barriers that African-American women face in accessing health information (Bishop, Bazzell, Mehra, & Smith, 2001; Bishop, Mehra, Bazzell, & Smith, 2000). Women participating in the project were directly involved in developing a set of health-oriented web-based resources, outreach efforts, and the research process itself. Alkalimat and Williams (2001) examined a community technology center in a predominately African-American populated section of Toledo, Ohio. Their research points to the need for community technology centers to connect with organizations in the community, such as churches and schools, when planning programming and conducting outreach efforts. They also point to the important role of community networks in increasing capacity within the local community by cultivating and sharing power with its users.

The next section describes the approach used in this study to examine technology use among community members taking part in a computer training and distribution program attempting to address the digital divide. A situated approach was used to understand how low-income users brought technology into their lives, problems that they encountered along the way, and the way they drew on their social networks to use technology to achieve their goals.

THEORETICAL FRAMEWORK

The goal of this study was to develop a model for studying technology use by marginalized users that starts from the premise that they are active and successful technology users that bring technology into their lives in meaningful ways. In using a situated approach, the analysis in this study is centered on: (a) documenting the everyday literacy activities that occur in people's homes and the meaning that technology holds in their lives, (b) describing the problems that the CNI participants experienced and how they drew upon people in their social network to solve these problems, and (c) accounting for the barriers that people encounter as they attempt to adopt new literacy practices.

Documenting Everyday Literacy Practices

This study takes a situated approach to studying technology use that emphasizes the vernacular literacy practices that occur in people's homes and communities (Barton & Hamilton, 1998). From this perspective, we are surrounded by literacy, and we carry out literacy activities as we carry out the details of our lives like paying bills, writing notes to a spouse, or drafting a shopping list. Previous work on the CNI project has described the way that CNI participants made use of the computers distributed through the program (Merkel, 2004). The participants used their computers to organize their lives, maintain their social networks, pursue leisure activities, document their lives, research topics of interest, and support community organizations of which they were members. The CNI data suggests that one new literacy practice that might be studied is child-rearing practices that occur in the home. The computer was used by parents to teach their children life lessons such as the need to take care of one's belongings and values like cooperation (Merkel, 2004).

Networks/Roles and the Development of Expertise

From a situated perspective, literacy is viewed as a collective resource rather than as an attribute or a set of skills that resides in an individual. Barton and Hamilton (1998), in their study of the reading and writing activities in the community of Lancaster, England, found that much of people's reading and writing was located in reciprocal exchange networks of friends, neighbors, and families. The people in their study relied on these networks for support and advice, and they in turn provided support and advice to others in their network. In the same way, it is possible to examine the kinds of activities that occur in people's networks to support technology use.

Identifying Barriers

Many studies point to the difficulties that people encounter as they adopt new literacy practices (Horsman, 1990; Klassen, 1991; Rockhill, 1987; Taylor & Dorsey-Gaines, 1988). From this perspective, the goal is to understand how factors like characteristics of the users, features of the technology, institutional roles and norms, and the set of practices surrounding use help to account for the differing ways that people bring technology into their lives (Bruce & Peyton, 1993; Bruce & Rubin, 1993). When looking at marginalized groups, additional factors come into play such as the extent to which people are made an active part of the decision making process (Bishop, Tidline, Shoemaker, & Salela, 1999) and the extent to which literacy programs create a climate in which people are treated as "knowers" rather than as people deficient in literacy skills (Horsman, 1990; Taylor & Dorsey-Gaines, 1988).

METHODS

The research site for this study was the Community Networking Initiative (CNI) project, a computer training and distribution program aimed at low-income residents of Champaign County, Illinois. Participants in the CNI program received a free computer and Internet training course, a refurbished computer, and dial-up Internet access. The project was a collaborative effort between Prairienet (a community computer network that serves East Central Illinois), the Urban League of Champaign County, and the Graduate School of Library and Information Science at the University of Illinois. Participation in the program was loosely based on income guidelines used by the federal government for participation in other aid programs. The participants in the program were primarily African-American women. The program served a diverse age range from those just out of high school to senior citizens.

This study adopts an "ethnographic perspective" with the goal of studying computer and Internet use in the context of people's daily lives (Barton & Hamilton, 1998; Green & Bloome, 1997). Data for this study was collected over a one-year period using a number of methods including interviews, observations, focus groups, and an analysis of support logs maintained by Prairienet staff members. Focus groups were conducted with people that completed the CNI program, with the goal of understanding how the community members were using their computers, the types of technical problems that they encountered, and how (and if) they solved these technical problems. Interviews were conducted with 11 participants to gather more specific examples of computer use and problem-solving. During this same period, observations were conducted during the CNI training classes and in the homes of eight of the participants that had been interviewed. More extended observations of computer use were conducted with two of the participants, Suzy and Elaine, who were key informants for the study. Data was collected using multiple methods to ensure the accuracy of the analysis. Member checking was also used to ensure the accuracy of the interpretations being made and to give the participants some control over the personal details of their lives that were revealed in the writing.

The data was collected and analyzed using the constant comparative method (Glaser & Strauss, 1967). The constant comparative method closely links data collection and analysis through theoretical sampling. In analyzing the focus group data and the early interviews, prior computer experience and the presence of children in the family appeared to influence technology use. The focus groups also revealed that those who volunteered with the program served an important role in helping other participants solve the technical problems that they encountered. As the study progressed, participants were selected that had a range of computer experiences (work, school, and computer novices); volunteers and non-volunteers; and those with varying family structures (families with young children, families with older children, seniors, single-parent families, and dual-parent families).

BEYOND ENSUING ACCESS: THE INTRACTABLE NATURE OF TECHNICAL PROBLEMS

This section draws on support logs maintained by the technology staff at Prairicnct that documented the technical problems that the CNI participants experienced. The support logs reveal that the CNI staff had contact with about 47% of the CNI community members over the course of the project (295 unique contacts, out of 628 adults completing the project). On average, there were at least three contacts or attempted contacts with each community member that received support through the CNI program in the first year, a point of frustration for both for CNI participants and staff members. This was caused by differences in schedules, disconnected or changed phone numbers, and the difficulties involved in diagnosing and repairing computer problems, especially on older equipment.

The overwhelming problem experienced by CNI participants was difficulty connecting to the Internet to access e-mail and the World Wide Web. This finding is consistent with the Homenet study that also documented the difficulties that new users experienced as they attempted to connect to the Internet (Kiesler, Kraut, Lundmark, Scherlis, & Mukhopadhyay, 1997; Kiesler, Lundmark, Zdaniuk, & Kraut, 2000). The problems that users experienced connecting to the Internet were tied to hardware and software problems such as modem failures, missing cables, or incorrect settings. The frequency with which this happened may be attributed to the fact that participants received refurbished equipment, making it more likely that they would experience a hardware failure. Difficulty connecting to the Internet was also tied to user inexperience. Novice users had difficulty setting up their computers to connect to the Internet, faced problems using software and entering login or password information correctly, and sometimes changed settings or deleted files, not realizing the impact that this would have on their systems. Training issues in some cases exacerbated these problems. The machines in the training lab were already connected to the Internet, so the program participants did not have to go through the dial-up procedure when using the Internet like they did at home. In addition, the systems in the training lab were used for a variety of purposes, so there were differences between the software available on the lab machines and the computers that the participants took home.

While the support log data were useful to get an overall sense of the most typical technical problems experienced by the CNI participants, they missed problems that did not get reported or other issues such as the intimidation involved in using new technology. This sentiment was best expressed by one of the CNI participants that was interviewed:

> When you don't know a lot about computers, it's kind of easy to get away from it. You get the computer, and it's nothing to keep you going with it, and you don't know anything about a computer, so you don't want to go in there because sometimes you get in there and do something wrong. Our teacher was talking about how people be calling down there, talking about I done messed up my e-mail. I done did this. I done did that. So, I don't know. I was thinking that maybe if they had some like classes to help them, like to keep something ongoing with them. Because the more you use it, because it really is a fun thing. It's really real interesting, but if you're intimidated by it, you're not going to mess with it.

It can be difficult to be viewed as a person who does not know how to do something or as someone who has "messed something up." Clearly, just having access to technology is not enough to ensure use. There is a need to try to find ways to keep people engaged with the technology until they get to the point where they see technology as fun, interesting, or at least potentially useful. The next section provides examples of the kinds of support needed to encourage technology use over time in one's social network.

VOLUNTEERISM AND SUPPORTING TECHNOLOGY USE: SUZY'S STORY

In contrast to the more formal help-giving provided by the CNI project, the work that the volunteers did to help others solve problems was important in encouraging the adoption of new literacy practices. As part of the CNI program, participants could volunteer to help during training classes, computer distributions, and other CNI program activities. In return for their volunteer work, the CNI participants could earn upgrades for their computer. The volunteers engaged in a number of different activities to help others make sense of the technology and to solve technical problems. These help-giving activities extended to members of the volunteers' family and friendship networks.

Suzy provides an example of the important work that volunteers did to encourage technology use and of the kind of social support needed to support computer and Internet use. Suzy is a White woman in her mid-fifties who moved to East Central Illinois when her husband was stationed at a local military base that currently is no longer in operation. She and her husband have since divorced, and she now lives on her own in a trailer home. She was working two full-time jobs until she cut herself on the job, suffering a staph infection that put her in the hospital for a month. She had to apply for public aid because she was denied worker's compensation for this injury. Soon after her job injury, Suzy was diagnosed with cancer and was undergoing chemotherapy right before participating in the CNI program. Learning to use the computer was important to Suzy because, despite her illness, she could "still be productive and be in contact with the outside world and not have to leave the house."

Suzy's story illustrates the importance of having a meaningful context in which to apply one's technology knowledge. An important theme that dominates Suzy's story is the importance of volunteerism and making a difference in her community. Suzy is the volunteer coordinator for a nonprofit food cooperative that works to get low cost food into people's homes. Suzy is in charge of organizing all aspects of the food distribution and handles the business end of the program. Since participating in the CNI program, she has converted many of her paper-based recording systems to computer-based systems, using her computer to create signs, sign-up sheets, raffle tickets and other paperwork needed to manage the day-to-day activities of the program.

Suzy's commitment to volunteerism carried over to a new activity—encouraging people in her social network to use computers and providing support to them as they encountered obstacles. Suzy has served an important intermediary role between people in her social network and the CNI program. Through her volunteer work at Prairienet, she has gained an understanding about how the organization works. This allowed her to give people she knows useful advice about the application process and the procedure for getting into classes. This is reflected in the way she encouraged a person she met through another volunteer activity, volunteer driving, in which she took people without transportation to doctor's appointments.

> Suzy: She became afflicted with MS, her husband left because he just couldn't handle it, and she seems to have a real fear of being alone. So her doctor, I think it was a psychologist, suggested that she get a computer. And I had taken her to that appointment and she was kind of talking about it when she came out to the car. She said, "My doctor wants me…," she was kind of almost crying. She said, "My doctor, tells me that I need to have a computer." She said, "Where can I get a computer? I can't even work." And I said, well…
>
> Researcher: (laugh), let me tell you
>
> Suzy: so yeah, that was on a Thursday. I came down to Prairienet. I got her the form. I took it to her. She called me up she said, I don't know how to fill this form out. So I went back over, we filled it out.

Suzy provided help in countless ways to those in her immediate friendship network and to those she met through her volunteer activities. She told people about the CNI program, brought applications for them to fill out, delivered computers to them when they completed the program, drove them to classes, and offered support and encouragement along the way.

Suzy also played an active role in supporting people in her immediate friendship network in their technology use. For example, she helped her friend Gund participate in the CNI program and helped her with the many technical problems she experienced along the way. Gund and Suzy met shortly after Suzy was diagnosed with cancer. At one time or another each has provided emotional support and care when the other was sick. They shared meals together. They did volunteer work together, including work through the CNI program and the food distribution program that Suzy ran. They knew each other's histories and life stories. There was an expectation that they would be there for each other. Suzy suggested to Gund that she participate in the CNI program, attended the training with her, and even used her volunteer hours to upgrade Gund's computer. Suzy helped Gund in a number of ways by providing resources, monitoring her progress, suggesting ways that she could use the computer to meet her goals, and helping her when she encountered obstacles along the way.

Suzy also acted as a "partner-in-use" and planned shared activities with others in her social network that used computers. For example, Suzy and her friend Laurie bought computers at roughly the same time so that they could "lean on each other" as they learned to use them.

> Suzy: My next door neighbor on the on the other side of me, she and I both got an E-machine, the very, like she got hers one night then I got mine like two or three days later. And we planned it that was so that we can kind of lean on each other and...but she has had some compu[ter] some college courses, plus her dad is really big into computers. So between Laurie and I, we kind of tried (laugh) [to] lead them through some of their problems.

In using the computer with a friend, there is a reason and a motivation to learn how to use the computer. This also speaks to the community members' abilities to add people to their social network. Suzy was adept at adding people to her social network, including the CNI staff.

There are some limits to the helpfulness of one's social network in distributing technical expertise. There may be people in one's social network who have technical expertise but not in the areas that are needed to solve a problem. Shifts in one's friendship, neighbor, and even family networks can influence a person's ability to give and receive help. In some cases, because the expert user was a member of one's family or friendship network, learning about computers was inhibited. Instead of actively learning how to resolve technical problems there was an expectation that the friend would always be available to solve problems that would arise. In addition, the shared history between people who are part of a social network may make it less likely that a person will provide help or share equipment. For example, Suzy talked about not sharing a piece of extra equipment that she had because she did not think that the friend would take care of it.

This section highlights the types of activities needed to support technology *use* rather than just ensuring *access* to computers. Volunteers, like Suzy, provided troubleshooting help and computer advice, taught others how to use their computers and what the computer could do, monitored progress, acted as a partner-in-use, provided resources to help novice users learn about and use their computers, and acted as an intermediary between the CNI project and friends and family members in their social network. Another important element of Suzy's story is that she had a meaningful context in which to apply her skills. The next section considers further the link between having access to technology and having access to the benefits connected to technology use, such as increased job and educational opportunities.

DECONSTRUCTING LITERACY CHOICES: ELAINE'S STORY

The digital divide literature assumes that there is a direct link between having access to technology and having access to the opportunities afforded to technology use. Elaine's experience with technology and her participation in the CNI program helps us to think through the impact of having access to technology and the complex choices that people make in integrating technology into their lives. Elaine is an African-American woman in her forties. She is originally from Tennessee and moved to East Central Illinois because her husband found a job at a local company. They have since divorced, but she decided to stay in the area to raise her children, who are now grown. Elaine is active in the lives of her children and her grandchildren; one of her daughters was living in her home with her own children during this study. Four years prior to participating in the CNI program, she injured her leg and has had trouble with it ever since, making it difficult for her to stand for long periods of time. She had some limited computer experience in a previous job that required her to do some data entry.

Elaine went through the CNI program in 1999. One of her motivations for going through the program was her strong connection to her children and to her grandchildren. One of the reasons that she wanted to get a computer was to keep up with her grandchildren.

> Elaine: I guess it made me realize too that, you know, here in a few years and stuff they [are] going to know quite a bit about computers and stuff. I'm not going to know anything....Because at the time, they were going through Head Start. That's what they did. They sit there and let the kids mess with the computer quite a bit more in the day time. And then like I said, as you know too, a whole lot of things now is computerized. I knew that if I wanted to keep up at all, if I wanted to keep [up] with my grandkids, or if it was something that they wanted to know that they didn't know, I couldn't tell them not unless I learned it. So that's kind of how I really got interested in doing this.

Elaine saw the potential of the computer to help her grandchildren get ahead. Since participating in the CNI program, she has purchased several computers and educational programs for her grandchildren. With great pride she described the kinds of learning programs that they used and how they were using programs at a higher level than their actual grade level.

As she used the computer more, Elaine became known in her social network as someone who could help solve technical problems, which helped to further her own skills. Once you become known in your network as a computer expert, there is an incentive to live up to that reputation. Being viewed as an expert "becomes a habit," and this encouraged those who were especially interested in computers to gain further computer expertise. Elaine described how people had problems that she did not know how to solve, so she would call someone to find out how to fix them, furthering her own computer knowledge and her role as expert within her social network. It was because of these efforts that the CNI project decided to hire her as a staff member to conduct training classes.

When Elaine first came to work at Prairienet, the hope was that she would be able to use the technical skills that she learned to start her own business. The director of Prairienet encouraged her to go through a special training class designed to help people start small businesses. Part of this training involved creating a business plan, and there was funding available through the program to start a small business. Elaine went through this additional training, but she has not finished the business plan for a computer-related business, and it appears this is not something she is going to pursue in a formal way for now.

While she has decided to put a computer business on hold, she has decided to start another business. She has obtained a childcare license and has begun offering childcare services in her home. One of the barriers that Elaine faced as she thought about starting a computer-related business was the fear of doing something "this big." She talked about being overwhelmed by all the steps involved in actually creating a computer business. Childcare, on the other hand, was familiar to her because she had raised her own children and she was actively involved in the lives of her grandchildren. Elaine insists that her grandchildren should not be taken care of by just anyone. By getting her childcare license, she could receive funding to watch her grandchildren while her daughter was at work, and she could watch other children as well.

It is important to note here that Elaine has made a perfectly valid choice about where to focus her attention and energy. She may decide that she does want to start up a computer business, or she may continue to do some work informally for people she knows. When we look at some of the reasons why Elaine has decided not to pursue a computer-related business, we begin to understand the messiness that comes between an intended effect of a program designed to increase literacy skills and the reality of people's lives. This gets at the heart of programs, like the CNI, that are designed to promote social change.

How should we interpret Elaine's use of technology? How should we evaluate the other participants' uses of technology? The key issue here is in the interpretation of the choices that the poor make in striving to adopt new literacy practices and in achieving these goals. From the point of view of researchers and policy-makers operating from an access model, all that is required is to provide the opportunities for literacy training and access to computers. From this perspective, if people do not choose to take advantage of these opportunities, then they lack the motivation to achieve a better life. This is in contrast to the poor for whom choice is constructed in a different way and for whom difficult decisions must be made about pursuing new literacy practices and accounting for the realities of everyday life.

The story not being told, when the details of people's lives are abstracted from the discussion about the digital divide, is the real way that material circumstances influence literacy. The CNI participants in the focus group and the interviews mentioned a number of barriers that made it difficult to participate in the CNI program, to participate in subsequent training classes, and even to volunteer. These issues included: a lack of transportation, the need for childcare, the busyness and exhaustion of every day life, the loss of telephone access, a lack of computer experience, and features of the training classes and the CNI program itself.

DISCUSSION

There is a disconnect between the lives of the CNI participants and the approach that is typically taken by researchers and policy-makers who remove the details of people's lives from discussions about technology use. In addressing this disconnect, this study argues that these are, in the end, the wrong questions to ask: whether or not the poor are like or unlike middle class Americans, whether or not their use of technology is empowering or disempowering, or whether the poor are inherently worthy or unworthy in terms of their pursuit of new literacy practices. Instead, in taking a situated approach, this study explores different questions by asking how marginalized users bring technology into their lives when given the chance, what barriers they encounter when trying to make technology part of their daily practice, and how they draw on their social networks and develop expertise to solve these problems. This means that having access to technology can be empowering, disempowering, or some complex combination of both, depending on the situation (Bruce & Hogan, 1998). This section considers some of the challenges involved in studying marginalized technology users and in evaluating the impact of programs such as the CNI project.

Impacts of Having Access to Technology are Not Direct

One of the implications of this study is that the impact of having access to technology is often indirect and can be difficult to measure. This is true in the sense that there is a difference between providing people with access to technology and ensuring that they can use technology. This is also true in the sense that there is frequently a gap between having access to technology and having access to all of the benefits associated with technology use. In this study, the user-support data revealed that the CNI participants encountered a number of problems when trying to connect to the Internet due to hardware and software failures, problems caused by a lack of experience with technology, and problems caused by the training that they received. Novice users also experienced a great deal of intimidation when it came to bringing technology into their lives. Even technically proficient users, such as Elaine, faced significant barriers when it came to gaining access to some of the presumed benefits associated with technology use.

The adoption of computer and Internet technology was not a linear process. CNI participants adopted technology in a stop-start fashion, using the technology, stopping their use, and picking up the technology again when they found a new use for the technology or when they found a way to solve a problem that they encountered. The meaning of technology in their lives was constantly being renegotiated. This suggests the need for prolonged engagement to capture some of the long-term impacts of having access to technology and to account for the shifts in use, identity, and learning that occur.

Connecting Technology Use to Practice

Technology use, like any form of literacy, is inseparable from social practice. Learning technology skills goes beyond just mastering the ability to use e-mail or a web browser. At a basic level, people need to find a meaningful context in which they can practice and develop their technology literacy skills. In this chapter, Suzy and Elaine found a meaningful way to develop their technical skills through their volunteer efforts. In connecting technology use to practice, it also becomes relevant to describe the ways that people draw on their social networks and develop expertise to address technology problems they encounter. Evidence of the support that is needed is seen when examining the work that the volunteers did to help people in their social network use technology. These support activities included: providing troubleshooting help and computer advice, teaching others how to use their computers and what the computer could do, monitoring the progress that people made as they adopted new practices, acting as a partner-in-use, and providing material resources that people needed to participate in the program (i.e. providing transportation to classes). This kind of ongoing support is often not addressed in public policy, research efforts, and training classes (including the CNI project), which focus on access rather than use.

Recognizing the Ideological Nature of Technology Use

As the data was further examined, it was realized that the way the problem was framed in the beginning of the chapter was only half right. It is not just that researchers tend to operate from a model in which the poor are seen as being deficient. Rather it is that technology and the pursuit of literacy practices is a site for the study of competing ideologies. The CNI participants saw the potential of the computer to help them gain economic security, be good parents, advocate for themselves and their family, be productive, and fit into a world that is increasingly requiring technical knowledge. It is in addressing the issue of how to achieve these goals that the two sides diverge. Those who operate from an access-oriented paradigm argue that once the technology is provided, any failure to achieve these goals is because the poor do not choose to do what it takes to achieve these goals. In contrast, when the lives of the poor are examined, it is apparent that a lack of material resources impinges on their ability to achieve these goals. Rather than dismissing these issues, the barriers that the participants experience due to a lack of material circumstances need to be fully accounted for.

This suggests new roles for researchers, policy-makers, and practitioners and a new criterion for evaluating the effectiveness of their roles. Research needs to be carried out in which marginalized groups are treated as "knowers" rather than as people who are deficient in acquiring literacy skills. The people that participate in literacy programs may still be working on learning new literacy practices, but they are experts in their own lives, in the lives of their families, and on issues that are important to them. The effectiveness of such efforts should be judged in terms of an individual's capacity to define the meaning of technology for themselves and how well an individual can use technology to achieve personally-relevant goals. Professors, researchers, and activists need to think carefully about the assumptions that are made about the poor and find ways to move away from a view of the poor as "other" towards a view of the poor as "us," appreciating the intrinsic value of all people.

REFERENCES

Alkalimat, A. & Williams, K. (2001). Social capital and cyberpower in the African American community: A case study of a community technology center in the dual city. In L. Keeble & B. Loader (Eds.), *Community informatics: Shaping computer mediated social relations* (pp. 177–204). London, UK: Routledge.

Barton, D. & Hamilton, M. (1998). *Local literacies: Reading and writing in one community.* New York, NY: Routledge.

Bishop, A. P., Bazzell, I., Mehra, B., & Smith, C. (2001). Afya: Social and digital technologies that reach across the digital divide. Retrieved from http://firstmonday.org/ojs/index.php/fm/article/view/847/756

Bishop, A. P., Mehra, B., Bazzell, I., & Smith, C. (2000). Socially grounded user studies in digital library development. Retrieved from http://www.firstmonday.org/issues/issue5_6/bishop/index.html

Bishop, A. P., Tidline, T., Shoemaker, S., & Salela, P. (1999). Public libraries and networked information services in low-income communities. *Libraries & Information Science Research, 51*(4), 361–390.

Bowker, G. C. & Star, S. L. (1999). *Sorting things out: Classification and its consequences.* Cambridge, MA: MIT Press.

Bruce, B. C. & Hogan, M. P. (1998). The disappearance of technology: Toward an ecological model of literacy. In D. Reinking, M. McKenna, L. Labbo, & R. Kieffer (Eds.),

Handbook of literacy and technology: Transformations in a post-typographic world (pp. 269–281). Hillsdale, NJ: Erlbaum.

Bruce, B. C. & Peyton, J. K. (1993). A situated evaluation of the ENFI. In B. C. Bruce, J. K. Peyton, & T. W. Batson (Eds.), *Network based classrooms* (pp. 33–49). New York, NY: Cambridge University Press.

Bruce, B. C. & Rubin, A. (1993). *Electronic quills: A situated evaluation of using computers for writing in classrooms.* Hillsdale, NJ: Lawrence Erlbaum.

Clark, L. S., Demont-Heinrich, C., & Webber, S. A. (2004). Ethnographic interviews on the digital divide. *New Media & Society, 6*(4), 529–547.

Connell, R. W. (1994). Poverty and education. *Harvard Educational Review, 64*(2), 125–149.

DiMaggio, P. & Hargittai, E. (2001). *From the "digital divide" to "digital inequality": Studying Internet use as penetration increases.* Princeton, NJ: Center for Arts and Cultural Policy Studies, Woodrow Wilson School, Princeton University.

Fox, S. (2005). *Digital divisions: There are clear differences among those with broadband connections, dial-up connections, and no connections at all to the Internet.* Retrieved from http://www.pewinternet.org/PPF/r/165/report_display.asp

Glaser, B. G. & Strauss, A. L. (1967). *The discovery of grounded theory: Strategies for qualitative research.* New York, NY: Aldine De Gruyter.

Green, J. L. & Bloome, D. (1997). Ethnography and ethnographers of and in education: A situated perspective. In J. Flood, S. B. Heath, & D. Lapp (Eds.), *Handbook of research on teaching literacy through the communicative and visual arts* (pp. 181–202). New York, NY: Macmillan.

Gurstein, M. (2003). Effective use: A community informatics strategy beyond the digital divide. Retrieved from http://firstmonday.org/ojs/index.php/fm/article/view/1107

Hargittai, E. (2002). Second-level digital divide: Differences in people's online skills. Retrieved from http://firstmonday.org/ojs/index.php/fm/article/view/942

Hoffman, D. L., Novak, T. P., & Schlosser, A. E. (2000). The evolution of the digital divide: How gaps in Internet access may impact electronic commerce. *Journal of Computer-Mediated Communication, 5*(3),1–55.

Horrigan, J. (2001). *Online communities: Networks that nurture long-distance relationships and local ties.* Retrieved from http://www.pewinternet.org/Reports/2001/Online-Communities.aspx

Horsman, J. (1990). *Something in my mind besides the everyday: Women and literacy.* Toronto, Ontario: Women's Press.

Katz, M. (1989). *The undeserving poor: From the war on poverty to the war on welfare.* New York, NY: Pantheon Books.

Katz, M. B. (1995). *Improving poor people.* Princeton, NJ: Princeton University Press.

Kiesler, S., Kraut, R., Lundmark, V., Scherlis, W., & Mukhopadhyay, T. (1997). Usability, help desk calls, and residential Internet usage. *Proceedings of the SIGCHI Conference on Human Factors in Computing Systems.* Retrieved from http://homenet.hcii.cs.cmu.edu/progress/usechipaper.html

Kiesler, S., Lundmark, V., Zdaniuk, B., & Kraut, R. E. (2000). Troubles with the Internet: The dynamics of help at home. *Human Computer Interaction, 15*(4), 323–351.

Klassen, C. (1991). Bilingual written language use by low-education Latin American newcomers. In D. Barton & R. Ivanic (Eds.), *Writing in the community: Vol. 6* (pp. 38–57). Thousand Oaks, CA: Sage.

Martin, P. S. (2003). Is the digital divide really closing? A critique of inequality measurement in a nation online. *IT & Society, 1*(4), 1–13.

Mehra, B., Merkel, C., & Bishop, A. P. (2004). The Internet for empowerment of minority and marginalized users. *New Media & Society, 6*(6), 781–802.

Merkel, C. (2004). Beyond deficit models of technology use: Viewing "have-nots" as active technology users. In M. Consalvo & M. Allen (Eds.), *Internet Research Annual: Selected Papers from the Association of Internet Researchers Conferences (AOIR) 2003: Vol. 2* (pp. 189–200). New York, NY: Peter Lang Publishing Group.

Millward, P. (2003). The "grey digital divide": Perception, exclusion and barrier of access to the Internet for older people. Retrieved from http://firstmonday.org/ojs/index.php/fm/article/view/1066

O'Conner, A. (2001). *Poverty knowledge*, Princeton, NJ: Princeton University Press.

Parker, E. B. (2000). Closing the digital divide in rural America. *Telecommunications Policy, 24*, 281–290.

Pinkett, R. (2003). Community technology and community building: Early results from the creating community connections project. *The Information Society, 19*(5), 365–379.

Rainie, L. & Horrigan, J. (2005). *A decade of adoption: How the Internet has woven itself into American life.* Retrieved from http://www.pewinternet.org/PPF/r/148/report_display.asp

Robinson, J. P., DiMaggio P., & Hargittai, E. (2003). New social survey perspectives on the digital divide. *IT & Society, 1*(5), 1–22.

Rockhill, K. (1987). Literacy as threat/desire: Longing to be somebody. In J. Gaskell & A. McLaren (Eds.), *Women and education: A Canadian perspective* (pp. 315–331). Calgary, Alberta: Detselig Enterprises Limited.

Stuckey, J. E. (1991). *The violence of literacy.* Portsmouth, NH: Boynton/Cook Publishers.

Taylor, D. & Dorsey-Gaines, C. (1988). *Growing up literate: Learning from inner-city families.* Portsmouth, NH: Heinemann.

UCLA Center for Communication Policy. (2004). *The digital future report: Surveying the digital future year four.* Retrieved from http://www.staticworx.com/assets/pdf/digital-future-report.pdf

U.S. Department of Commerce. (1995). *Falling through the net: A survey of the "have nots" in rural and urban America.* Retrieved from http://www.ntia.doc.gov/ntiahome/fallingthru.html

U.S. Department of Commerce. (1998). *Falling through the net II: New data on the digital divide.* Retrieved from http://www.ntia.doc.gov/ntiahome/net2/

U.S. Department of Commerce. (1999). *Falling through the net: Defining the digital divide.* Retrieved from http://www.ntia.doc.gov/ntiahome/fttn99/FTTN.pdf

U.S. Department of Commerce. (2002). *A nation online: How Americans are expanding their use of the Internet.* Retrieved from http://www.ntia.doc.gov/legacy/ntiahome/dn/nationonline_020502.htm

U.S. Department of Commerce. (2004). *A nation on-line: Entering the broadband age.* Retrieved from http://www.ntia.doc.gov/reports/anol/index.html

Warschauer, M. (2003). *Technology and social inclusion, rethinking the digital divide.* Cambridge, MA: MIT Press.

Wellman, B. & Hampton, K. (1999). Living networked on and off line. *Contemporary Sociology, 28*(6), 648–654.

Wellman, B., Quan Haase, A., Witte, J., & Hampton, K. (2001). Does the Internet increase, decrease, or supplement social capital? Social networks, participation, and community commitment. *American Behavioral Scientist, 45*(3), 436–455.

CHAPTER 7

SUPPORTING READING-TO-LEARN IN SCIENCE

The Application of Summarization Technology in Multicultural Urban High School Classrooms

Kimberley Gomez, Samuel Kwon, Louis Gomez, and Jennifer Sherer

ABSTRACT

This study contributes to the growing body of research and professional literature about classroom integration of literacy support technologies, like Summary Street.[1] The results of this study suggest that summarization, in general, and a summarization tool, Summary Street, in particular, can be useful and effective tools to supplement teachers' content-area reading support, encourage students to read texts more carefully, work well for students at all reading skill levels, and provide individual attention that students find useful and appealing. This work offers insights into technology integration and the specific challenges and benefits that may be applicable to other classroom settings.

INTRODUCTION

Imagine that you are a ninth grade regular education environmental science teacher, and it is the first week of the new school year. You look around your classroom

Research on Technology Use in Multicultural Settings, pages 139–157.

and realize that 80% of your 32 students are Latino and, though they speak to you in English, they speak to their peers, and when they think you're not looking, pass notes written in Spanish. Imagine that they turn in their first science assignment. They have been asked to locate several important facts about aquifers in the science text, locate the main ideas and supporting evidence presented by the author, paraphrase the main and supporting ideas, and write a short summary. Understanding the basic ideas underlying a scientific concept is critical for students. The text the students have been asked to read has a Lexile grade level of tenth grade that, though slightly above grade level, should not be too difficult for ninth grade students to handle, and you look forward to their first graded responses.

When you receive their responses you are troubled. Aside from the numerous grammatical and spelling errors, which signal second language learners' challenges in writing, many of the students have either (a) copied large amounts of the text, word for word, in an apparent broad swath effort to identify the main and supporting ideas, or (b) attempted to paraphrase sentences in the text that originally represented the main and supporting ideas, yet in the paraphrase have lost the key element or elements that conveyed the author's message. You spend the next week during your evenings writing individual feedback to the students about their performance on the summarization assignment and trying to think of a way to instructionally support their ability to locate the main idea (or argument) and supporting ideas (or evidence) and to give substantive feedback in a timely fashion.

A few interrelated points will be made in this chapter:

- Many high school students, and especially second language learners, need to develop their reading comprehension skills if they are to learn the complex concepts of a subject area like science. "Beyond the primary grades, students need to grapple with texts that are expository, dense, and full of new, more difficult vocabulary, especially in math, science, and social studies" (Allen, 2000, p. 83). Readers who comprehend what they read have well-developed reading-to-learn skills that they apply as they read domain-specific text. Students who have poorly developed reading-to-learn skills likely experience science as a confusing, patchwork discourse not unlike participating in a cellular phone conversation when the signal fades in and out.

- Content-area teachers often have little experience with supporting reading comprehension in their subject areas while teaching subject-area concepts. Science and other content-area teachers at the high school level have a great deal of material that must be addressed during a school year. In school, they present students with content, usually from textbooks or from trade book texts, and move through it fairly quickly. Science teachers rarely think about themselves as teachers of reading in science (Gomez & Madda, 2005; Williams & Gomez, 2002), although recent research indicates that science teachers identify reading as a frequently used form of science instruction (Craig & Yore, 1995; Yore, 1991; Yore, Craig, & Maguire, 1998; Yore & Shymansky, 1991).

- A key reading-to-learn metacognitive strategy that both supports students' monitoring of their reading comprehension and helps them to read texts more critically is summarization (Pressley, 2000). When students summarize the text, their content understanding improves, and they retain the information longer. Summarization as a reading-to-learn strategy has proven to be a successful tool for developing the reading comprehension skills of students as young as fifth grade as well as for college students (Wade-Stein & Kintsch, 2005).

- Children who have poor reading-to-learn skills, and/or who are second language learners, need regular and multiple opportunities to develop their reading comprehension in content-area reading. A critical element of learning to extract and apply information derived from the text is the opportunity to have frequent exposure to text.

- Students need regular, clear, and usable feedback about their comprehension of the text. Students with limited reading comprehension skills, in particular, need specific feedback about where they need more help in improving their acquisition of knowledge through text-based materials. They benefit from timely feedback about their performance on a reading comprehension task. What is needed is a supportive literacy technology that provides readers who have limited reading comprehension skills frequent opportunities to read domain-specific text and to receive feedback that is specific to their performance level.

After these points are made, we will describe our response to the need for better reading comprehension support for second language learners in urban high school science classrooms. We will describe our effort to integrate a literacy technology support tool, Summary Street, into ninth grade science and social studies classrooms in two "small schools" within a large urban high school. We will discuss several challenges to the successful integration of the tool and share our findings regarding the benefits that the use of the tool provided for teachers and for students. Finally, we will explore implications of this effort for teachers and researchers interested in integrating literacy technologies in multicultural content-area high school classrooms.

CONCEPTUAL FRAMING

Wanted in Content-Area Learning: Good Reading Comprehension Skills

The National Reading Panel (2000) defines reading comprehension as "an active process that requires an intentional and thoughtful interaction between the reader and the text" (p. 13). In science, like most other disciplines, accomplished readers are aware of their purpose in reading, are continually monitoring and regulating their approach, and are adjusting their reading effort to the complexity of the text (Pressley, 2000; Pressley, Johnson, Symons, McGoldrick, & Kurita, 1989). There are at least three important characteristics of accomplished science readers. First, accomplished readers are always sensitive to the fact that they are engaged in a meaning-making task (Berieter & Scardamalia, 1986). In this sense, accomplished readers are constantly seeking connections to prior knowledge and paying attention to the current situational purpose in contrast to simply decoding the text and attending to the most surface level features of vocabulary. Second, attention to meaning-making implies that readers are always engaged in a second task of monitoring metacognitive awareness of their comprehension. When good readers encounter intellectual roadblocks in the text, they note them. Poor readers, on the other hand, simply ignore them and press on (Clay, 1991). Third, accomplished readers have at their disposal multiple strategies that support their meaning-making and metacognitive awareness. For example, when they encounter a claim in the text that they don't understand or concepts that are confusing, they may make notes in the margins, underline difficult vocabulary words, or simply put a question mark beside a difficult passage (Zywica & Gomez, 2008). In short, accomplished readers are aware of their level of understanding of the text.

Supporting Reading Comprehension in Science: More Information Please

Secondary teachers often feel that they lack the expertise to teach reading. Allen (2000) and others (Cziko, 1998) have argued that this perception of lack of knowledge often results in teachers enabling students not to read. That is, teachers may lift out important material and discuss the materials with students rather than having students closely read and strategically interact with the text. Teachers often "wing it," calling upon their previous instructional experiences, their assumptions and beliefs about students' abilities, and, when available, utilizing information obtained through one-shot or short-term professional development to supplement their instructional practices (Gomez & Madda, 2005). Given the growing numbers of second language learners in U.S. classrooms, it seems clear that leaving teachers in the classroom to "wing it" is not a viable solution for educating diverse urban and bilingual students.

Reading-to-Learn Metacognition: The Route to Accomplished Reading in Science

To paraphrase Michael Pressley (2000), we teach students to read because we want them to gain knowledge through texts. That is, we want students to comprehend what they read. In order to gain knowledge through texts, students must have a tool kit of resources available to them whenever they read. Many adolescents in this country do not have such a tool kit available. They fail to learn how to make meaning from the text, how to recognize the organizational structures of various genres, and how to communicate meaningfully about what they have encountered through reading in their science classrooms. In short, they do not read in a strategic manner. Literature addressing the differences in metacognitive skills of good versus poor readers (e.g. Allen, 2000; Schoenbach, Greenleaf, Cziko, & Hurwitz, 2000; Wilhelm, 1995) suggests that it is essential that adolescent readers learn not only the content, during reading, but also the structural features of text, and then, with this information actively apply appropriate strategies (Allen, 2000) if they are to read-to-learn.

For us, reading-to-learn encapsulates the set of skills that allows a learner to develop from an ineffective reader to an accomplished reader. Reading-to-learn is an ensemble of cognitive approaches that support learners who have mastered the problems of reading as decoding but are still mastering the problem of reading for knowledge. Following Guthrie (2001) and others (Romance & Vitale, 2005; Yore, Shymansky, Henriques, Chidsey, & Lewis, 1997), we believe that the cognitive components of reading-to-learn include activating background knowledge, questioning to construct meaning, question answering, summarizing, and comprehension monitoring within a self-regulating system.

Teachers and students need a tool kit of strategic approaches for reading instruction in science. The forms, purposes, and processing demands of science require that teachers show, demonstrate, and make visible to students how literacy operates within the content. There is evidence to suggest that adolescents benefit from explicit instruction in strategies to improve reading comprehension. These strategic reading approaches are successful when they are explicit, embedded in authentic learning tasks, and motivate the learner to own the information (Pressley et al., 1989; Yore et al., 1997).

Summarization: An Important Reading-to-Learn Metacognitive Strategy

Our approach to supporting reading-to-learn development in high school students is through summarization, specifically using a tool called Summary Street. Summarization, as a reading comprehension strategy, has been identified as having particular benefits for readers (Wade-Stein & Kintsch, 2005). Studies have found that writer-based summaries not only improve students' comprehension, but also help them monitor their understanding (Hare & Borchardt, 1984; King, 1992; O'Donnell & Dansereau, 1992; Wittrock, 1990). First, summarization encourages students to identify the main idea and supporting ideas in the text. Second, summarization requires that students understand the essence of a topic (Kintsch, Steinhart, Matthews, Lamb, & LSA Research Group, 2000). This means that students must understand the relationship of ideas to each other in support of an argument or explanation. Finally, summarization requires students to put the text in their own words. Students must understand the text's semantics sufficiently well to be able to draw on their personal corpus of similar terms and phrases.

Several studies (Frey, Fisher, & Hernandez, 2003; Radmacher & Latosi-Sawin, 1995; Wade-Stein & Kintsch, 2005) have examined the effectiveness of summarization as a reading comprehension strategy in middle school and college classrooms and have concluded that summarization, under certain conditions, is effective in supporting reading comprehension. These conditions include: effective instruction (including modeling of how to write a summary), consistent feedback on students' summaries, and regular opportunities to write summaries. There has not been a great deal of discussion, however, about the use of summarization in high school settings and particularly in urban high school settings.

Summarization Technology: Quick, Direct Feedback about Reading Comprehension

In high school science classrooms, the diversity and complexity of students' reading levels, coupled with the necessity of teaching content, render direct support for reading improvement challenging. One response to this challenge is the deployment of summarization technologies in classrooms to provide diverse learners with explicit feedback about their reading comprehension of science text. Though summarization technologies have been employed in suburban and middle grade classrooms (Herman, Perkins, Hansen, Gomez, & Gomez, 2010), these technologies have not been used in the linguistically complex and culturally diverse environments of urban high school settings. The current study is based on previous research, which used latent semantic technology to support students' summarizations through the use of a tool called Summary Street (Landauer, 1998; Landauer, Foltz, & Laham, 1998).

Latent Semantic Analysis and Summarization

Summary Street is a Web-based system that provides an environment in which students can prepare multiple drafts of a summary with feedback about the adequacy of what they have written. The feedback is generated by latent semantic analysis (LSA), which is a machine-learning method that constructs semantic representations that in many ways mirror human semantics. Summary Street uses LSA (Landauer et al., 1998) to judge how close a student-generated summary captures the ideas in a target text. LSA creates a statistical profile of the student summary article and judges it with respect to statistical characteristics of the target article. A LSA study (Kintsch et al., 2000) found LSA statistical feedback to be highly correlated with teachers' judgments of content adequacy.

The goals of Summary Street project are to infuse Summary Street seamlessly: (a) to provide students extended, guided practice in expository writing and revision without adding to their teachers' workload; (b) to integrate Summary Street into teachers' curricular plans and instruction; and (c) to make students responsible for improving their own writing and revision skills.

To engage with Summary Street, the student first reads the target article and types a summary into the Summary Street interface. The student then submits the summary for scoring and analysis. Summary Street provides immediate feedback to students and their teachers about the adequacy of a summary across several dimensions. They receive a detailed report of the student's performance, including analysis of the summary's length, redundancy, evidence of plagiarism, spelling, and content coverage. The tool provides immediate feedback to students and their teachers about the adequacy of a summary. Summary Street allows students to revise their summaries and tracks students' progress in improving the summary from draft to draft. Its designers report several positive results and benefits of use, including increased student engagement (Kintsch et al., 2000; Wade-Stein & Kintsch, 2005), closer reading of text (Wade-Stein & Kintsch, 2005), and high scoring accuracy when compared to teacher scored summaries (Wade-Stein & Kintsch, 2005). Kintsch and colleagues (2000), along with Wade-Stein and Kintsch (2005), conducted controlled, counterbalanced, in-school studies of Summary Street software in sixth-grade suburban classrooms. Students spent more time voluntarily revising text when they received Summary Street feedback, as compared with times when feedback from the software was not present. Overall, the results of Kintsch's classroom trials suggested that the tool had a broad application in support of reading comprehension and that classroom use motivated students to work longer on their summaries. There is relatively little data about the utility of the Summary Street technology for second language learners and with poor readers (an exception is a study by Bogart, Kintsch, Visvader, Clark, and Riorda, 2005, who piloted Summary Street with students with disabilities). In addition, Summary Street has not been piloted with high school students in urban classroom environments. Furthermore, although writing summaries has been shown to be an effective reading comprehension strategy, little is known about the kind of preparatory instruction and follow-up support that is necessary to use summarization technology to support adolescents' reading comprehension.

This study looks at the use of Summary Street and its implementation in an urban, predominately Latino, high school. Our aim was to understand the affordances of a summarization technology, in general, and the Summary Street technology, in particular, as an effective tool in support of reading comprehension in diverse, urban high school content-area classrooms. Specifically, we asked (a) whether the technology would be useful in supporting high school students' reading comprehension through summarization, (b) whether students would be engaged by the technology, and (c) whether teachers would find utility in integrating the tool into classroom planning, instruction, and assessment.

METHODS

Setting

Our research was conducted in four ninth-grade classrooms in an urban high school in Chicago. Three teachers in the school piloted or supported the piloting of Summary Street with approximately 125 of their students. The study was conducted during the fall and spring semesters of the school year. The teachers included a science lab teacher, a social studies teacher, and a reading specialist. The reading specialist provided support for the content-area teachers' integration and use of Summary Street. Two researchers worked closely with the teachers to design materials to introduce summarization (e.g., how to write a summary) and Summary Street technology, to support students' use of the tool in the computer labs, to help the teachers select content-area text for summary writing, and to query students about the tool.

Data Sources

This study employed a multi-methodological approach in its pilot research design. The data sources included:

- teacher interviews,
- focus group interviews (students),
- field notes of classroom observations related to summarization instruction,
- field notes of computer lab use of Summary Street,
- student talk-aloud protocol responses,
- students' summarization scores, and
- student post-activity surveys.

We employed teacher interviews to learn more about teachers' perceptions of the value of the tool in classroom use. We also included student focus group interviews to learn more about students' perceptions and experiences with using Summary Street. The teacher and focus group interviews and student talk-aloud responses were subjected to thematic analysis during which patterns were identified and coded and categories were created representing themes. We also used post-activity surveys to learn more about students' perceptions of Summary Street use on a just-in-time basis. We used this information to inform our understanding of students' experiences and to inform our ongoing support efforts. We coded the surveys using descriptive statistics. Teachers and researchers compared students' summaries to their same-grade peers' non-machine-scored summaries. Handwritten, teacher-graded summaries were analyzed according to content (presence of main ideas and supporting ideas), length, and plagiarism. Field notes of classroom observations were coded with respect to the teacher's framing of summarization, Summary Street, and the teacher's modeling of summarization for students. Field notes of computer lab use were coded with respect to computer and tool use challenges and students' questions about tool use.

Setting

This study examined a large urban high school in Chicago that served approximately 2,100 students. Approximately 90% of the student body was considered low-income, and 86% qualified for free or reduced price lunch. Approximately 82.4% of the student population was Hispanic, 14.6% African-American, 2.5%

Caucasian, and 0.4% Asian. Just over 11% of the student body was designated as limited-English-proficient (LEP).[2] Of the approximately 700 incoming eighth grade students for the 2003–2004 school year, 11.1% received test scores indicating that they were at or above the 50th percentile in reading.[3] In 2003, 16.3% of juniors scored at or above grade level in reading on the state's Prairie State Achievement Examination (compared to 36.2% citywide and 56.4% statewide). The average ACT reading score in 2003 was 15.0 (compared to 17.1 citywide and 20.1 statewide).[4]

Chicago Summary Street Implementation Overview

Seven teachers participated in summer meetings discussing the support of reading through the use of Summary Street in classrooms. Three ninth-grade teachers (a social studies teacher, an environmental science teacher, and a reading teacher) agreed to pilot the use of Summary Street during the school year.

The environmental science teacher and reading teacher were members of a team of teachers with a common group of 100 students and worked together. Organizationally, they are members of a "small school" (School A) within the larger high school. The social studies teacher was a teacher in another "small school" (School B) within the same larger high school and had her own group of approximately 100 students. All three teachers had a history of working together on university research projects, planning activities, and in professional development activities. All three teachers met with researchers to discuss planning and implementation issues, and to debrief afterwards.

The teachers used Summary Street in their classrooms on multiple occasions, for a combined eight times during the school year (four implementations for each small school). The social studies teacher used a summarization activity and Summary Street with one of her classes (approximately 25 students), while the environmental science teacher did the same with four of her classes (approximately 100 students). All classroom implementations were supported by one of the authors (Kwon), who assisted teachers in helping students get online and also helped students use the Summary Street interface.

First Trial Implementation

Our trial one implementation plan seemed very straightforward. We arranged with the classroom teachers and the computer lab technologists to schedule opportunities for students to use the computer lab for Summary Street. We had several tacitly held assumptions about students' and teachers' expectations of the tool and experiences with the ease of use of the tool. For example, we assumed that students, who had varied keyboarding skills, might have challenges with logging in to Summary Street. Therefore, Kwon volunteered to be present at every Summary Street lab implementation in order to provide extra support for the teachers. We also assumed that the teachers, having practiced using Summary Street, and having been apprised of the tool's focus on content (using LSA technology) and

not grammar or syntax, would understand that a poorly written text did not constitute lack of adequate comprehension of the science text. We assumed that teachers
would focus their attention on the content of the summaries and less on the written
form of the summaries. Finally, we assumed that the rapid feedback would be engaging for students and would encourage them to keep revising their summaries.

There were several issues brought up by teachers that needed to be addressed
in order to make the use of Summary Street in their setting beneficial to the students:

1. There were concerns about students' weak summary-writing skills. The
    inability to write a summary would make using Summary Street very
    difficult.
2. There were logistic computer lab access issues. Demand for lab time was
    high in the school, while resources were limited. Classroom activities
    had to be structured so that when computer lab time was scheduled, it
    would be used as efficiently as possible.
3. There were questions about instructional efficacy and assessment. Being
    new to the tool and its use in class, teachers were unsure of how helpful
    students would find using the tool for learning, and they were unsure of
    how to use activity products for assessment purposes.

To address the above issues, the components of summary writing instruction,
pre-lab reading and writing, and complementary content examination were added
to the Summary Street activity.

Summary Writing Instruction

All three teachers felt that summarizing was a skill with which students might
not be very familiar. High school students often are inexperienced with summary
writing as a reading-to-learn strategy. They have had little exposure to explicit
instructional guidelines for writing a good summary. To help maximize the benefit
of using a tool like Summary Street, it was felt that students should receive some
instruction about writing summaries just prior to an activity using the Summary
Street tool. For one small school, the reading teacher provided summary-writing
instruction for all 100 students just before using Summary Street. In the other
small school, the social studies teacher provided summary-writing instruction
during an academic issues class where she saw students outside of her social
studies class.

Summary-writing instruction included summarizing an article together as a
class and evaluating strong and weak points of the class attempt. Once teachers
were satisfied that students understood the steps of summary-writing, students
were asked to write a summary about aquifers (a subject they'd been covering as
a part of their environmental science unit).

Pre-Lab Reading and Writing

Many students had weak typing skills, and teachers were concerned that going straight to the computer lab would result in the inefficient use of time. As a result, students were asked to read the target article and write a draft of their summary on paper before going to the computer lab. This practice seemed to go well and was repeated for all subsequent uses of Summary Street.

Complementary Content Examination

One of the challenges of integrating Summary Street into the classroom was teachers' concerns about its instructional value. There were questions about how effective an activity using Summary Street would be for helping students learn subject-specific content. Teachers asked "Could students' performance using Summary Street provide specific information about what students understand or fail to understand about key science concepts?" In addition, there were concerns

---

Name: _____   Period: _____ Date: _____

Choose the best-fit answer (1 pt each)

1. What is the name given to the movement of carbon?
(a) carbon movement (b) oxygen movement (c) global warming (d) carbon cycle

2. Beside carbon dioxide, what are some other heat-holding gases in the atmosphere?
(a) CFCs, methane, and oxygen   (b) CFCs, nitrous oxides, and oxygen
(c) CFCs, methane, and nitrous oxides   (d) oxygen, methane, and nitrous oxides.

3. Which of the following activities add carbon dioxide to the atmosphere?
(a) Plants release carbon dioxide through photosynthesis (b) planting trees
(c) Animals breathe out carbon dioxide (d) not using electrical appliances

4. Which of the following activities take in carbon dioxide from the atmosphere?
(a) Animals breathing   (b) plants photosynthesizing
(c) Cutting down trees   (d) burning fossil fuels

5. What do these gases, water vapor, CFCs, CO_2, nitrous oxide, and methane have in common?
(a) They are all naturally formed gases.   (b) They all keep the earth cool.
(c) They are all heat-holding gases.   (d) They are all human-made chemicals

Write a 1-2 sentence answer to your CHOICE OF THE 2 OF THE FOLLOWING QUESTIONS. (5 points each)

   1. What human activities are increasing the amount of carbon dioxide in the atmosphere?
   2. What is the problem with adding fertilizers to grow crops or keep the grass green?
   3. CFCs is a chemical created by humans. What is the purpose of CFCs?

FIGURE 7.1.   Content examination

about how the Summary Street activity student output should be used for assessing student learning. Teachers wondered whether the tool would be useful as a measure of student learning that would be as reliable as traditional assessments (e.g., multiple choice and short answer) about the same content. After the initial trial using Summary Street, and after carefully reading students' summaries and attempting to grade them, one of the teachers who had very positive comments about the tool expressed disappointment in Summary Street's score of her students' summaries. While the quick feedback seemed to provide clear motivational advantages for students, the instructional value of the feedback remained in question for her because the accuracy/type of the feedback did not appear to match what she would give to students if grading and commenting manually.

In response to her concerns, a complementary content examination (See Figure 7.1) was used for a few of the implementations to provide another measure of student learning. The choice to use a complementary exam proved to be a good decision because students who scored well using the tool also scored well on the content examination. This comparison demonstrated for the teacher and her colleagues that while the written output seemed poorly written (lack of acceptable grammar and syntax), the tool measured comprehension.

RESULTS

Using Summary Street: Views from the Computer Lab

Outcomes from the first trials were positive and provided useful feedback. Students seemed very engaged with the computer activity. This was both visible to the teacher and researcher as they walked around in the computer lab helping students and seen in the number of times students tried modifying their summaries in Summary Street (see Table 7.1).[5] Student interaction patterns showed that students were making multiple revisions to improve their summaries with Summary Street. Their in-class behavior seemed to indicate an interest in the activity and in the use of the computer tool.

Figure 7.2 illustrates students' interaction patterns and strategies in using Summary Street. The tool's progress tracking indicates that students modified words to increase their scores and, for group 1, increased the average number of words overall. Laboratory observations indicated that students frequently re-read the original article after receiving feedback from Summary Street. They also frequently asked an adult (Kwon or the teacher) about how they might improve their sum-

TABLE 7.1. Number of Times Students Tried Modifying Their Summaries in Summary Street

	Avg number of attempts	Avg words first attempt	Avg words last attempt	Avg spell checks
Group 1	4.46	135	180	2.0
Group 2	3.72	114	134	3.8

Steady Improvement	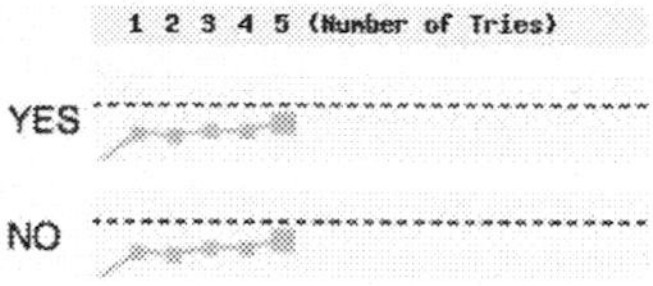 1 2 3 4 5 (Number of Tries) YES NO
Almost random wandering	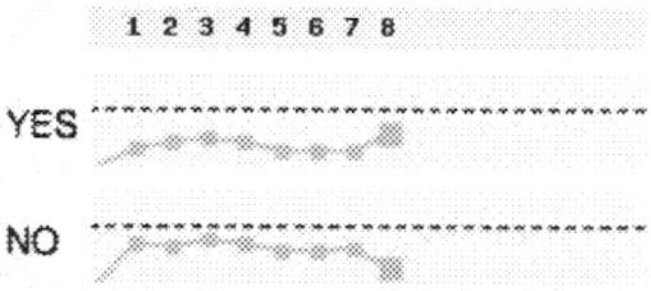 1 2 3 4 5 6 7 8 YES NO
Using to get interim feedback while typing summary	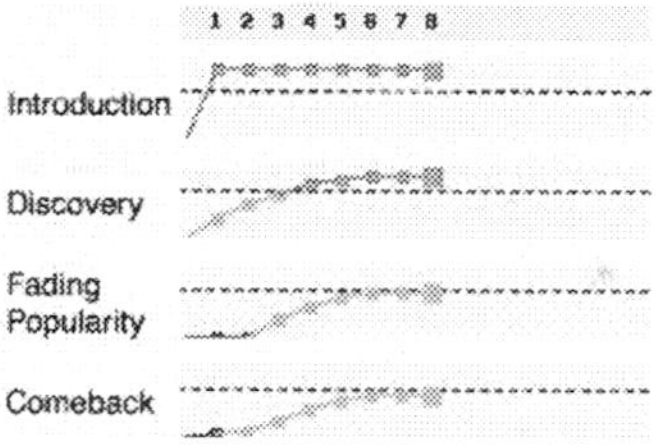 1 2 3 4 5 6 7 8 Introduction Discovery Fading Popularity Comeback
Summary writing with quick feedback motivates persistence in some students	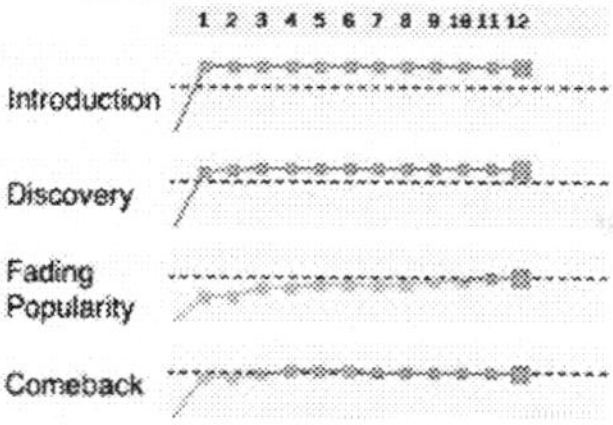 1 2 3 4 5 6 7 8 9 10 11 12 Introduction Discovery Fading Popularity Comeback
Teacher assistance	1 2 3 4 5 6 7 YES NO

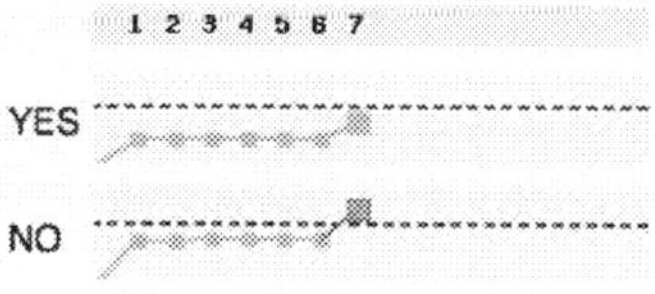

FIGURE 7.2. Students' progress (dotted line is the target to get above) on various sections of an article (the "yes" and "no" section) over several attempts.

mary, and occasionally they asked peers for assistance. In Figure 7.2 one section of the Summary Street feedback is displayed as an example of the students' approaches to revising their summaries. The charts indicate the amount of progress that students have made in covering content in their summaries for each section. The charts also indicate how long their responses are, across multiple requests for feedback. Each colored dot represents one scored response. The colored dot that is furthest to the right of the line represents the most recently scored response. The shading indicates the passing threshold. The dark shading in the top portion indicates passing, while the lighter shading indicates below passing. In the section represented here (Figure 7.2), students were to have provided reasons (derived from the main argument and supporting details in the original text) for the use of aquifers in the Southwest. Some readers, perhaps those with somewhat stronger comprehension skills, displayed steady improvement in this section. They were able to make the necessary modifications to their summaries, although the original summaries may have been poorly connected to the content. Other students

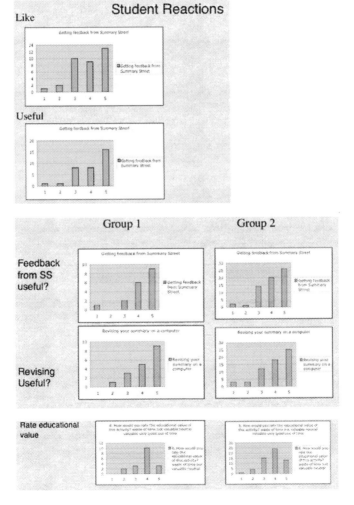

FIGURE 7.3.   Student survey results about the effectiveness of Summary Street

displayed a sort of random wandering. These students seemed to be guessing in their modification to the summary. Students who we classified as getting interim feedback from the tool displayed a particularly interesting strategy. Rather than randomly guessing, these students seemed to be more deliberate in their efforts. For example, when the tool gave feedback about redundancy or plagiarism, the students would delete a word or an entire sentence and then press for feedback from the tool. Based on that feedback they would continue this process or add the word or sentence back into the summary.

For supporting student reading skill development, quick individualized feedback is important for students, and Summary Street provided that. Feedback from students through post-activity surveys (see Figure 7.3) and focus group interviews supported researcher observations. In interviews, students said they found the activity with Summary Street to be engaging enough to use frequently. Furthermore, in post-activity student surveys, in which students were asked to rate the tool on a five-point scale (1 being least useful to 5 being most useful), almost 90% of students said they found the feedback from Summary Street to be useful, and a large majority said the tool helped them improve their written summary and check their understanding of the text.

Post-activity teacher interviews revealed that the teachers were very pleased with the Summary Street trial. Shortly after the first implementation, the reading teacher offered a very positive assessment:

> The kids really like it, and it does force them to read carefully. It provides a form of individual attention that they don't always get. It works well for students at all levels. I will definitely want to use it again, and I am encouraging the other teachers in my core to try it.

However, after reading the students' Summary Street summaries, the reading teacher felt concerned about their use of a tool that did not correct grammar and syntax. She felt particularly concerned because many of the students were second language learners or speakers of American dialects, and she feared that they would get the message that poor grammar was acceptable in writing.

Similar to the findings of previous studies (Kintsch et al., 2000; Wade-Stein & Kintsch, 2005), the content-area teachers felt that the activity caused their students to read (and re-read) their texts more carefully. They felt that it worked well for students at all reading skill levels and that the tool provided a form of individual attention that students found useful and appealing. Both content-area teachers wanted to use Summary Street again and planned to suggest its use to colleagues.

DISCUSSION

In recent years, reading researchers and practitioners have increasingly focused on the dearth of research-based information about how to effectively support adolescent literacy in high schools. The results of this study suggest that summarization, in general, and a summarization tool, Summary Street, in particular, can be useful and effective tools to supplement teachers' support for content-area classroom reading. Teachers and researchers can benefit from learning more about the conditions under which technologies can help teachers improve students' interaction with content-area text.

Previous research (Doering & Beach, 2002; Holum & Gahala, 2000) has investigated the affordances of supporting literacy practices through the use of literacy technologies, but relatively few have examined the challenges of integrating literacy support technologies, especially in high school classrooms. Even fewer still have investigated the integration of literacy support technologies in multicultural high school classrooms. This study identifies several benefits of integrating a literacy support technology to develop students' reading-to-learn skills in high school science and social studies classrooms. The findings may be useful to other classroom researchers who are seeking ways to integrate literacy support technologies in high school. In particular, our finding that students in our study were engaged by the technology and repeatedly revised their summaries in order to obtain a high score suggests that students are willing to use it, and the tool may be successfully integrated into multicultural high school content-area classrooms. Further, our finding that content-area teachers believed that the tool encouraged students to read and re-read text more carefully is particularly promising. If the tool can facilitate closer reading of content-area text, perhaps, combined with the reading-to-learn summarization activity, students' reading comprehension will increase over regular and repeated uses of the technology.

The study also illustrates challenges with integrating a literacy support technology like Summary Street into high school content-area classrooms. We found that while students' are willing to use the tool, some students used revision strategies that were less than productive. These students appeared to randomly revise their text without rhyme or reason. They did not appear to connect the summarization instruction received prior to interaction with the tool to their active use of the tool and revision strategy. Perhaps the summarization instruction needs to be more explicit and provide more examples. Perhaps some students needed more practice with writing summaries prior to using the technology. What is clear is that instruction in summarization and the explicit use of the tool should be improved in order to be useful to a wider range of students.

We also found that the teachers needed concrete and measurable assurances of the fidelity of the tool as a reading comprehension assessment. In this study, we employed a multiple choice, short answer content-area assessment to both provide evidence for the teachers and to contribute to previous findings in the Summary Street-related literature (Kintsch et al., 2000) that argues that summaries graded as passing by the tool would also be considered passing by teachers. Since students who scored well using traditional reading assessment instruments also scored well using Summary Street, we suggest that Summary Street is an effective tool for assessing reading comprehension.

We will need to consider how to best address the concerns of teachers, like the reading teacher in our study, who believed that the written output of the tool was at best a fairly good gauge of students' knowledge, but at worst, sent a message to students with poor literacy skills and second language learners that grammar and syntactical errors were permissible. Perhaps this challenge can be addressed through better designed professional development, or other mechanisms might need to be included as part of a suite of reading- and writing-to-learn tools that support students' written production.

This study contributes to the growing body of research and professional literature about the integration of literacy support technologies, like Summary Street, into classrooms. This work offers insights into the integration of technology and the specific challenges and benefits that may be applicable to other classroom settings. We have offered suggestions for responding to these challenges. In the future, we will report on further efforts to build on understandings developed from the study described here.

NOTES

1. Summary Street is now trademarked as WriteToLearn® Pearson Publishing Corporation.
2. Source: 2003 Illinois School Report Card.
3. Source: Degrees of Reading Power (DRP) Test 2003 Fall Administration.
4. Source: 2003 Illinois School Report Card.
5. Summary Street monitors common statistics like number of revision attempts, summary score changes, and summary length.
6. Williams is the former surname of K. Gomez.

REFERENCES

Allen, R. (2000). Before it's too late: Giving reading a last chance. *Curriculum Update*. Alexandria, VA: Association for Supervision and Curriculum Development. Retrieved from http://www.ascd.org/publications/curriculum-update/summer2000/Before-It%27s-Too-Late.aspx

Bereiter, C. & Scardamalia, M. (1986). Levels of inquiry into the nature of expertise in writing. In E. Z. Rothkopf (Ed.), *Review of research in education* (vol. 13, pp. 259–282). Washington, DC: American Educational Research Association.

Bogart, R., Kintsch, A., Visvader, P., Clark, R., & Riorda, J. (2005). Virtual ramps for invisible disabilities: One district's approach to assistive technologies for students with disabilities. *Closing The Gap, 24*, 1–4.

Clay, M. (1991). *Becoming literate: The construction of inner control*. Auckland, New Zealand: Heinemann Education.

Craig, M. & Yore, L. (1995). Middle school students' metacognitive knowledge about science reading and science text: An interview study. *Reading Psychology, 16*, 169–213.

Cziko, C. (1998). Reading happens in your mind, not in your mouth: Teaching & learning "academic literacy" in an urban high school. Retrieved from http://www.wested.org/stratlit/prodevel/happens.shtml

Doering, R. & Beach, A. (2002). Preservice English teachers acquiring literacy practices through technology tools. *Language Learning & Technology, 6*(3), 127–146.

Frey, N., Fisher, D., & Hernandez, T. (2003). "What's the gist?" Summary writing for struggling adolescent writers. *Voices from the Middle, 11*, 43–49.

Gomez, K. & Madda, C. (2005). Vocabulary instruction for ELL Latino students in the middle school science classroom. *Voices in the Middle, 13*, 42–47.

Guthrie, J. (2001). Contexts for engagement and motivation. In M. L. Kamil, P. B. Mosenthal, P. D. Pearson, & R. Barr (Eds.), *Handbook of reading research* (vol. 3, pp. 403–422). New York, NY: Erlbaum.

Hare, V. & Borchardt, K. M. (1984). Direct instruction of summarization skills. *Reading Research Quarterly, 21*, 62–78.

Herman, P., Perkins, K., Hansen, M., Gomez, L., & Gomez, K. (2010). The effectiveness of reading comprehension strategies in high school science classrooms. In K. Gomez, L. Lyons, & J. Radinsky (Eds.), *Learning in the disciplines: Proceedings of the 9th International Conference of the Learning Sciences* (pp. 857–864). Chicago, IL: International Society of the Learning Sciences.

Holum, A. & Gahala, J. (2000). *Using technology to enhance literacy instruction.* Retrieved from http://www.ncrel.org/sdrs/areas/issues/content/cntareas/reading/li300.htm

King, A. (1992). Comparison of self-questioning, summarizing, and note taking review as strategies for learning from lectures. *American Educational Research Journal, 29*, 303–323.

Kintsch, E., Steinhart, D., Matthews, C., Lamb, R., & LSA Research Group. (2000). Developing summarization skills through the use of LSA-based feedback. *Interactive Learning Environments, 8*(2), 87–109.

Landauer, T. K (1998). Learning and representing verbal meaning: The latent semantic analysis theory. *Current Directions in Psychological Science, 7*, 161–164.

Landauer, T. K., Foltz, P. W., & Laham, D. (1998). An introduction to latent semantic analysis. *Discourse Processes, 25*, 259–284.

National Reading Panel. (2000). *Teaching children to read: An evidence-based assessment of the scientific research on reading and its implications for reading instruction.* Washington, DC: National Institute of Child Health and Human Development.

O'Donnell, A. M. & Dansereau, D. F. (1992). Scripted cooperation in student dyads: A method for analyzing and enhancing academic learning and performance. In R. Hertz-Lazarowitz & N. Miller (Eds.), *Interaction in cooperative groups: The theoretical anatomy of group learning* (pp. 120–141). New York, NY: Cambridge University Press.

Pressley, M. (2000). What should comprehension instruction be the instruction of? In M. L. Kamil, P. B. Mosenthal, D. P. Pearson, & R. Barr (Eds.), *Handbook of reading research* (pp. 545–561). Mahwah, NJ: Lawrence Erlbaum.

Pressley, M., Johnson, C., Symons, S., McGoldrick, J., & Kurita, J. (1989). Strategies that improve children's memory and comprehension of text. *The Elementary School Journal, 90*, 3–32.

Radmacher, S. A. & Latosi-Sawin, E. (1995). Summary writing: A tool to improve student comprehension and writing in psychology. *Teaching of Psychology, 22,* 113–115.

Romance, N. & Vitale, X. (2005, May). *A knowledge-focused multi-part strategy for enhancing student reading comprehension proficiency in Grade 5.* Paper presented at the Annual Meeting of the International Reading Association, San Antonio, TX.

Schoenbach, R., Greenleaf, C., Cziko, C., & Hurwitz, L. (2000). *Reading for understanding: A guide to improving reading in middle and high school classrooms.* San Francisco, CA: Jossey-Bass.

Wade-Stein, D. & Kintsch, E. (2005). Summary Street: Interactive computer support for writing. *Cognition and Instruction, 22,* 333–362.

Williams[6], K. P., & Gomez, L. M. (2002). Presumptive literacies in technology-integrated science curriculum. In G. Stahl (Ed.), *Proceedings of the Conference on Computer Support for Collaborative Learning: Foundations for a CSCL Community* (pp. 599–600). Mahwah, NJ: Erlbaum.

Wilhelm, J. F. (1995). *"You gotta BE the book": Teaching engaged and reflective reading with adolescents.* New York, NY: Teachers College Press.

Wittrock, M. C. (1990). Generative processes of comprehension. *Educational Psychologist, 24,* 345–376.

Yore, L. (1991). *Secondary science teachers' attitudes toward and beliefs about science reading and science textbooks.* Journal of Research in Science Teaching, 28, 55–72.

Yore L. D., Craig M. T., & Maguire T. O. (1998). Index of science reading awareness: An interactive-constructive model, test verification, and grades 4–8 results. *Journal of Research in Science Teaching, 35,* 27–51.

Yore, L. & Shymansky, J. (1991). Reading in science: Developing an operational conception to guide instruction. *Journal of Research in Science Teaching, 35,* 27–51.

Yore, L., Shymansky, J., Henriques, L., Chidsey, J., & Lewis, J. (1997). Reading-to-learn and writing-to-learn science activities for the elementary school classroom. In P. Rubba, P. Kieg, & J. Rye (Eds.), *Proceedings of the Annual International Conference of the Association for the Education of Teachers in Science* (pp. 40–72). Hoboken, NJ: Wiley Periodicals.

Zywica, J. & Gomez, K. (2008). Teaching science with annotation. *Journal of Adolescent and Adult Literacy, 52*(2), 155–165.

CHAPTER 8

BUILDING CAPACITY IN COMMUNITY CONTEXT

Studying the Impact of Technology on Low-Income Immigrant Spanish-Speaking Families

Hector H. Rivera and David J. Francis

ABSTRACT

This study is focused on examining the impact of an intervention technology program (Centros Communitarios de Aprendizaje [CCA]) designed to assist Spanish-speaking parents in learning and using technology for family advancement. The study is based on a sample of 377 participants of the program. In general, participants reported positive attitudes on what they perceived to be the impact of the CCA program for their lives. Participants were also of the opinion that what they learned in the CCA would be helpful for assisting their children with school-related activities at home as well as for their involvement in the classroom. Overall, pre- and post-survey data suggests that the program is achieving its objective of providing technology literacy to parents as well as the means by which they can become participants in the education of their children.

Research on Technology Use in Multicultural Settings, pages 159–175.

INTRODUCTION

The persisting technology gaps between the mainstream population and Hispanics results in differential access to educational and economic opportunities (U.S. Department of Commerce, 1999). It contributes to inequitable social outcomes and to fewer economic opportunities for Spanish-speaking immigrant communities. Research shows that fifty-five percent of the Hispanic immigrants in Houston, Texas do not have a high school education, placing the area's fastest-growing ethnic group in a perilous position in our knowledge-based economy (Klineberg, 2005). According to the Houston Area Survey, the educational attainment of Hispanics (who comprise one third of Houston's population) lags far behind that of Anglos, African-Americans, and Asians (Klineberg, 2005). The educational attainment of Hispanics is an economic and a social issue that will affect the future of Houston's Hispanic communities as a whole as well as other communities across the nation.

The low education level among Hispanic immigrants is exacerbated by a modern proliferation of technology that has made basic computer knowledge fundamental to a person's academic and occupational success (President's Advisory Commission on Educational Excellence for Hispanic Americans, 2003). Among the many challenges facing Hispanics in the United States is a widespread lack of familiarity with basic computer technology and a lack of access to computers and the Internet at home. Because many Hispanic immigrants have neither higher education nor computer knowledge, they not only experience severely curtailed employment opportunities, but they also lack the resources necessary to assist with and participate in their children's education (President's Advisory Commission on Educational Excellence for Hispanic Americans, 2003; U.S. Department of Commerce, 1999).

Prevalent in Hispanic families is what the Mexican Institute has termed the "upside-down model," a social paradigm in which the children of immigrants become the de-facto leaders in the family because they speak English and receive ongoing education that often includes computer training. This de-facto model devastates healthy family dynamics and completely undermines parental authority. Hispanic parents are unable to navigate the U.S. school system or are unable to help their children with homework, and the children, in turn, cease to view their parents as role models. Furthermore, the lack of access to computer technology in Hispanic communities is manifested in two ways: lack of infrastructure/ connectivity in these communities and the fact that computer instruction, where available, is not provided in Spanish.

A significant response to the above challenges has come from the Mexican Institute of Greater Houston. They have accepted the challenge and demonstrated that given the right conditions, Spanish-speaking parents from underrepresented communities can also achieve their educational goals through the use of technology. Uniquely, the Mexican Institute focuses on Hispanic parents as the key figures in family advancement. To provide innovative education opportunities for these parents, the Institute is collaborating with the Texas-accredited Tecnológico de Monterrey, in Mexico, to offer distance-based computer education programs to Hispanic adults (in Spanish) across Houston. In partnership with the Houston Independent School District and numerous community based organizations, the Institute has established Community Learning Centers (Centros Comunitarios de Aprendizaje—CCAs) where Hispanic parents can take computer technology courses and receive tutorial help in Spanish via the Internet. These CCAs have proved to be a realistic means of empowerment for Hispanic parents, providing them with opportunities for self-improvement through education, which in turn allows them to become positive role models who influence their children to stay in school.

The CCAs provide Spanish-language classroom instruction and online tutorials in computer technology, allowing Hispanic parents, many of whom never finished primary school and cannot operate a computer, to learn marketable computer skills in a non-threatening, peer group setting. The diploma obtained at the completion of the 100-hour program that keeps parents at the schools for 16 weeks is the first education certificate many of these parents have ever received. This capacity-building program has encouraged many of the graduates to continue their online education by taking other free courses offered by the Mexican Institute, such as Webpage design in order to advertise their small businesses and basic statistics or health related courses. By partnering with local schools and other organizations in establishing CCAs, the Mexican Institute has developed a cost-effective, easily-duplicable approach to adult online education. The program uses the Internet connectivity, classroom facilities, and computer resources already in place at the schools, and in turn, it works to foment parental involvement in their children's education at home and in the classroom.

In the past, research has shown that family aspirations and expectations for children's academic success differ due to the fact that some parents are not able to aide their children in school-related activities or assist them in their educational paths (Gallimore, Reese, Balzano, Benson, & Goldenberg, 1991). However, the CCAs are not only training parents on the use of technology but are also connecting their technology training to meaningful ways in which parents may be a positive influence on their children. For example, a survey participant expressed her opinion about the usefulness of the program, "Yes, I will have more opportunities to find a job, and I will be able to help my children with their school work." A post-survey evaluation of the program indicated that, across time, parents did not change their positive perception on the usefulness and positive impact of the program. Parents are beginning to develop a sense of self-efficacy through their participation in the CCAs despite the fact that most of the parents who come into the centers are computer illiterate. In most cases, they do not even know how to turn on a computer or how to use the computer's mouse. By the time they finish the program they are equipped and empowered to action. For example, a survey participant stated, "I wish to work on my own business, and I needed to prepare myself for it. So I can achieve a better business and use the Internet to manage it from my computer."

Significance of Parents' Training and Capacity Building

Spanish-speaking parents face many obstacles in order to be effectively involved in the education of their children. The focus of many immigrant, Spanish-speaking parents is on working one or two jobs in order to provide their children with the essentials for life. As children mature and continue to move along their educational path, the need arises for more direct parental involvement that would allow parents to exercise a direct influence on their children's academics. Compounding the situation is the parents' lack of education that may be an obstacle to their upward mobility or in securing a better job in the future. The financial and educational demands faced by Spanish-speaking parents represent an at-risk community ecology that serves to perpetuate a cycle of poverty, lack of knowledge, and lack of involvement in guiding their children's schooling (Bronfenbrenner, 1986). Therefore, capacity-building in the form of education in their native language and the development of technology skills are key components that parents need in order to effectively participate in their children's education as well as to advance as a family. It is not our claim that parents have nothing to contribute to their children's education; as a matter of fact, there is plenty of research that suggests that parents have much to contribute to their children's education, such as the value they place on academic achievement or cultural practices that aide children towards a positive identity formation (Gallimore, Boggs, & Jordan, 1974; Gallimore et al., 1991; Moll, Amanti, Neff, & Gonzalez, 1992). However, parents also want the opportunity to be able to do more for their children, such as guiding their educational development through informed decisions and assisting their children with school-related activities at home.

The significance and the complexity of parental involvement in their children's academic development has been well documented (Bronfenbrenner, 1979; Gallimore et al., 1991). A four-year study conducted by Delgado-Gaitan (1991) examined a school district's attempt at incorporating parent-involvement activities to encourage isolated Spanish-speaking parents to participate more fully in their children's schooling. The findings suggest that conventional avenues for involving parents in school were closed to many parents because specific cultural knowledge and language were required in order to participate effectively. It was concluded that when socio-cultural congruency exists between home and school settings, children have a greater chance of succeeding in school. Further findings suggest that parents who are knowledgeable about the school's expectations and the way in which the schools operate are better advocates for their children than parents who lack this knowledge (Delgado-Gaitan, 1991). To make matters more difficult, many Spanish-speaking parents also face a digital divide that further separates them from being involved in their children's classrooms and also separates them from their children's academic activities at home. In order to reduce the gap in overall parental involvement, it is necessary to develop capacity-building programs that are contextual to the needs of the schools and classroom teachers as well as to the needs and social reality of the parents and children within their neighborhoods (Barton, Drake, Perez, St. Louis, & George, 2004; Padrón, Waxman, & Rivera, 2002).

The literature on the development of effective prevention programs also suggests that strong families and effective parenting are critical to children's future developmental outcomes. Parents need more than ever to know how to effectively guide their children (Kumpfer & Alvarado, 2003). In a longitudinal study, researchers also concluded that parents have a larger impact on their children's future behavior than previously thought. Therefore, parents' involvement in their children's education is an important point of leverage for any program seeking to improve children's academics (Resnick et al., 1997). In general, researchers have also found that parents' training and capacity-building programs are most effective when: (a) the training focuses on assisting younger children (three- to ten-year-olds), (b) the training can be generalized to the home setting, and (c) the capacity-building approach is contextual to family and community needs (Kumpfer & Alvarado, 2003). Overall, research also suggests that the road to greater success includes prevention programs that are based on scientific findings and community-based models of accountability and technical assistance systems that build capacity in socio-cultural contexts (Braun, 1997; Cochran, 1988; Israel et al., 2000; Wandersman & Florin, 2003).

METHODS

Characteristics of CCA Participants

Overall, there were 34 CCAs participating in the survey study. The study was conducted during the first semester of 2004. From those centers, 377 Hispanics consented to participate in the study. Descriptive analysis of the data revealed important characteristics of the participants. Overall, 17% of the participants were males, and 83% were females. People participating in the CCAs came from diverse backgrounds. The majority of participants were from Mexico (79%), but there were 17% that included participants from Central America, South America, and the Caribbean and 4% who represented Hispanics born in the U.S. On average, participants reported having lived in the U.S. for 13 years (answers ranged from one year to 62 years). The age of those participating in the program ranged from 14 to 63 years old. There was one 14 year-old student who also decided to take the technology course with his mother. However, the mean was 35 years, and the mode was 32 years of age. Of those participating in the program, 83% of the parents reported having children in school, and 17% reported not having children in school. In general, the grade levels of their children were 42% in elementary school; 13% junior high and high school; 40% reported having children at multiple levels of school, such as elementary, junior high, high school or college; and

5% reported having sons and daughters in college only. Participants were also asked about their educational background. Overall, 77% reported having studied in their country of origin, with 8% in the U.S. only, and 15% having studied in both countries. Overall, some participants reported having achieved a high school level of education (11%); however, their answers varied from starting their freshmen year in high school to actually finishing high school. The majority of participants (68%) reported having achieved a middle school level of education or less.

Instrument

The study included two questionnaire/surveys. The first questionnaire contained 21 items addressing the ethnic background of participants as well as sociohistorical information on the participants' educational and work experiences and their experiences with technology. A second survey was developed for the purpose of assessing participants' attitudes, beliefs, and perceptions about technology and their technology skills. This second survey contained a total of 91 items; 67 of the 91 items were rating scales on participants' opinions, beliefs, and values. This second survey was administered as a pre- and post-assessment instrument (all instruments were developed in Spanish). Overall, the surveys had mostly structured questions, but they also included follow-up open-ended questions for participants to provide a thicker description of their views and opinions about the program.

Two other instruments were used for constructing a description of the community and its resources. This was done in an attempt to exemplify the ecology of the community as illustrated by one neighborhood. The data presented from these two instruments is archival data collected during previous studies of the same community and neighborhoods carried out at the Texas Institute for Measurement, Evaluation, and Statistics (TIMES), with which both authors are associated. The instruments used were the School Attendance Area Survey-Literacy (SAAS-L) and the School Attendance Area Survey-Drive (SAAS-D). Both instruments were focused on providing an inventory of the resources available in the communities/neighborhoods where the CCAs were located. The SAAS-L was focused on assessing the presence of literacy resources as well as the general look of the neighborhood where Hispanics reside. The SAAS-D involved the process of driving through every street in a neighborhood in order to document the general look of the neighborhood, including visible resources and services within the community, as well as language preponderance (e.g., Spanish, English, or other). These instruments were developed as part of a large-scale longitudinal study of early reading development among Spanish-speaking students in California and Texas, along with instruments of home language use and early reading skills (Branum-Martin, Mehta, Carlson, Francis, & Goldenberg, in press; Francis et al., 2005; Reese, Linan-Thompson, & Goldenberg, 2008).

Procedure

In this study we engaged primarily in two data collection activities in order to assess the extent to which the program produced the broad scale changes envisioned and to examine the efficacy of the strategies. First, we conducted a needs assessment in order to gather information on past activities as well as to guide the future course of the formative and summative aspects of the study. To accomplish this task, archival data (from the Mexican Institute) were examined in order to assess past accomplishments by the institution. Second, we began the development of questionnaires intended primarily for the formative and summative components of the study. This process involved formal meetings with the program's executive director and personnel. It also involved participant observations of their annual activities, such as two of their community conferences and the inauguration of one of their CCAs. Researchers also visited two of the CCAs located within the public schools. During these two visits, informal conversations were carried out with some of the parents participating in the program in order to inform researchers on parents' perceptions about the program. As a final procedure, focus groups were conducted in order to assess several levels of validity for the survey instruments.

Items from the pre-survey, administered at the beginning of the program, are explored in this study ($n = 377$). For the purpose of general description of the program participants, this larger sample was used for the analysis of descriptive variables such as ethnicity (nationality), gender, level of education, and so on. Also, the first procedure in the quantitative data analysis involved a multivariate analysis of variance (MANOVA). The goal was to examine potential differences due to age, gender, nationality, level of education, and language among program participants. For items related to differing values and beliefs across time (e.g., pre and post), regarding technology, we used a sub-sample of the population that agreed to participate in the post survey ($n = 49$). For this sub-sample, the quantitative procedure involved paired sample *t*-tests to examine pre- and post-survey differences on technology skills gained.

This study is limited to answering the questions pertaining to the success/impact of the program on the parents' technology skills as well as on their values, beliefs, and attitudes towards the importance of technology and education for their families. The direct effect of the program on children's academic achievement was proposed as part of a more comprehensive program evaluation, but that project was not completed due to lack of funding.

RESULTS

The Ecology of the Community

Families attending the CCAs live in neighborhoods that in many respects lack the resources and the infrastructure for family improvement and social advancement. In the following section, a typical neighborhood is described to illustrate some of the needs within some of the communities where the CCA program is being implemented. The SAAS-D and the SAAS-L surveys were used within a defined set of criteria on what represents a neighborhood. In this case, a neighborhood represented the school zone with clear boundaries as established by zip codes that would let parents know which school their children were assigned to attend. This also helps in understanding the resources available (e.g., libraries, bookstores, community centers, and others) for families within a certain school zone.

La Mission (pseudonym) is a neighborhood located in the eastern part of the city of Houston. Historically, it has been a predominantly Hispanic area. This section of Houston is comprised of many blue-collar businesses, an industrial area, and a residential area. Some Hispanic families have lived here for two or three generations. There is also a preponderance of Spanish-speaking immigrants whose children attend the local public schools. As a whole, the community's infrastructure looks old and dirty, as illustrated by piles of junk and trash that are found around the area (SAAS-D, observers' field notes). Overall, the residential area is comprised of old homes with a few exceptions where a new home is found in between the older homes.

In general, the commercial area of this neighborhood includes car dealerships and stores that serve as multi-purpose stores, which include check-cashing services, sending money to Mexico, and immigration/legal services. There are also two industrial subsections within the neighborhood. In the industrial areas, there are big warehouses for the import and export of industrial parts and products. Overall, the neighborhood seems to represent a working class neighborhood, which historically has had a high concentration of Latinos/Hispanics within its boundaries. No major chain stores or general bookstores are present in the neighborhood. Within the two mom-and-pop convenience stores visited, there were signs displayed in both English and Spanish, and the range of literacy resources was limited to greeting cards and free local newspapers in Spanish. No books for children, no books for adults, magazines, or other children consumables were found (SAAS-L, field notes).

Overall, resources seem to be limited in this neighborhood. The survey of the community resources also indicated that there are only two churches located in this neighborhood. The churches are nested within the residential area. No other facilities or social service centers were observed in the neighborhood. There are no parks or recreational facilities within the neighborhood area. Observers familiar with the area reported that there were two parks outside of the school neighborhood zone (e.g., Turtle Park and Selena Quintanilla Park) that residents of La Mission neighborhood use as recreational facilities. It may be the case, however, that some families are not able to use these resources due to a lack of transportation.

The type of facilities and services found within the community seem to suggest that the target clientele are members of the Latino community. The two churches around the area were both advertising services in Spanish. The small mom-and-pop stores also had signs in Spanish, and one of the clerks indicated that it was necessary to speak Spanish in order to conduct a successful business in the community. Also the type of consumables found inside the stores suggested a focus on catering to the Hispanic community. However, both surveys revealed a lack of resources or facilities focused on providing educational training for family advancement and social improvement. The type of resources, or lack of resources, in the neighborhood represents the social reality of this community as well as other neighborhoods where the SAAS surveys were also conducted. The neighborhood surveys paint a grim picture of the ecology of the community, and it is indicative of how a cycle of poverty is perpetuated in such a social context. It also provides an understanding on the points of leverage for community development and capacity-building. Hispanic immigrants are highly motivated to learn, and given the opportunities and resources, they are capable of improving their lives and the lives of their children.

The Work Environment of CCA Participants

This section on the work environment represents an effort to understand the ecology of the family in reference to access to and opportunities for literacy and technology use. Of the 377 who participated in the survey, 144 reported having jobs, 201 reported not working, and 32 did not answer the question. In general, of those not working, 82% reported not working for six months or more, and 18% reported not having a job for less than six months.

Participants who reported having a job ($n = 144$) were asked about the language most often used at work. Overall, 16% reported using English, 36% reported using Spanish, and 48% reported using both languages (Spanish/English). In reference to their use of literacy skills at work, only 37% of the participants reported having to do some type of reading at work, and only 33% reported doing some sort of writing at work (e.g., writing/reading work orders or filling out inventories at work).

Participants were also asked if they use computers at work. Only 27% indicated using computers at work. It is important to note that as we inquired about activities requiring literacy or the use of technology, the general trend indicated that fewer participants were involved in some type of technology activities at work. This may be indicative of the lack of resources and opportunities available to the Spanish-speaking community, which, in turn, do not allow for their upward mobility.

Addressing Key Community Needs

Within the Hispanic neighborhoods, the Mexican Institute identified a lack of access to technology in the communities as the main barrier that needed to be overcome. This lack of access manifested itself in two forms. First of all, there

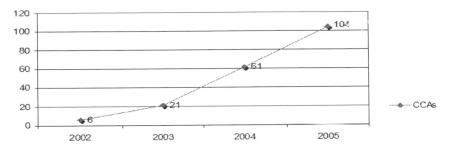

FIGURE 8.1.   Number of operating Community Learning Centers

is a lack of infrastructure or technology connectivity in Hispanic neighborhoods. Secondly, there is a lack of opportunities to learn computer skills in the community's native language.

Examining the Impact of the Program at the Community Level

Overall, the findings show that in a brief period of three years (when this study was conducted), the Mexican Institute had experienced a dramatic increase in the number of CCAs operating in Houston's public schools. For example, in 2002 there were six centers operating in Houston. In 2003, 14 new centers were added, and by May of 2004, there were 25 new centers added to their network, bringing the total number of centers to 39. However, since the time this study was conducted, the number of CCAs across Texas has grown to 100. This is indicative

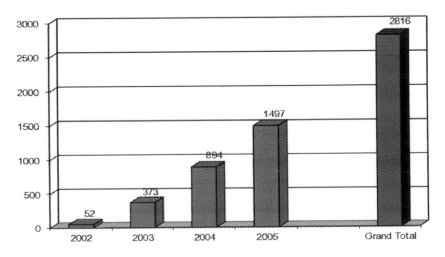

FIGURE 8.2.   CCA total graduates per year

of the impact and success of the program (see Figure 8.1). On average, each center supported 15 participants per class. The Mexican Institute and its partnership with the Tecnológico de Monterrey, in Mexico, offered two technology-training courses per year. The rapid growth of the program points to the needs within the community; furthermore, it points to the program's positive impact on the community on how these needs can be ameliorated (see Figure 8.2).

Another point of leverage for community building has been their concentrated effort to reduce the digital gap within the homes by making computer technology available and affordable to the families. The Mexican Institute, in collaboration with Genesys IT, acquires refurbished computers at a very low price (ranging from $150 to $350), which in turn are sold to the participants after completion of the program. These computers are equipped with all of the software and hardware required for the parents to continue their education online and to work with their children on school-related activities at home. During the time of the study, 57 computers had been sold to families. Currently, a total of 126 computers have been sold to families, and 20 participants have continued their education online by taking new courses such as HTML for web page design, health-related courses, and basic statistics through the Tecnológico de Monterrey's web portal. In the next sections, we begin to address the impact of the program on individual participants as well as potential impacts on the family unit, as perceived by program participants.

Examining the Impact of the Program on Individual Participants

A MANOVA was used to examine participants' differences on attitudes, opinions, and beliefs about technology ($n - 377$). The dependent variables were a set of 67 structure questions focused on examining the efficacy of the intervention program as well as examining participants' beliefs on the impact of the program to their lives and their children. These dependent variables were subsequently analyzed with a set of independent variables including level of education, gender of participants, and language (whether participants spoke Spanish only, or both Spanish/English). The analysis examined if participants' attitudes towards using computers, the importance of the program, and future aspirations were significantly different as a function of the above independent variables. Overall, the findings show no statistically significant main effects for level of education, gender, and language. Also, no significant interactions were found among these variables. This analysis of the pre-survey data ($n = 377$) suggests a degree of homogeneity among participants in their perceptions of the program.

Participants' Perceptions on the Worth and Merit of the CCA Program

Participants were asked about their attitudes and perceptions in reference to learning and using technology. Overall, 83% perceived the CCA program as a useful learning experience to improve their current job status. Additionally, 98% of the participants were of the opinion that the CCA training would provide better opportunities for future employment. Eighty-one percent of the participants believed that what they were learning about technology at the CCA would be helpful for assisting their children with homework. For example, a parent expressed that "the program will be useful for many things. Primarily, it is motivating for my son to see me taking this course." In general, the participants' comments seemed to suggest that they were making clear connections to the usefulness and importance of computer training not only for their immediate jobs but also for their future employment. They were also making connections in reference to the implications that their computer training and other learning activities may have had in their involvement in the education of their children.

Participants were also asked whether their participation in the program would increase the chances of employment. Ninety-one percent agreed that it would increase chances of employment. Also, 93% expressed that what they were learning at the CCA was applicable in many areas of their lives. In general, they also had a positive attitude about technology. Overall, 98% indicated that what they were learning at the CCA was worth learning. These findings suggest that the program was connecting to participants' lives and was meeting their expectations and needs. Overall, no pre- and post-program differences of opinions and beliefs were found. This suggests that participants finished the program with the same positive attitudes and perceptions with which they had started.

Immigrant Parents Are Learning Technology Skills

Paired sample t-tests were used to examine pre- and post-survey data on participants' technology gains at the end of the program. In the pre-assessment survey participants reported that using computers was a difficult task for them to perform. In the post-assessment survey, they reported that using computers was not a difficult task any longer ($t(48) = 2.40$, $p = .02$). This is indicative of their growth in learning how to use computers. To further examine participants' gains on the use of computer technology, other paired sample t-tests were carried out. Items were focused on determining what participants did not know when they entered the program and what they knew at the end of the program. The scale used gave participants the option of identifying the skills or procedures they "could not do," those they "could do with the help of someone else," and those skills and procedures they "could do by themselves," making the scale similar to the learning processes as described by Vygotsky (1978) in reference to the zone of proximal development. Overall, on the use of Microsoft Word, participants reported significant gains ($t(47) = 3.86$, $p = .0001$) on being able to use the program beyond the basics (e.g., paste photos, or to import or paste text from other files). Figure 8.3 shows the magnitude of the effect on learning how to use Microsoft Word. Half of the participants seemed to be able to use the program during the pre-assessment, but this is mainly due to the fact that in some centers the pre-assessment was given after participants were already learning to use the Word application.

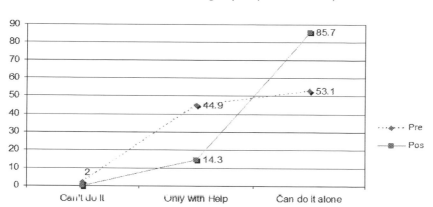

FIGURE 8.3.   Parents are learning to use Microsoft Word.

Other significant gains were observed on the use of Microsoft Excel. On the pre-assessment, 69.4% of the participants indicated that they could not use Excel or they could only do it with the assistance of an expert other; however, in the post-test 81.6% reported being able to perform Excel tasks by themselves ($t(47) = 5.28, p = .0001$) (see Figure 8.4).

Significant gains were also observed on the use of Microsoft PowerPoint ($t(45) = 7.23, p = .0001$). Overall, at the beginning of the program 83.7% of the participants reported that they could not use the program or they could only do it with the assistance of an expert other; however, in the post-assessment 85.7% reported being able to perform PowerPoint tasks by themselves (see Figure 8.5).

Overall, participants reported having gained an understanding of the operations of computers such as creating a folder, copying a file onto a disc, opening/

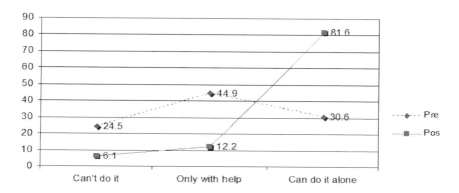

FIGURE 8.4.   Parents are learning to use Excel.

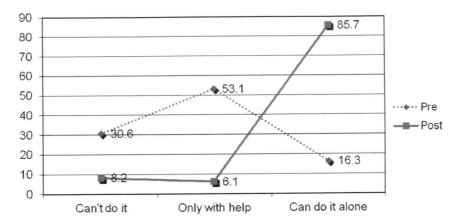

FIGURE 8.5. Parents are learning to use PowerPoint

using email accounts, and using the World Wide Web to conduct Internet search-es. Participants moved from having difficulties using the computer as measured on the pre-assessment survey to a point where they were performing difficult tasks such as designing PowerPoint presentations or developing databases in Microsoft Excel. For example, in one school, a group of seven mothers, after graduating from the technology program, went to their children's teacher and began to volunteer in the classroom. In collaboration with the teacher, they developed a class unit on the ABCs, recognition of colors, and dollars and cents for kindergartners. Using their newly acquired PowerPoint application skills they were able to assist the teacher in the development of this particular lesson.

The applicability and significance of the program is not only measurable by its success in teaching participants computer skills. Many of the program graduates have also obtained more gainful employment or pursued continued education opportunities as a result of the computer course. A growing archive of success stories can be found at the Mexican Institute's website (www.mexico-info.com/institute). These accounts include the story of a CCA graduate, from Mexico, who went on to become a highly skilled, highly paid computer technology instructor; a hotel cook whose new computer skills landed him a job in the hotel's main administrative office; and another Mexican woman who now works as a secretary for a phone-card company whose calling cards she used to hawk on city streets. Over the last three years, fifty-five graduates have been trained as CCA coordinators/facilitators and others as tutors/mentors for the Mexican Institute itself. These job opportunities have created new avenues for better employment and professional development for these individuals, at the same time that many of them are also empowered to participate in the education of their children in ways previously not available to them.

CONCLUSION

The study suggests that given the appropriate resources and capacity-building support, Hispanic immigrants will make significant gains educationally and socio-economically. The Mexican Institute is providing valuable resources that serve as a technology pipeline for Spanish-speaking parents. Their CCAs program involves a series of coordinated efforts affecting a number of different components on the education and development of the Hispanic community. Parents reported a sense of self-efficacy, and the findings suggest that they have been empowered by the processes within the CCA. There is also a legacy left behind in the number of centers currently operating within the public schools. For example, today there are over 100 CCA centers operating in Texas. New districts, new cities, and new states are being added to what is likely to become a national community-building network.

The lessons learned from this study represent a guiding mechanism in an effort to inform future delivery of services to Hispanic immigrants. The study also pinpoints that under the right conditions, the digital divide that seems to threaten the future of Hispanic immigrant families can be overcome when the needs of the community are addressed appropriately.

We hope that this study, identifying the activities and the importance to place community needs in a socio-cultural context, will have a modest impact on the trajectory and shape of the educational process for underrepresented communities such as Hispanics. Overall, efforts to better the lives of Hispanic immigrants have moved program practices in a direction that is generally considered to be an improvement for the Hispanic community. This improvement has begun to occur at the individual level for some families as well as in some communities. The evidence also shows that the process of involving parents in their children's education has, in fact, left behind a legacy of new and improved frameworks for parental involvement in their children's education. It has also aided in establishing a technology network within the public schools and partnering arrangements in order to increase the number of access points in the communities. We hope that this study will have a positive impact on educational policy and on future efforts for providing technology education and technology access for the Spanish-speaking community across the nation.

REFERENCES

Barton, C. A., Drake, C., Perez, G. J., St. Louis, K., & George, M. (2004). Ecologies of parental engagement in urban education. *Educational Researcher, 33*(4), 3–12.

Branum-Martin, L., Mehta, P. D., Carlson, C. D., Francis, D. J., & Goldenberg, C. (in press). The nature of Spanish versus English language use at home. *Journal of Educational Psychology.*

Braun, D. (1997). Parent education programmes. In K. N. Dwivedi (Ed.), *Enhancing parenting skills: A guide for professionals working with parents* (pp. 91–121). New York, NY: John Wiley and Sons.

Bronfenbrenner, U. (1979). Beyond the deficit model in child and family policy. *Teachers College Press, 81,* 95–104.

Bronfenbrenner, U. (1986). Ecology of the family as a context for human development: Research perspectives. *Developmental Psychology, 22,* 723–742.

Cochran, M. (1988). Between cause and effect: The ecology of program impacts. In A. R. Pence (Ed.), *Ecological research with children and families: From concepts to methodology* (pp. 143–169). New York, NY: Teacher College Press.

Delgado-Gaitan, C. (1991). Involving parents in the schools: A process of empowerment. *American Journal of Education, 100,* 20–46.

Francis, D. J., Carlson, C. D., Fletcher, J. M., Foorman, B. R., Goldenberg, C. R., Vaughn, S.,... Papanicolaou, A. (2005). Oral/literacy development of Spanish-speaking children: A multi-level program of research on language minority children and the instruction, school, and community contexts, and interventions that influence their academic outcomes. *Perspectives, 31*(2), 8–12.

Gallimore, R., Boggs, W. J., & Jordan, C. (1974). *Culture, behavior and education: A study of Hawaiian-Americans.* Thousand Oaks, CA: SAGE Publications.

Gallimore, R., Reese, L., Balzano, S., Benson, C., & Goldenberg, C. (1991, April). *Ecocultural sources of early literacy experiences: Job-required literacy, home literacy environments, and school reading.* Paper presented at the annual meeting of the American Educational Research Association, Chicago, IL.

Israel, B., Shulz, A., Parker, E., Becker, A., Allen, A., & Guzman, R. (2000). Critical issues in developing and following community based participatory research principles. In M. Minkler & N. Wallerstein (Eds), *Community-based participatory research in health: From process to outcomes* (pp. 556–573). San Francisco, CA: Jossey Bass.

Klineberg, S. (2005). *Public perceptions in remarkable times: Tracking change through 24 years of Houston Surveys.* Retrieved from http://houstonareasurvey.org/RE-PORT-2005.pdf

Kumpfer, K. & Alvarado, R. (2003). Family-strengthening approaches for the prevention of youth problem behaviors. *American Psychologist, 58*(6/7), 457–465.

Moll, L., Amanti, C., Neff, D., & Gonzalez, N. (1992). Funds of knowledge for teaching: Using a qualitative approach to connect homes and classrooms. *Theory into Practice, 31,* 132–141.

Padrón, Y., Waxman, H., & Rivera, H. (2002). Issues in educating Hispanic students. In S. Stringfield & D. Land (Eds.), *Educating at-risk students* (pp. 66–88). Chicago, IL: University of Chicago Press.

President's Advisory Commission on Educational Excellence for Hispanic Americans. (2003). From risk to opportunity: Fulfilling the educational needs of Hispanic Americans in the 21st century. Retrieved from http://www2.ed.gov/about/inits/list/hispanic-initiative/from-risk-to-opportunity.pdf

Reese, L., Linan-Thompson, S., & Goldenberg, C. (2008). Variability in community characteristics and Spanish-speaking children's home language and literacy opportunities. *Journal of Multilingual and Multicultural Development, 29,* 271–290.

Resnick, M., Bearman, P. S., Blum, R. W., Bauman, K. E., Harris, K. M., & Jones, J. (1997). Protecting adolescents from harm. *Journal of the American Medical Association, 278,* 823–832.

U.S. Department of Commerce. (1999). *Falling through the net III: Defining the digital divide.* Washington, DC: Author.

Vygotsky, L. S. (1978). *Mind in society: The Development of higher psychological processes.* (Edited by M. Cole, V. John-Steiner, S. Scribner, & E. Souberman). Cambridge, MA: Harvard University Press.

Wandersman, A. & Florin, P. (2003). Community interventions and effective prevention. *American Psychologist, 58*(6/7), 441–448.

CHAPTER 9

STRATEGIES TO ENGAGE FEMALE AND HISPANIC YOUTH IN ROBOTICS IN THE SOUTHWESTERN UNITED STATES

Tirupalavanam G. Ganesh

ABSTRACT

Informal learning settings offer the potential to stimulate interest, initiative, experimentation, discovery, play, imagination, and innovation in learners. Engaging adolescents in activities where they are free to design and innovate on their own can be useful in sparking their curiosity and interest in new fields. Female and minority youth used robotics kits to engage in technological problem-solving experiences. Learners were presented with an engineering design challenge focused on an authentic life-science context and introduced to technologies where solutions are achieved via an actual project. This chapter offers an alternative approach to engaging students traditionally under-represented in the STEM fields.

Research on Technology Use in Multicultural Settings, pages 177–193.

INTRODUCTION

Over the last several years, robotics-based educational programs have become a popular activity in the United States (Gura & King, 2007) and around the world. With the increasing popularity of programs such as For Inspiration and Recognition of Science and Technology Lego League (U.S. FIRST, 2011), many children and youth of ages nine to 17 have had opportunities to build their own robots using programmable kits like Lego Mindstorms and VEX Robotics. A typical robotics program may engage students in designing and building robots that are modeled after those recommended in the print material accompanying the robotics kits. For example, print material in some versions of the Lego robotics kits included instructions to build a "battle tank"-like robot. As an introduction, students are usually asked to build a robot by following instructions in the manual that accompanies the kit. Also, building vehicles and navigating mazes are common activities in many robotics-based programs and competitions. While one may argue that there is nothing inherently wrong in introducing robotics in formal and informal K–12 learning settings by giving students the task of building a robotic vehicle or engaging students in science and engineering competitions, such efforts may be limiting, especially if we are to engage non-traditional students in Information and Communication Technology (ICT) and Science, Technology, Engineering, and Mathematics (STEM) subjects (see Sadler, Coyle, & Schwartz, 2000). In order to attract youth who would not otherwise engage in robotics, a different approach is needed. Such an approach would give learners the opportunity to define the problem and create their own solutions, where there is no single correct answer to the problem, allowing students to find personal relevance in their learning experience (Eccles & Wigfield, 2002). Many researchers (Resnick & Silverman, 2005; Rusk, Resnick, Berg, & Pezalla-Granlund, 2006) have put forth ideas and materials (Druin, 1999; Druin & Hendler, 2000) to broaden the appeal of robotics as an educational tool.

OBJECTIVES

This chapter describes strategies used to engage Hispanic and other traditionally under-served junior-high school students in an activity where robotics was introduced using non-typical techniques rooted within the tradition of arts-based approaches and the sciences. These programs were conducted in Houston, Texas and Phoenix, Arizona. In Houston, the program was offered: (a) as an after-school program in a middle school through a community science workshop offered in collaboration with a children's museum and (b) as a summer university/industry partnership for ninth-graders. In Phoenix, the program was offered as a university/school collaborative after-school program for seventh graders.

Research Objectives

The research objectives of the study as reported in this chapter are to understand students' (a) pre-conceptions of robots; (b) attitudes about engineers and self-efficacy about "tinkering," in other words, the ability to build, take apart, and put things together; and (c) learning resulting from the reported informal life-science based robotics program.

THEORETICAL FRAMEWORK

Adolescents seldom lack curiosity, but as they go into teenage years their enthusiasm for learning ICT and STEM subjects appears to decline (National Academy of Engineering, 2008). Many drop out before the end of required schooling. Others continue to turn up for school but make the minimum effort. These problems take on new meaning in a period when a fundamental survival tool for individuals, and nations, is a willingness to engage in life-long learning (Organisation for Economic Co-operation and Development, 2000). Low-skill jobs are disappearing, people are switching jobs more often, and demands for highly skilled professionals in developed nations are growing rapidly (National Academy of Sciences, National Academy of Engineering, and Institute of Medicine, 2007). Significant differences in educational attainment remain with regard to ethnicity, origin, age, and sex (U.S. Department of Commerce, 2011).

Engineering is among the least gender-equitable professions with a workforce that was only 13% female in 2008, and ICT/STEM programs continue to have low minority enrollment (National Science Board, 2012). The cause has psycho-sociocultural roots that create barriers to female and minority participation in these fields (Meinholdt & Murray, 1999). Informal learning settings outside the framework of schooling offer the potential to stimulate interest, initiative, experimentation, discovery, play, imagination, and innovation in learners (National Research Council, 2009). Engaging adolescents in an imaginative activity where they are free to design and innovate on their own, without the aid of print material or instructor prompts on what to do, can prove to be useful in sparking young minds' curiosity and interest in new fields.

The workplaces of today and tomorrow demand skills that are not merely exemplified as technological skills (logical, analytical, and technical), but also those represented as value skills (creativity, critical thinking, ability to see the big picture, and work with diverse learners) (Collins, Brown, & Holum, 1991). Educational experiences within K–12 settings need to engage youth in content knowledge as well as these technological and value skills. The National Science Foundation (NSF, 2003) reported that current curricular approaches appear outdated and de-contextualized. Students need to be exposed to inquiry-oriented learning environments as a means of increasing their interest in ICT/STEM fields. The case for fundamentally changing how we introduce students to these fields and careers is strong.

METHODS

Students who find the traditional in-school science/mathematics curricula uninteresting and disconnected from their lives need to be engaged in learning by doing (Schank & Cleary, 1995). In this research effort, the critical issue at hand was to enthuse urban youth, particularly traditionally under-represented students, females and ethnic minorities, in ICT/STEM fields by engaging them in learning that emphasizes both useful and inquiry-based motivations.

The Participants

Urban female and minority youth were recruited to take part in informal learning in Houston and Phoenix. The programs were multifaceted and not merely robotics-based. This chapter focuses primarily on how robotics was introduced to these students. Participant demographics are noted in Table 9.1.

The Curriculum Model

Project-based learning is an instructional strategy that helps students apply content knowledge to authentic problems that require critical thinking and increase their responsibility for learning. This approach has as its foundations the curricular and psychological research work of Dewey (1902), Kilpatrick (1918, 1921), Stevenson (1928), Piaget (1969, 1970), and Vygotsky (1978, 1986). It was Dewey (1902) who advocated that the most natural way for children to learn is by doing. He said that for children to develop a habit of "critical examination and inquiry" (p. 29), they need to be provided with appropriate learning experiences and guidance. Kilpatrick (1921) defined *project* to refer to any unit of purposeful experience or activity "where the dominating purpose, as an inner urge, (1) fixes

TABLE 9.1. Robotics-Based Program Participant Demographics

Program	Houston #1	Houston #2	Phoenix
Type	After-School	Summer	After-School
Demographics	Percentage (*n*=22)	Percentage (*n*=21)	Percentage (*n*=20)
Race/Ethnicity			
Hispanic	77% (17)	24% (5)	55% (11)
Black	9% (2)	76% (16)	5% (1)
White	14% (3)	0% (0)	30% (6)
Asian-American	0% (0)	0% (0)	5% (1)
Native American	0% (0)	0% (0)	5% (1)
Sex			
Female	45% (10)	48% (10)	60% (12)
Male	55% (12)	52% (11)	40% (8)

the aim of the action, (2) guides its process, and (3) furnishes its drive, its inner motivation" (p. 283). Vygotsky (1978, 1986) described learning as a social process that takes place in the context of culture, community, and prior experiences that is further enhanced when learners work collaboratively on challenging tasks.

Projects embedded in engineering design give learners the opportunity to explore: a) design, b) testing, and c) the production of tools, technology, structures, and materials. This approach is ideally suited for addressing engineering design projects, which are by definition open-ended with alternative solutions, where the problem acts as the catalyst that initiates the learning process (Duch, Groh, & Allen, 2001). Learners were presented with an engineering design problem that focused on an authentic life-science context and were introduced to technologies where solutions are achieved via an actual project. Participants had access to a wide range of resources that included human and content-rich media, an art museum, science and engineering laboratories, and a number of different types of hardware and software technologies. The *project* therefore is the culmination of the learning *process,* and the solution is the finished *product* (Lesh & Kelly, 2000; National Research Council [NRC], 2000; Thomas, 2000). Using a project-challenge that is analogous to complicated tasks encountered in today's ICT/STEM workplaces, student teams were confronted with a project that acts as a focus for teamwork and a catalyst for multidisciplinary learning. The informal learning experience incorporated problems that gave context to and served as supports to learning (Hmelo, 2004; Hmelo & Ferrari, 1997). Projects extended over time to allow students to acquire new knowledge and skills (Blumenfeld et al., 1991).

In Houston the engineering design project was to design and build a robot that would mimic selected behaviors of the sea turtle. In Phoenix the engineering design project was to design and build a robot that would mimic selected behaviors of the desert tortoise. Art, storytelling, and poetry were used to engage participants. The study was grounded around the protection of an endangered species (*Lepidochelys kempii, the* Kemp's ridley sea turtles along the United States Gulf Coast) and a protected species (*Gopherus agassizii*, the desert tortoise in the southwestern United States) as a means to consider conservation of natural resources for future generations.

Integration of Life Sciences

In Houston, the program objectives were to develop knowledge of sea turtles (Harrison, 2005), their behaviors, and habitats along the Gulf of Mexico (Galveston, Texas) and simulate their behaviors using MicroWorlds EX software and Lego Mindstorms. To begin their inquiry about sea turtles, participants visited the National Oceanic and Atmospheric Administration facility where a sea turtle conservation effort exists. In Phoenix, the program objectives were to develop knowledge of desert tortoises (Brennan & Holycross, 2006), their behaviors, and habitats in the southwestern United States (Phoenix, Arizona) and to simulate their behaviors using MicorWorlds EX and Lego Mindstorms. Students visited habitats in local eco-preserves facilitated via the Arizona Game and Fish Department to study desert tortoises. Students then built robots simulating the behaviors of desert tortoises.

Integration of Art and Local Context

In Houston's third ward there exists Project Row Houses, a neighborhood-based art and cultural organization inspired by the work of African-American artist Dr. John Biggers (1924–2001). Dr. Biggers painted fantastic murals illustrating the strength and breadth of African-American culture (Wardlaw, 1995). Houston was his home and primary workshop from 1958 to 2001, and Houston has been gifted with John Biggers' outstanding legacy of art. In his art, we can find sea turtles amidst railroad tracks and shotgun houses. This local context connected our participants' experience of studying and simulating sea turtles' behaviors using software and robotics kits with their history. Participants reviewed John Biggers' murals and artwork and visited Project Row Houses to become aware of their local culture through which program activities were linked to their own futures.

In Phoenix, the Navajo people and their way of life have influenced the culture and history of the place. Students read books about the southwest, its native people, culture, and bio-diversity. This allowed students to engage in story-telling as they developed scenarios for their projects. These included *The Desert is Theirs* (1975) and *Desert Voices* (1981) by Byrd Baylor. The books contain folklore and facts about the southwestern U.S. region in poetry form. They describe how the land is to be shared and how people and many desert animals reside in harmony in the desert. The poems describe the desert through the voices of its many inhabitants: the jackrabbit, rattlesnake, cactus wren, desert tortoise, lizard, coyote, and human being.

Participants were posed with the engineering design-based project challenge of building a robot that would mimic selected behaviors of the sea turtle/desert tortoise. They were provided with access to print material and opportunities to observe the animals—sea turtles/desert tortoises—in person, and learn about the natural habitats of these animals. This focus on life sciences gave students plenty of opportunities to understand the animals' life cycles, their habitats, threats to the animals' existence, and the animals' relevance to our lives as related to how humans interact with the environment.

Students (grouped in small teams of two to three) identified one or two behaviors of the sea turtle/desert tortoise that they wanted to mimic using robotics. As students explored the Lego robotics kit, they began to experiment with the various sensors provided to them to understand their functions and begin to relate how the sensors could be used to simulate specific animal behaviors. For instance, students related the use of the light sensor to the behavior of the young sea turtle that follows a light source. And in the case of the desert tortoise, students related the use of the temperature sensor to the behavior of the desert tortoise that goes into its burrow for shade from the high temperatures in the Sonoran Desert. Student teams had the freedom to define their problem—which meant that they could identify the specific sea turtle/desert tortoise behavior that they wanted to mimic using the robotics kit. Students were also able to determine for themselves whether their solution responded to the challenge. Students had to justify their design choices by describing the specific animal behavior they wanted to mimic. Creative solutions offered included the use of the sound sensor to detect loud noises (e.g., a bird's call indicating the predator's presence or the noise of a vehicle on a beach or desert tortoise habitat indicating human activity); the use of the light sensor to detect darkness/brightness (e.g., a bird's shadow indicating the approaching predator); the use of the temperature sensor to detect increase in temperature (e.g., the desert tortoise hides in its burrow to escape from the high temperature in the Sonoran Desert); and so on. Student teams also constructed artificial habitats for their sea turtle robots and desert tortoise robots and developed posters to describe their understanding of the animals and their habitats. Thus the introduction of robotics was embedded as an ICT tool to model animal behaviors in the larger context of a project where students developed in-depth knowledge about the sea turtle/desert tortoise through first-hand experiences with the animals, interactions with experts such as herpetologists and conservationists, and through print materials and other resources.

Instructional Planning

The *learning cycle* is an inquiry approach to instruction and is a popular science instructional planning tool (Atkin & Karplus, 1962; Bybee, 1997). This approach has been researched for its impact on learning (Abraham & Renner, 1986; Beeth & Hewson, 1999; Gerber, Cavallo, & Marek, 2001). Its origins can be traced to Bruner (1960), who introduced the notion of "discovery learning" where students interacted with their environment to discover new ideas. Initially described in the *Science Curriculum Improvement Study* (Karplus & Their, 1967), the learning cycle was based on three phases of instruction: exploration, concept introduction, and concept application. Since its initial description, the learning cycle has undergone a number of variations. A more recent variation offered by Bybee (1997) is known as the 5-E model—engage, explore, explain, elaborate, and evaluate. The learning experiences designed and offered to students in this study used the 5-E model.

The *engage* phase was deliberately designed to capture learners' interest and attention and access student's prior knowledge and conceptions while connecting it to the current learning experience. The learning activity had to be interesting so it could retain and sustain the learner's attention for the duration of the experience. Giving students access to the animals (the sea turtle/desert tortoise) and access to experts and information sources about the animals and their habitats were essential aspects of the engage phase. Furthermore, students maintained their interest as they began to learn about the animals and their relevance to the local context of where the students lived.

The *explore* phase was designed to provide the learners with activities wherein the current concepts, processes, and skills were identified, and conceptual change was facilitated. Learners were encouraged to draw upon prior knowledge to generate ideas and questions, and explore them with their peers, teachers, and mentors who were engineers and scientists, professionals from industry, and also undergraduate/graduate science and engineering students. The exploration took the form of testing out ideas through experimentation by trying different sensors provided in the robotics kits to better understand their functions. Exploration began with students being given ample time to play with the robotics kits by themselves before any specific activities were offered to introduce the programming necessary to operate the robot.

The *explain* phase provided participants with opportunities to describe their understanding of knowledge, processes, or skill. Small sized whiteboards (11" x 17") and dry-erase markers were provided to each student to share her ideas with peers and adult mentors or to exchange ideas in small groups. This is also the phase where facilitators could explain a concept, process, or skill or the curriculum materials could be used to guide the learner to a deeper understanding of the concept. Experts such as a herpetologist and sea turtle/desert tortoise conservationists were available to explain content knowledge related to the animal behaviors, habitats, and threats to their survival. In addition, specific programming skills were introduced through deliberate activities. Students were also provided with opportunities to explain to their peers, family members, and other adults associated with the informal science program their content knowledge related to the project.

The *elaborate* phase provided participants with experiences to develop deeper and broader understanding, more information, and adequate skills through additional activities. For instance, these included specific activities that allowed students to experience in context the use of sensors in the robotics kits such as the light, touch, sound, and temperature sensors.

The *evaluate* phase provided learners with the opportunity to reflect and assess their understanding and skills, while also providing facilitators with the opportunity to evaluate learners' progress. Evaluation occurred throughout the learning experiences. Various non-digital tools were used to evaluate student learning. It is important to note that the 5-E phases are by no means linear; rather they are cyclic. In this study, the learning cycle was deliberately used in the design of learning experiences with careful attention to each phase (Brown & Abell, 2007; Colburn & Clough, 1997; Maier & Marek, 2006).

Tools such as personal sized whiteboards/dry erase markers, word walls, and engineering notebooks were used for the facilitation and demonstration of student learning throughout the school year. Assessment was focused on learning what students knew and were able to do (NRC, 2001; Schneider, Krajcik, Marx, & Soloway, 2002).

Personal sized whiteboards (11"x 17") and dry erase markers were provided to each team of participants so they could record their ideas, sketches, and what they had learned. These ideas and sketches were then shared with peers during learning activities. They were also used for informal presentations to the parents, teachers, and other visitors associated with the informal science program. The personal sized whiteboards permitted participants to pass the whiteboards around to other teams. This facilitated easy exchange of ideas and knowledge.

Word walls were used at each program site and integrated into the project's learning activities. Science vocabulary word walls have been used in elementary, middle, and high schools as an important tool in scaffolding and facilitating student learning (Staires, 2007; Vallejo, 2006). Gee (2004) noted that children need to be supported so they can deal with the academic language of science, mathematics, and so on in order to be successful in school. Additionally, researchers who study adolescent and adult literacy have advocated word walls as effective literacy tools that hold the potential for enhancing vocabulary learning with older learners when used with effective instructional practices (Harmon, Wood, Hedrick, Vintinner, & Willeford, 2009). An interactive word wall was accessible for students to add any new and interesting words they had learned throughout the learning experience. This tool helped enhance students' understanding of how words work as new vocabulary related to the STEM fields were visible not only for program participants, but also for other users and visitors of the media center (library and computer lab) where activities were held.

Each participant was provided with an engineering notebook. Laboratory or science notebooks have been used for a long time in science education (Gilbert & Kotelman, 2005; Livingston, 2005; Shepardson & Britsch, 2001). Literacy and science content experts have recommend the use of learning logs in K–12 education, especially with bilingual and English language learners (Amaral, Garrison, & Klentschy, 2002; Klentschy & Molina-De La Torre, 2004; Rivard, 1994). In pre-engineering education, Poole, deGrazia, and Sullivan (2001) advocated using a notebook as an embedded assessment tool. Here the idea was that not only would the notebook serve as a place for students to record notes, but also to include goals, objectives, performance criteria, pre- and post-activity questions, and other specifics related to the project-based challenge. Participants recorded their journal entries, sketches, designs, and organized materials such as resource handouts and information organizers in the notebook. Journal prompts were provided to participants that served to facilitate: (a) recording data collected during observations and field trips, (b) information collected during content exploration activities essential for the project-based challenge, and (c) reflection on the learning activities.

Accessing Student Pre-conceptions of Robots: Imagine a Robot

Participants were asked to draw a robot from their imagination and describe their robot's functions. This activity was conducted before participants were ever exposed to the Lego Mindstorms kits so they would not be influenced by related print material or the materials themselves. Students were given the following prompt on a sheet of paper:

> Close your eyes and imagine a Robot. Think about the purpose of this Robot and the functions that the Robot can perform. On the attached sheet of art paper, draw what you imagined. In the space below respond to the following questions: (1) Describe what the robot in your picture can do. (2) List three words that come to mind when you think of the robot you imagined and designed above. (3) What do you know about robots?

This form of exploration of students' prior knowledge was key in accessing students' preconceptions about robots and was also a means to engage students in imaginative expression of their notions of robots.

Data Sources

Data collection included the use of a pre- and post-survey of participants' "tinkering and technical self-efficacy." This survey was adapted for use with youth from an instrument that was validated by Yasar, Baker, Robinson-Kurpius, Krause, and Roberts (2006), where a sample of 200 engineers' responses were used to develop the items. Students' drawing and description of a robot from their imagination were collected and analyzed. It was surprising to note that none of the participants had ever seen or used a robotics kit prior to this experience. However, many had knowledge of robots from popular culture (e.g., *I, Robot*, 2004; *The Iron Giant*, 1999). Three observers observed small teams of two participants while teams engaged in activities. An observation protocol that focused on the nature and quality of student interactions with each other and the tools was developed and used. Participants were interviewed at the start and end of the program in small focus groups about program impact, content knowledge, and interest in STEM fields. Interviews lasted 15 minutes each and were audiotaped and transcribed. Students were taught to maintain science notebooks (Rivard, 1994), which were collected and analyzed. Notebooks and interview transcriptions were examined using qualitative procedures. Text was coded for changes in understanding content, design, engineering, and programming. We looked for text that reflected changes in interest in ICT/STEM careers and educational goals and developed a codebook that was refined on subsequent readings of the data corpus (Ganesh, 2011a).

RESULTS

What We Learned about Participants

Pre-conceptions of Robots

Ninety-eight percent of the students made robots that were humanoid objects. Most designs indicated a social or helpful use to family, elderly, disabled, or others. Students said things like, "My robot has a few restrictions: it cannot kill"; "Coming in 2029: A robot for the disabled, and for use in retirement homes, so it can get to hard-to-reach places; can hear calls for help from even 3 miles away…"; "Can help clean, cook, wash, make beds,. . ."; "Can conduct surgery…". There were a couple of exceptions to the norm in the group where participants designed a tank-like robot "that could drop soldiers and arms in enemy territory." Further probing revealed that family members of these participants were serving in the U.S. armed forces.

Attitudes about Engineers and Self-Efficacy about "Tinkering"

In focus group discussions, many described scientists and engineers as predominantly male: "I think of an engineer as a man, White, in his 40s, wearing khakis" and "A scientist would be a White male, around 30 years old, wears a lab coat and would have taken physics in high school." Almost all female participants, with the exception of two females, indicated that engineers and scientists would be males. Prior to starting the program, 42% of participants overall felt that women and minorities don't do well in science and engineering; however, only 7% maintained this attitude after the program. Pre-program, 30% of participants felt that they did not understand how parts work together to make the whole device work, but only 1% maintained this feeling post-program.

Resultant Learning

Students expressed knowledge of:

- robots as being human-controlled via programming;
- modeling and mimicry from nature as an engineering design activity;
- enhanced awareness of the impact of human activity on the environment;
- sea turtle behaviors (hatch on land and newly born turtles go towards light and water; are small and can fit on the palm of an adult's hand when they are newly born; hatchlings are most vulnerable to predators; take 40 years to become sexually active; human activities such as coastal driving, construction, and lighting are the main cause for the decline in the Kemp's ridley population; fishing activity that can cause entanglement in fishing gear, pollution and trash, and collision with boats are threats to sea turtles' survival; the Kemp's ridley sea turtles along the Gulf Coast are an endangered species; and shrimp fishermen in the U.S. and Mexico are required to use devices that allow turtles to escape from the nets); and
- desert tortoise behaviors (go underground when the temperature goes above 90F; are small and can fit on the palm of an adult's hand when they are newly born and are most vulnerable then to predators; survival of juveniles is low as only two to three per 100 hatched may live to become adults; burrows are crucial to their survival; desert tortoises have the ability to store water in their bladders; adult desert tortoises can survive a year or

more without access to water; succulents are crucial to their survival in the desert in the absence of other foliage; reach sexual maturing between 15 and 20 years of age; increased urban development throughout the southwestern United States has reduced the desert tortoise habitat; and off-highway vehicles within the desert tortoise habitat are a threat to its survival).

In general, students expressed detailed and in-depth knowledge of the life-science content as well as programming and robotics as evidenced by the use of light sensors in robotic sea turtles that moved forward when a flashlight was flashed at the light sensor in the turtle, or when the temperature sensor registered a specific temperature in robotic desert tortoises that moved into a burrow seeking shade from the high temperature. Students needed guidance on specific programming tasks, such as conditional blocks like the "for" and "while" loops to repeat actions while or until a specific condition was met.

In this study, participants had no first-hand experience with robotics kits prior to their informal science learning experience. Participants' preconceptions of robots were around the idea of robots as humanoid in form. However, during the program, students learned that humans deliberately program robots to perform specific functions. Post-program, students identified pre-programmed functions that exist in our taken-for-granted technical devices, such as the kitchen microwave and the garage door opener, as examples of programming that are ubiquitous. Furthermore, students recognized that their use of robotics was to build a toy or a device that would mimic specific animal behaviors.

I found that by engaging youth in learning that emphasizes inquiry-based motivation, where learning is made relevant to students' lives, the outcome leads to enhanced learning in content areas (see Center for Cooperative Research and Extension Services for Schools [CRESS], 2003). In specific, participants in Houston found the local context of the sea turtle along the U.S. Gulf Coast and Mexico and the art of John Biggers relevant to where they lived and engaged in the afterschool program with interest. Similarly, participants in Phoenix found the local context of the desert tortoise and its habitat in the Sonoran Desert relevant to where they lived, specifically that they themselves lived on land that is essentially a place "paved over the desert." Participants also found the native culture of the Navajos and enhanced awareness of the natural desert habitat relevant and interesting. These local contexts and culture were important design elements in the project curricula that allowed students to engage in the learning experiences and find social relevance in their activities.

I also learned that systematic efforts are needed to dispel misunderstandings regarding STEM subjects and professions. For instance, female participants did not begin to demonstrate change in their perceptions that engineers were male until they had several opportunities to interact with female engineering students and professionals (Ganesh, 2011b). Students need to interact with STEM professionals over time in both professional and informal settings to develop their own understandings of these professionals and their roles in society. Seeking volunteers from local industries and STEM professional societies to visit with students during the after-school programs and work side-by-side with the students in the informal setting facilitated this. This helped students learn first-hand from the professionals about their education and career pathways. In addition, the project included visits to university engineering research laboratories and to local industry work places where students saw and interacted with STEM professionals. Undergraduate and graduate students in science and engineering also interacted with participants. This strategy of including professionals and undergraduate/graduate students from the STEM fields as mentors to participants within the context of the project challenge provided for cognitive apprenticeship (Brown, Collins, & Duguid, 1989). Cognitive apprenticeship has at its heart the idea of learning in context where the activity being taught is modeled in real-world situations. Brown, Collins, and Duguid (1989) proposed that skills and concepts are best learned in their real-world contexts and situations. Cognitive apprenticeship is situated within the social constructivist paradigm, which advocates that humans generate knowledge and meaning from their experiences (Collins, Brown, & Newman, 1989; Vygotsky, 1978). Lave (1988) said that learning is a social process and that skills are best acquired through authentic situations by communicating with peers and experts about those contexts. An example of a situated learning activity is more "apprentice like," and the learning activity is designed such that it is just beyond what a learner can attain on her or his own, but not at a level of difficulty where it is impossible to achieve with the help of peers and experts.

Coordinated and carefully designed in-depth and long-term experiences are needed to provide students and their families with knowledge of STEM education and career pathways. The critical issue for our nation is to enthuse all youth, particularly traditionally under-represented students—*females and ethnic minorities*—in STEM subjects. Results from this study will be useful for others who are interested in informal learning strategies and studying the impact of such efforts.

EDUCATIONAL IMPORTANCE OF STUDY

Through this project, we explored ways to advance discovery and understanding for learning. This study offers an alternative approach to engaging learners with robotics-based tools. The introduction of robotics by building a vehicle to navigate a maze was supplanted with an approach where robotics became the means to demonstrating understanding of biological resources. Thereby students who typically did not demonstrate interest in robotics-based competitions in their school districts and cities were attracted to the informal science education programs described in this study. Both formal and informal educators will find approaches described in this chapter to be useful in engaging learners with robotics-based tools employed in the service of inquiry. This effort was consciously designed so activities were not about "robotics for the sake of robotics" but about engaging youth in local conservation efforts. In this case, art and culture were used within the context of encouraging civic responsibility. Study and understanding of an endangered or protected species was enhanced through active learning that employed software and hardware to further student interest in information technology and science, technology, engineering, and mathematics fields.

NOTE

Portions of this material are based upon work supported by the *Learning through Engineering Design and Practice: Using our Human Capital for an Equitable Future*, National Science Foundation Award# 0737616, PI: Tirupalavanam G Ganesh. Opinions, findings, conclusions or recommendations expressed in this material are those of the author and do not necessarily reflect the views of the National Science Foundation (NSF).

REFERENCES

Abraham, M. R. & Renner, J. W. (1986). The sequence of learning cycle activities in high school chemistry. *Journal of Research in Science Teaching, 23*(2), 121–143.

Amaral, O., Garrison, L., & Klentschy, M. (2002). Helping English learners increase achievement through inquiry-based science instruction. *Bilingual Research Journal, 26*(2), 213–239.

Atkin, J. M. & Karplus, R. (1962). Discovery or invention? *Science Teacher, 29*, 45–51.

Baylor, B. (1975). *The desert is theirs.* New York, NY: Macmillan.

Baylor, B. (1981). *Desert voices.* New York, NY: Macmillan.

Beeth, M. & Hewson, P. (1999). Learning goals in exemplary science teacher's practice: Cognitive and social factors in teaching for conceptual change. *Science Education, 83*, 738–760.

Blumenfeld, P. C., Soloway, E., Marx, R. E., Krajcik, J. C., Guzdial, M., & Palincsar, A. (1991). Motivating project-based learning: Sustaining the doing, supporting the learning. *Educational Psychologist, 26*(3 & 4), 369–398.

Brennan, T. C. & Holycross, A. T. (2006). *A field guide to amphibians and reptiles in Arizona.* Phoenix, AZ: Arizona Game and Fish Department.

Brown, J. S., Collins, A., & Duguid, P. (1989). Situated cognition and the culture of learning. *Educational Researcher, 18*(1), 32–41.

Brown, P. L. & Abell, S. K. (2007). Project-based science. *Science and Children, 45*(4), 60–61.

Bruner, J. (1960). *The process of education.* Cambridge, MA: Harvard University Press.

Bybee, R. W. (1997). *Achieving scientific literacy: From purposes to practices.* Portsmouth, NH: Heinemann.

Center for Cooperative Research and Extension Services for Schools (CRESS). (2003). *A closer look at California's high performing, high poverty and/or high minority schools and learning supports.* Davis, CA: University of California, Davis.

Colburn, A. & Clough, M. P. (1997). Implementing the learning cycle. *The Science Teacher, 64*(5), 30–33.

Collins, A., Brown, J. S., & Holum, A. (1991). Cognitive apprenticeship: Making thinking visible. *American Educator, 15*(3), 6–11.

Collins, A., Brown, J. S., & Newman, S. E. (1989). Cognitive apprenticeship: Teaching the craft of reading, writing, and mathematics. In L. B. Resnick (Ed.), *Knowing, learning, and instruction: Essays in honor of Robert Glaser* (pp. 453–494). Hillsdale, NJ: Lawrence Erlbaum Associates.

Dewey, J. (1902). *The child and the curriculum.* Chicago, IL: University of Chicago Press.

Druin, A. (1999). *The design of children's technology.* San Francisco, CA: Morgan Kaufmann Publishers, Inc.

Druin, A. & Hendler, J. (2000). *Robots for kids: Exploring new technologies for learning.* San Francisco, CA: Morgan Kaufmann Publishers, Inc.

Duch, B., Groh, S., & Allen, D. (2001). *The power of problem-based learning: A practical "how to" for teaching undergraduate courses in any discipline.* Sterling, VA: Stylus Publication.

Eccles, J. S. & Wigfield, A. (2002). Motivational beliefs, values, and goals. *Annual Review of Psychology, 53,* 109–132.

Ganesh, T. G. (2011a). Children-produced drawings: An interpretive and analytic tool for researchers. In E. Margolis & L. Pauwels, (Eds.). *The Sage handbook of visual research methods* (pp. 214–240). Thousand Oaks, CA: Sage.

Ganesh, T. G. (2011b). Analyzing subject produced drawings: The use of the draw-an-engineer in context. *Proceedings of the American Society of Engineering Education (ASEE) 2011* (Paper no. AC 2011-2655; pp. 1–25). Washington, DC: ASEE Publications.

Gee, J. P. (2004). Language in the science classroom: Academic social languages as the heart of school-based literacy. In E. W. Saul (Ed.), *Crossing borders: Literacy and science instruction* (pp. 13–32). Newark, DE: International Reading Association/ National Science Teachers Association.

Gerber, B. L., Cavallo, A. M. L., & Marek, E. A. (2001). Relationship among informal learning environments, teaching procedures, and scientific reasoning abilities. *International Journal of Science Education, 23*(5), 535–549.

Gilbert, J. & Kotelman, M. (2005). Five good reasons to use science notebooks. *Science and Children, 43*(3), 28–32.

Gura, M. & King, P. K. (Eds.). (2007). *Classroom robotics: Case stories of 21ˢᵗ century instruction for millennial students.* Charlotte, NC: Information Age Publishing.

Harmon, J. M., Wood, K. D., Hedrick, W., Vintinner, J., & Willeford, T. (2009). Interactive word walls: More than just reading the writing on the walls. *Journal of Adolescent & Adult Literacy, 52*(5), 398–408.

Harrison, M. (2005). *The kid's times: Kemp's Ridley Sea Turtle.* Silver Spring, MD: NOAA's National Marine Fisheries Service, Office of Protected Resources.

Hmelo, C. E. (2004). Problem-based learning: What and how do students learn? *Educational Psychology Review, 16*(3), 235–266.

Hmelo, C. E. & Ferrari, M. (1997). The problem-based learning tutorial: Cultivating higher order thinking skills. *Journal for the Education of the Gifted, 20,* 401–422.

Karplus, R. & Their, H. D. (1967). *A new look at elementary school science.* Chicago, IL: Rand McNally.

Kilpatrick, W. H. (1918). The project method. *Teachers College Record, 19,* 319–335.

Kilpatrick, W. H. (1921). Dangers and difficulties of the project method and how to overcome them: Introductory statement: Definition of terms. *Teachers College Record, 22,* 282–288.

Klentschy, M. & Molina-De La Torre, E. (2004). Students' science notebooks and the inquiry process. In W. Saul (Ed.), *Crossing borders in literacy and science instruction: Perspectives on theory and practice* (pp. 340–354). Newark, DE: International Reading Association Press.

Lave, J. (1988). *Cognition in practice.* New York, NY: Cambridge University Press.

Lesh, R. & Kelly, A. (2000). Multitiered teaching experiments. In A. Kelly & R. Lesh (Eds.), *Research design in mathematics and science education* (pp. 197–230). Mahwah, NJ: Lawrence Erlbaum Associates.

Livingston, J. (2005). Journals of discovery. *Science and Children, 43*(3), 52–55.

Maier, S. J. & Marek, E. A. (2006). The learning cycle: A re-introduction. *The Physics Teacher 44*(2), 109–113.

Meinholdt, C. & Murray, S. L. (1999). Why aren't there more women engineers? *Journal of Women and Minorities in Science and Engineering, 5*, 239–263.

National Academy of Engineering. (2008). *Changing the conversation: Messages for improving public understanding of engineering.* Washington, DC: The National Academies Press.

National Academy of Sciences (NAS), National Academy of Engineering (NAE), & Institute of Medicine (IOM). (2007). *Rising above the gathering storm: Energizing and employing America for a brighter economic future,* Washington, DC: National Academies Press.

National Research Council. (2000). *How people learn: Brain, mind, experience, and school: Expanded edition.* Washington, DC: The National Academies Press.

National Research Council. (2001). *Knowing what students know: The science and design of educational assessment.* Washington, DC: National Academy Press.

National Research Council. (2009). *Learning science in informal environments: People, places, and pursuits.* Washington, DC: National Academies Press.

National Science Board. (2012). *Science and engineering indicators 2012.* Arlington, VA: Author.

National Science Foundation (NSF). (2003). *The science and engineering workforce: Realizing America's potential.* Retrieved from http://www.nsf.gov/nsb/documents/2003/nsb0369/start.htm

Organisation for Economic Co-operation and Development (OECD). (2000). *Where are the resources for lifelong learning?* Paris, France: Author.

Piaget, J. (1969). *The psychology of the child.* H. Weaver (Trans.). New York, NY: Basic Books.

Piaget, J. (1970). *Science of education and the psychology of the child.* New York, NY: Viking Press.

Poole, S., deGrazia, J. L., & Sullivan, J. F. (2001). Assessing K–12 pre-engineering outreach programs. *Journal of Engineering Education, 90*(1), 43–48.

Resnick, M. & Silverman, B. (2005). *Some reflections on designing construction kits for kids.* Retrieved from http://llk.media.mit.edu/papers/IDC-2005.pdf

Rivard, L. P. (1994). A review of writing to learn in science: Implications for practice and research. *Journal of Research in Science Teaching, 31*, 969–984.

Rusk, N., Resnick, M., Berg, R., & Pezalla-Granlund, M. (2006). *New pathways into robotics: Strategies for broadening participation.* Retrieved from http://web.media.mit.edu/~mres/papers/NewPathwaysRoboticsLLK.pdf

Sadler, P., Coyle, H., & Schwartz, M. (2000). Engineering competitions in the middle school classroom: Key elements in developing effective design challenges. *Journal of The Learning Sciences, 9*(3), 299–327.

Schank, R. C. & Cleary, C. (1995). *Engines for education.* Hillsdale, NJ: Lawrence Erlbaum Associates.

Schneider, R. M., Krajcik, J., Marx, R. W., & Soloway, E. (2002). Performance of students in project-based science classrooms on a national measure of science achievement. *Journal of Research in Science Teaching, 39*(5), 410–422.

Shepardson, D. & Britsch, S. (2001). The role of children's journals in elementary school science activities. *Journal of Research in Science Teaching, 38*(1), 43–69.

Staires, J. (2007). Word wall connections. *Science Scope, 30*(5), 64–65.

Stevenson, J. A. (1928). *The project method of teaching.* New York, NY: Macmillan.

Thomas, J. (2000). *A review of research on project-based learning.* Retrieved from http://www.bobpearlman.org/BestPractices/PBL_Research.pdf

U.S. Department of Commerce. (2011). *Education supports racial and ethnic equality in STEM.* Washington, DC: Author.

U.S. FIRST (For Inspiration and Recognition of Science and Technology). (2011). *The FIRST tech challenge and the FIRST robotics competition cross program evaluation executive summary.* Retrieved from http://www.usfirst.org/aboutus/impact

Vallejo, B., Jr. (2006). Word wall. *The Science Teacher, 73*(2), 58–60.

Vygotsky, L. S. (1978). *Mind in society: The development of higher psychological processes.* M. Cole, V. John-Steiner, S. Scribner, & E. Souberman (Eds.). Cambridge, MA: Harvard University Press.

Vygotsky, L. S. (1986). *Thought and language.* A. Kozulin (Ed.). Boston, MA: MIT Press.

Wardlaw, A. J. (1995). *The art of John Biggers: View from the upper room.* New York, NY: Harry N. Abrams, Inc.

Yasar, S., Baker, D., Robinson-Kurpius, S., Krause, S., & Roberts, C. (2006). Development of a survey to assess K–12 teachers' perceptions of engineers and familiarity with teaching design, engineering, and technology. *Journal of Engineering Education, 95*(3), 205–216.

CHAPTER 10

UNDERSTANDING THE SHAPE OF LEARNING IN THE CONTEXT OF TECHNOLOGICAL INNOVATION

Finbarr Sloane, Jennifer Oloff-Lewis, and Anthony E. Kelly

ABSTRACT

Quantitative researchers in technology education investigate student learning as an outcome of the technological interventions they develop and deploy. However, we regularly substitute simple measures of achievement as proxies for the complexity of learning. Here we argue that quantitative researchers need to clarify what they mean by "learning" and how they quantify and model such learning. The goal of the chapter is to explore the meaning (and shape) of learning as a quantified entity (which is often hidden). We do so by being purposefully argumentative in the hope that the chapter generates a platform for important discussion within the research community.

INTRODUCTION

All educational research involves design choices. For researchers in technology education, the nature of the choice is most explicitly about the character of a de-

Research on Technology Use in Multicultural Settings, pages 195–208.

signed artifact (e.g., software or learning environment) or to support a student's intellectual navigation of some content-specific content terrain (e.g., force) (diSessa, Gillespie, & Esterly, 2004). Less obvious, and perhaps unconscious, are the education researcher's beliefs about the nature and shape of the change or learning under investigation. These beliefs affect the researcher's choice of theoretical framework (e.g., conceptual change, socio-cultural, and critical), choice of measure, and choice of analytic tool. These choices interact one with another and fundamentally affect the way inferences are drawn (either qualitatively or quantitatively). The goal of this chapter is to highlight some of the defining features of change implicit and hidden in technology education research, either from the perspective of instructional design or that of a design researcher, which guide researchers as they move to quantify and then model student growth over time. Furthermore, we highlight a series of questions pertinent to the study of change when equity is a central feature of the research. We note that the challenges posed to technology education researchers in modeling change afflict, equally, the modeling of change even by those with mastery of current statistical modeling formalisms. Models of change over time intersect with and are grounded in larger construct validity issues facing all education researchers that are not resolved (but at least made more explicit) by quantitative techniques (AERA, 2007).

ASSESSING CHANGES PRODUCED BY TECHNOLOGICAL INNOVATIONS

In some areas of educational research, such as those in developmental and cognitive psychology (e.g., Carey, 1999), the concept and assessment of change is explicitly the focus of study. In much technology education research, the concept of change over time is quite explicit in qualitative work (diSessa, 2006). In other parts of the field, particularly when quantification is indulged, the concept is much less explicit but no less fundamental. In both cases, change over time is fundamental. Accordingly, it is important that technology education researchers possess a good grasp of the basic, but often ignored, issues relating to its conceptualization and measurement from a quantification perspective.

STANDARD PRE-POST TESTING MODELS

The standard model for measuring change in educational research is the pre-post testing model. Generally, pre-post testing models are two time-point models and are found in many studies of learning (e.g., Shadish, Cook, & Campbell, 2002) and in technology education research studies (e.g., Fishman, Marx, Blumenfeld, Krjcik, & Soloway, 2004). Data from such a design are often analyzed by some two-wave analytic technique such as computing a difference (or change) score, a residual change score, or a regression estimate of true change.

TECHNICAL CONCERNS

The ubiquity of two-wave analytic techniques in applied educational research would suggest that these techniques are uncontroversial. Actually, the difference score has been criticized on technical and substantive grounds (Singer & Willett, 2003). The difference score frequently has a negative correlation with initial status (i.e., the change score is often negatively correlated with the pretest score). Its relatively low reliability is related to a number of factors including measurement error. The lesson for technology researchers is that unreliability of a measurement (and consequently its validity) poses problems even for quantitative researchers with sophisticated instruments. The measures used by technology design researchers (sometimes using a very small number of items or subjective judgments based on observations of complex classroom processes) cannot be assumed to be either reliable or valid. This clouds the quality of the claims that emerge at each time point, and the change (or learning) that occurs over time.

SUBSTANTIVE ISSUES

Two time-point designs generate problems because these data provide no precise information on intra-individual change over time. As Willett (1989) noted, it is a conceptualization that views individual learning, not as a process of continuous development over time, but as a quantized acquisition of skills, attitudes, and beliefs. It is as though the individual is delivered a quantum of learning in the time period that intervenes between the pre-test measure and the post-test measure, and that our only concern should be with the size of the acquired chunk.

Framed analytically, with only two snapshots, individual growth curves cannot be characterized with certainty (Bryk & Weisberg, 1977). The simplest approach is to assume that any growth from time one to time two is linear (thus allowing the difference score calculation). Mathematically, however, an infinite number of curves could pass through two points. Yet, some technology in education (TE) researchers may find reasons to challenge the simple linear model by demonstrating changes over time in terms of apparent mastery by students of increasingly difficult content (e.g., learning trajectories).

CONSIDERING MORE THAN TWO TIME POINTS

Multi-wave (three or more time points) repeated measurement within a longitudinal design allows for the possibility of better mapping to intra-individual change as it unfolds (Singer & Willett, 2003). The majority of published methodological work in this area, however, is highly technical, requiring quantitative methodological expertise and valid, reliable quantitative measures of learning, which typically are not always available. To bridge the gap between these statistical advances and TE research in substantive areas of conceptual change, we present a non-technical presentation of several fundamental questions concerning the conceptualization and analysis of change over time. Then we describe the basic building blocks of multilevel modeling in the context of change, in particular the hierarchical linear model (Raudenbush & Bryk, 2002) graphically and in written form. We close with a simple summary statement regarding the potential for TE researchers to better understand the learning supported by the technological environments they build.

FUNDAMENTAL QUESTIONS REGARDING THE UNDERSTANDING OF CHANGE

An adequate methodology for building and assessing a theory of change can be evaluated in terms of the extent to which the theory and commensurate methodology can address the following problems.

Problem 1

Do researchers assume the measure of change to be systematic or random? Change can refer to interpretable systematic differences or random fluctuation. As educational and TE researchers, we are always substantively interested in interpretable systematic change (as opposed to making sense of random fluctuation). Most, if not all, measuring instruments used in educational research, however, have measurement error. That is, they are not perfectly reliable or valid, and as such there are many discrepancies between the constructs and the measures used to operationalize them. As we noted, the difficulty of establishing high reliability in measures can create difficulties for the field in conceptualizing an adequate model of change. An adequate change assessment methodology should account for measurement error and allow observed variance to be partitioned into true construct variance, nonrandom (systematic) error variance, and random error variance.

When the same student or set of students is measured, repeatedly, then time-specific and time-related errors have to be considered carefully. When consecutive measurements, or measurement occasions, are closely spaced, as in design research experiments, measurement errors will also be correlated. This is especially true when the same measurement tool or set of items is used by the researcher. Researchers need to be cognizant of these possible dilemmas (e.g., the problem that repeated measurements over time are not independent of each other) and ways to deal with these issues in the analyses. Where sound quantitative measures are available, auto-correlated error regression models can be used to address this problem (Hedeker & Gibbons, 1997). The solution for mixed method or TE research studies is not yet clear. Researchers in each methodological tradition will likely find unique but somewhat similar answers.

Problem 2

Do researchers consider the change to be a reversible model? This assumption or realization has important implications for the functional form of the growth curves to be modeled. While it is simple to assume that the growth trajectory may be monotonically increasing or decreasing (e.g., linear), perhaps most psychological or developmental interest resides in U-shaped learning curves. These curves may show growth-decline-growth shape and cannot be captured in two time point designs. Learning scientists are also interested in curves with plateaus (e.g., stages in growth; see Liu & McKeough, 2005) or curves that display cubic growth (growth-plateau-further growth). Additionally, an adequate change assessment methodology should allow for two things. First, the researcher should be able to specify a priori one or more functional forms. Second, the researcher should be able to assess the goodness-of-fit of each form and the incremental fit of one form over another. The learning theory helps the researcher specify the anticipated functional form of the learning to be measured and modeled. Moreover, such a theory also helps the researcher specify an adequate number of measurement occasions and the spacing of such measurements.

Problem 3

Change may be assumed to be proceeding in a fixed pathway between sampled time points. Multiple paths may also occur as students proceed from one timepoint to another. For example, some students may follow a linear trajectory, while others follow a quadratic trajectory. An adequate theory of learning should be able to identify and describe why certain subgroups of students follow different paths. In parallel, an adequate assessment methodology should also be able to identify these subgroups and when data should be optimally collected for each group. Qualitative studies bring these concerns to our attention. Technology education research studies that purposefully (re)intervene to effect changes in learning can be assumed to promote multi-pathway growth, adding complexity to the statistical and theoretical modeling problems.

Problem 4

Do researchers view change: (1) to be continuous and gradual, (2) to have large magnitude shifts on quantitative variable(s), or (3) to progress through a series of qualitatively distinct stages (Case, 1985)? Gradual or large shifts can be captured by multi-point analyses. Where there are sharp qualitative shifts in the conceptualization of the phenomenon being measured between time-points (as may be expected with researcher-induced interventions), continuous metric models may be inadequate. One candidate approach to handling such eventualities is Wilson's *Saltus* model (for Piagetian and other stage dependent developmental theories). This model allows for the detection of stages when these stages have been built into the careful writing and testing of the item pool (Wilson, 1989). A theory for such discrete changes would need to be developed and articulated before the measurement items can be developed, piloted, and tested. Even here the discrete shifts are embedded as an extra parameter in the Rasch (1980) model, a psychometric model that forces continuity for fit to the psychometric assumptions of the model to occur.

Sharp, qualitative, and substantive changes in the assumed measurement construct pose significant problems for quantitative modeling. Under certain conditions, not discussed here, growth models can be used to analyze change in noncontinuous outcomes such as counts, dichotomies (whether a student persists in a content area or not), and ordinal outcomes. These models are decidedly more sophisticated and draw on the statistical theory of generalized linear models (McCullagh & Nelder, 1989). Methodologists have recently extended these generalized statistical models to allow for the analysis of nested data structures (Raudenbush & Bryk, 2002).

Problem 5

Is student growth occurring in what Golembiewski, Billingsley, and Yeager (1976) would consider as *alpha, beta*, and *gamma* change? Alpha change is assumed to be measured against a reasonably constant knowledge base—one that is reliably and validly measured. Measurement invariance across time exists when the numerical values across time are on the same measurement scale. Alpha change refers to changes in absolute differences given a constant conceptual domain and a constant measuring instrument—much like data gathered in the Longitudinal Study of American Youth (Miller, Kimmel, Hoffer, & Nelson, 2000) and the NAEP science trend tests.

Beta change refers to changes in the measuring instruments given a constant conceptual domain. Beta change occurs when there is recalibration of the measurement scale. That is, in beta change the observed change results from an alteration in the respondent's subjective metric rather than from actual change in the construct of interest. When beta change occurs, there is a stretching or shrinking of the measurement scale, making direct pre-test/post-test comparisons problematic.

Gamma change refers to changes in the conceptual domain, for example, those involving dramatic qualitative shifts in understanding by the students. Lord (1963) highlights this problem in the context of multiplication: "he argued that a multiplication test may be a valid measure of a mathematical skill for young children, but it becomes a measure of memory among teenagers" (Singer & Willett, 2003, p. 14). Gamma change can take a variety of forms. For example, in the context of factor analysis, the number of factors assessed by a given set of measures may change from one point in time to another. Alternatively, the number of factors may remain constant across time, but a differentiation process may occur so that the factor inter-correlations vary over time. When there is gamma or beta change over time, it is unlikely that a simple growth model will provide usable insight.

Problem 6

Do researchers consider the change to be a shared characteristic of a group of individuals over time, what occurs within individuals over time, or both? This question originally derives from Allport's (1937) distinction between the nomothetic research orientation, which focuses on lawful relations that apply across individuals, and the idiographic research orientation, which focuses on the uniqueness of individuals. In TE research, this issue of coordinating analyses at the individual and group levels poses significant methodological challenges, particularly when it is difficult to characterize contingent versus the necessary processes affecting learning (Kelly, 2004).

Problem 7

Do researchers assume that there are systematic inter-individual differences in the values of the individual growth parameters (e.g., initial status and rate of change) that define the individual trajectory (Huttenlocher, Haight, Bryk, Seltzer, & Lyons, 1991), assuming that all individuals have trajectories of the same functional form (e.g., linear, quadratic, etc.)? If so, how can we predict and increase our understanding of these inter-individual differences? The rate of change is a critical individual growth parameter that has been, until recently, neglected in the conceptualization and measurement of inter-individual differences. In the many sub-content domains of TE research the rate of change in a student's learning of content is of theoretical and practical importance, and is in need of further study. Moreover, as was shown in Sloane (2008), these rates can now be carefully analyzed.

Problem 8

Do researchers assume that there are cross-domain relationships (e.g., issues among content, content knowledge for teaching, and teacher instructional performance) that change over time? Is the relationship between inter-individual differences and intra-individual change over time and the predictors of those differences invariant across domains? These questions can only be addressed statistically with a multivariate, multilevel type analytic tool (see Thum, 1997).

Problem 9

Finally, in order to draw differential claims, the models of change assumed in a group of students under scrutiny may need to be compared to the behavior and learning of students in some other group (e.g., matched comparison students or students in a randomized cohort). The question of interest is whether a specific change pattern found in one group is equal to or differs from (in either magnitude or form) the change pattern found in the comparison group. The drawbacks of non-randomized controls or even matched groups have been documented elsewhere in advocacy pieces for randomized clinical trials in education (Sloane, 2008).

Taking the lead from Willett (1989), a simple resolution to these nine (somewhat overlapping) problems resides in the number and spacing of the measures the TE researcher is willing to collect. Specificity of the growth trajectory occurs through the gathering of high quality data across numerous time points (much like time series data collected by economists and other researchers in the business community). When the growth trajectory is in place, recent advances in the modeling of change can be invoked to improve intellectual insight and the theoretical understandings of why and how learning technologies support student content learning and under what conditions.

MODELING CHANGE: RECENT ADVANCES

Over the past 25 years, longitudinal modeling has become increasingly popular in the social sciences because the tools to support these analyses have improved significantly (Hedeker, 2004). For example, the hierarchical linear model, a tool described by Sloane (2008), allows for irregularly spaced measurements across time, time-varying and time-invariant covariates, accommodations of person-specific deviations from the average time trend, and the estimation of population variance associated with these individual effects. Longitudinal data analysis, however, requires the researcher to be explicit about the outcomes of the designed technological intervention and how they will be measured. We do not take up this issue in this chapter other than to note the need for high quality measurement tools that work well at single and multiple time-points.

In longitudinal models, subjects are measured on a number of occasions (three or more), and the researcher is interested in the shape of the learner's development (or growth) over time and what predicts differences across learners in their respective growth curves. Specifically, the researcher is interested in answers to two separate, but entwined questions (Singer & Willett, 2003): How does the measured outcome change over time for individuals (or groups)? and Can we predict or model the character of these differences that occur over time? These two questions are central to design researchers in technology innovation who iteratively build artifacts to positively affect student learning. Moreover, they sit at the core of every study of change.

The first question is descriptive in its nature, asking us to characterize each subject's pattern of change over time. Is the change linear or non-linear? Is the pattern of change consistent or not? The second question is relational and predictive. Here attention is focused on the association between independent variables and patterns of change in the sampled data. Does participation in the design study change one's pattern of learning? Additionally, do all subjects experience the same pattern of change? For example, do males and females share the same pattern of change? The first question requires the formulation of a within-person model (the intra-individual growth model); the second question requires a between-person model (the inter-individual model).

LONGITUDINAL OR MULTIWAVE ANALYSIS

We define longitudinal studies as studies where subjects are measured repeatedly and where the research interest focuses on characterizing subject growth across time. Traditional analysis of variance methods for such repeated measures models are described by Bock (1975). These traditional methods are of limited use to TE researchers conducting studies in real classrooms because of their restrictive assumptions concerning missing data across time and the variance-covariance structure of the repeated measures. The univariate "mixed-model" analysis of variance assumes that the variances and covariances of the dependent variable are equal across time. This is rarely sustainable in practice. The multivariate analysis of variance for repeated measures is also quite restrictive. Models of this variety force the researcher to omit from the analysis subjects without complete data across all time points. In general, these two procedures focus attention on the estimation of group trends across time and provide little by way of assistance to understanding specific individuals' change over time. For these reasons, hierarchical linear models (HLMs) have become the method of choice for quantitative growth modeling of longitudinal data.

Several features make HLMs especially useful to the longitudinal researcher. First, subjects are not assumed to be measured on, or at, the same number of time-points. Consequently, subjects with incomplete data across time are included in the analysis. The ability to include subjects with incomplete data across time is an important advantage relative to procedures that require complete data for all children across all time points because all the collected data can be included, increasing the statistical power of the analysis. Further, complete case analysis suffers from biases to the extent that children with complete data are not necessarily representative of the larger population of children. That is, many children miss days during the school year—this is particularly true of lower SES children—and when we exclude these children from our analysis, our results reflect only those students who happened to always attend when data were collected. This bias would reflect very unrealistic school- and technology-driven classrooms or school-based research settings.

Second, because time is treated as a continuous variable in HLMs, individuals do not have to be measured at the same time-points. In general, this is useful for analysis of longitudinal studies in which follow-up times are not uniform across all participants. This is particularly useful to design researchers, as it is unlikely that student interviews or testing, for example, will occur on the same day for all children.

Third, time-invariant and time-varying covariates can be included in the longitudinal model, providing a conceptually rich framework for analysis, a framework that better maps to the realities of schools and classrooms. Put simply, changes in student learning may be due to characteristics of the individual that are stable over time (e.g., student gender) as well as characteristics that change across time (e.g., individual interactions with a curricular innovation).

Traditional approaches estimate average change in a group (across time); HLMs can also estimate individual change for each subject. These estimates of individual change are particularly useful when proportions (or groups) of students exhibit change that differs from the average trend. That is, HLMs afford richer insight when different groups of students are expected to grow at differing rates because these differences can be modeled. Raundebush and Bryk (2002) note that the HLM modeling technique affords the longitudinal researcher the opportunity to:

- specify the structure of the mean growth trajectory,
- model the extent and character of individual variation around the mean growth,
- estimate the reliability of the measures for studying both status and growth,
- estimate the correlation between entry status and growth rate, and
- model correlates of both status and growth.

In the next section, we describe the general structure of the hierarchical linear model when used to investigate change. It should come as no surprise that its features parallel the two basic questions we have posed about change, the former descriptive and the latter predictive. We first present the need for the structure graphically and follow this introduction with our summary of the general structure algebraically. Finally, we close by noting the potential for technology researchers to investigate the impact of their designed innovations on student learning more fruitfully.

A HIERARCHICAL MODEL FOR GROWTH: GRAPHICAL AND ALGEBRAIC RENDERINGS

HLMs can be used to estimate change over time with longitudinal data. By using an HLM, the following types of question can be addressed: "How do individuals change over time on a measure of choice (e.g., the learning of mathematics supported by technological innovation), and what predicts differences in these individual growth curves?" (Singer & Willett, 2003, p. 8). In general, HLMs use nested data, such as students within classrooms, classrooms within schools, schools within districts, and so forth. In the longitudinal setting, an HLM nests individual growth within the construct of time.

Level-1 looks at within-individual change over time, or "learning" over time. By looking at individual empirical growth curves, one can observe the general shape of change over time and how individuals vary around this average growth trajectory. Do individuals differ in their intercepts, slopes, or both? Put simply, do students start at the same level of ability or achievement, and do they grow,

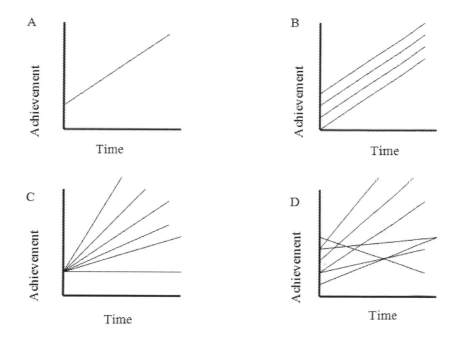

FIGURE 10.1.   Four different possible relationships between intercepts and slopes at Level-1

change, or develop at the same rate? These questions are presented graphically below.

In Figure 10.1a, there is no difference in the intercept or the slope of a set of individuals in this group. This graph indicates that students develop at the same rate and start at the same place. In Figure 10.1b, the slopes are the same, but the intercepts vary. In effect, this graph indicates that students develop at the same rate, but start at different points. If a treatment were being studied, it would be noted that it had the same effect on each participant, no matter where he or she started.

In Figure 10.1c, the intercept is the same, but the slopes differ, and in Figure 10.1d, the intercepts and the slopes are different. In both Figures 10.1c and 10.1d, access to a technological innovation appears to have different effects on the student learning—in Figure 10.1c, all of the students start at a given point of achievement, whereas in Figure 10.1d, the students start at different points. The differences displayed in Figures 10.1b, 10.1c, and 10.1d lead us to questions about individual variability that can be better answered in the Level-2 model. Level-1 models are written in the form:

Level-1: $$Y_{ti} = \pi_{0i} + \pi_{1i}X_{ti} + e_{ti} \tag{1}$$

Where:

Y_{ti} = the outcome measure at time t for individual i,

π_{0i} = the growth rate for individual i,

π_{1i} = the ability of individual i at ,

X_{ti} = the value of the predictor at time t for individual i, and

e_{ti} = error, which is normally distributed with a mean of zero and constant variance.

At Level-2, different people's pattern of change can be examined, and these differences based on person characteristics (or treatment assignment) can be modeled. In Figure 10.1d, individuals have different slopes and intercepts; it would be of interest to examine if differences by gender, race, and SES, for example, explain this variability in intercepts and slopes. In general, the predictors that account for this variability could be investigated. Together, these two levels make up a multilevel model. A Level-2 model is written in the form:

Level-2a: $$\pi_{0i} = \beta_{00} + \beta_{01}W_i + r_{0i} \tag{2}$$

Level-2b: $$\pi_{1i} = \beta_{10} + \beta_{11}W_i + r_{1i} \tag{3}$$

Where:

W_i = an individual-level variable/predictor,

β_{00} and β_{10} = the second-level intercept terms (fixed effect), and

$\beta_{01} = \beta_{11}$ the slopes relating W_i to the intercept and the slope terms from the Level-1 equation (fixed effects), and

r_{0i} = the Level-2 residuals.

A GENERAL TWO-LEVEL GROWTH MODEL

Many individual change phenomena can be represented through a two-level HLM. At Level-1, each subject's development is represented by an individual growth trajectory that depends on a unique set of parameters and some error. As a set, these individual parameters become the outcome variables at Level-2, where their variability can (possibly) be accounted for by a set of between-person characteristics. Formally, the repeated measures on each subject are considered nested within each individual over time. As a consequence, this model is less restrictive than the multivariate repeated measures model, allowing for uneven spacing of measures and missing data in the Level-1 model.

It is assumed that the Y_{it}, the observed status at time t for individual i, is a function of a systematic growth trajectory (or growth curve) plus random error. It is convenient to assume that systematic growth over time can be represented as a polynomial of degree P. Then, the Level-1 model is:

Y_{it} (Subject i's response at time t) = f (Growth parameters + error)   (4)

In the Level-2 model, it is asked if the growth parameters, estimated in the Level-1 model, vary across subjects. This parameter variation in the between-subject model is represented as:

Growth curve of subject = f (Subjects' background characteristics + error)   (5)

These two equations are used to structure longitudinal investigations. The first equation forms the basis for descriptive questions. The second equation supports predictive explorations of the variation that occurs across individuals in the first equation. Consequently, the two models map in one-to-one correspondence with the two questions posed earlier: How does the measured outcome change over time? and Can differences in these changes be predicted? The shape of the growth curve is central to the understanding, and estimation, of the designed innovation. Moreover, the shape of the growth curve is fundamentally related to the number of time points used to describe it and estimate it, particularly when moving from two to more time points.

In sum, measurement and modeling techniques for longitudinal data have changed dramatically over the past 25 years, affording the educational design researcher more opportunity to map to the practical (and often) critical realities of classrooms and schools. These advances afford technology researchers access to a set of analytic tools they normally do not use but that are now robust to the daily life of the learning settings in which their designed artifacts serve to support student learning.

REFERENCES

AERA. (2007). Dialogue on validity (with commentary). *Education Researcher, 36*, 437–484.

Allport, G. W. (1937). *Personality: A psychological interpretation*. New York, NY: Holt.

Bock, R. D. (1975). *Multivariate statistical methods in the behavioral research*. New York, NY: McGraw-Hill.

Bryk, A. & Weisberg, H. (1977). Use of non-equivalent control group design when subjects are growing. *Psychological Bulletin, 104*, 396–404.

Carey, S. (1999). Sources of conceptual change. In E. K. Scholnick, K. Nelson, & P. Miller (Eds.), *Conceptual development: Piaget's legacy* (pp. 293–326). Mahwah, NJ: Lawrence Erlbaum.

Case, R. (1985). *Intellectual development: Birth to adulthood*. New York, NY: Academic Press.

diSessa, A. (2006). A history of conceptual change research: Threads and fault lines. In K. Sawyer (Ed.), *Cambridge handbook of the learning sciences* (pp. 265–281). Cambridge, UK: Cambridge University Press.

diSessa, A., Gillespie, N., & Esterly, J. (2004). Coherence versus fragmentation in the development of the concept of force. *Cognitive Science, 28*, 843–900.

Fishman, B., Marx, R., Blumenfeld, P., Krjcik, J., & Soloway, E. (2004). Creating a framework for research on systemic technology innovations. *Journal of the Learning Sciences, 13*, 43–76.

Golembiewski, R. T., Billingsley, K., & Yeager, S. (1976). Measuring change and persistence in human affairs: Types of change generated by OD designs. *Journal of Applied Behavioral Science, 12*, 133–157.

Hedeker, D. (2004). An introduction to growth modeling. In D. Kaplan (Ed.), *The Sage handbook of quantitative methodology for the social sciences* (pp. 215–234). Thousand Oaks, CA: Sage Publications.

Hedeker, D. & Gibbons, R. (1997). Applications of random effects pattern mixture models for missing data in social sciences. *Psychological Methods, 2*, 64–78.

Huttenlocher, J., Haight, W., Bryk, A., Seltzer, M., & Lyons, T. (1991). Early vocabulary growth: Relation to language input and gender. *Developmental Psychology, 27*, 236–248.

Kelly, A. E. (2004). Design research in education: Yes, but is it methodological? *Journal of the Learning Sciences, 13*, 115–128.

Liu, X. & McKeogh, A. (2005). Developmental growth in students' concept of energy: Analysis of selected items from the TIMSS data base. *Journal for Research in Science Teaching, 42*, 493–517.

Lord, F. (1963). Elementary models for measuring change. In C. W. Harris (Ed.), *Problems in the measurement of change* (pp. 21–39). Madison, WI: University of Wisconsin Press.

McCullagh, P. & Nelder, J. A. (1989). *Generalized linear models* (2nd ed.). London, UK: Chapman and Hall.

Miller, J. D., Kimmel, L., Hoffer, T. B., & Nelson, C. (2000). *Longitudinal study of American youth: User's manual*. Chicago, IL: International Center for the Advancement of Scientific Literacy, Northwestern University.

Rasch, G. (1980). *Probabilistic models for some intelligence and attainment tests* (expanded ed.). Chicago, IL: University of Chicago Press.

Raudenbush, S. W. & Bryk, A. S. (2002). *Hierarchical linear models* (2nd ed.). Thousand Oaks, CA: Sage Publications.

Shadish, W., Cook, T., & Campbell, D. (2002). *Experimental and quasi-experimental designs for generalized causal inference*. New York, NY: Houghton Mifflin.

Singer, J. & Willett, J. B. (2003). *Applied longitudinal data analysis: Modeling change and event occurrence*. Oxford, UK: Oxford University Press.

Sloane, F. (2008). Through the looking glass: Experiments, quasi-experiments, and the medical model. *Educational Researcher, 37*(1), 41–46.

Thum, Y. M. (1997). Hierarchical linear models for multivariate behavioral data. *Journal of Educational and Behavioral Statistics, 22*, 77–108.

Willett, J. B. (1989). Some results on reliability for the longitudinal measurement of change: Implications for the design of studies of individual growth. *Educational and Psychological Measurement, 49*, 587–602.

Wilson, M. (1989). Saltus: A psychometric model of discontinuity in cognitive development. *Psychological Bulletin, 105*, 276–289.

CHAPTER 11

ALTERNATIVE MODELS FOR EVALUATING TECHNOLOGY USE IN SCHOOLS

Jacqueline R. Stillisano, Danielle B. Brown, and Hersh C. Waxman

ABSTRACT

The number of technology-based programs implemented in schools and classrooms has increased exponentially in recent years, in part to address the need to improve science, technology, engineering, and mathematics (STEM) education. Very few systematic approaches or models of evaluation have been developed or used to evaluate the effectiveness of these projects, however. The current chapter addresses this concern by describing five models appropriate for evaluating programs implementing technology-based enhancements or interventions in schools: (1) the experimental model, (2) the CIPP model, (3) the AEIOU model, (4) the logic model, and (5) the classroom observation model. The strengths and weaknesses of each of these models are described, as well as critical issues and assumptions associated with the respective models.

INTRODUCTION

Several major reports have addressed the importance of improving science, technology, engineering, and mathematics (STEM) learning in order to prepare stu-

Research on Technology Use in Multicultural Settings, pages 209–224.

209

dents with the technology and problem-solving skills needed to succeed in today's workforce (National Academies of Sciences, National Academy of Engineering, & Institute of Medicine, 2007; National Research Council, 2011; President's Council of Advisors on Science and Technology, 2010). Several of these reports argue that to achieve these goals, federal, state, and local educators need to collaborate in order to "provide resources to acquire, integrate, support, and evaluate the use of technology in the classroom" (Gayl, 2007, p. 1). These reports also discuss the need to adequately evaluate the efficacy of STEM initiatives in order to improve STEM education (Drew, 2011; State Educational Technology Directors Association [SETDA], International Society for Technology in Education [ISTE], & Partnership for 21st Century Skills [P21], 2007).

Over the last few decades, school districts have tried to acquire, integrate, and support technology in the classrooms. In most cases, however, districts have not effectively evaluated the use of technology, and vast amounts of money have been spent on technological programs and innovations that were never rigorously examined (Drew, 2011). Moreover, the literature contains few published reports or articles highlighting the results of evaluation studies examining the effectiveness of technology use in schools.

This paucity of evaluation studies may be attributed to several underlying factors. First, the cost associated with conducting research and evaluation is often considered to be an extravagant expense. Second, even if some type of research or evaluation has been conducted on the implementation and results of a technology project, the reports are often not effectively communicated or disseminated. Finally, Collis and Carleer (1993) and others suggest that educators may face a number of problems in finding appropriate theoretical and methodological approaches for examining technology-enriched projects or technology use in schools.

Addressing the previously described concerns, the current chapter discusses several appropriate models for evaluating programs that implement technology-based enhancements or interventions in schools. Since many such programs have been implemented or are currently in the process of implementation, it is important to clarify some of the critical issues and assumptions associated with their respective evaluations. Although the models or approaches discussed in this chapter are appropriate for evaluation of many different types of educational programs, they were chosen for inclusion in the chapter based on their particular applicability for evaluation of technology-based programs and technology use in schools.

MODELS OF EVALUATION

Program evaluation is generally considered to be more appropriate than educational research for addressing issues related to effectiveness of technology use, given that most technology is typically used in a particular school or classroom where (a) feasibility would dictate data collection, (b) control of most relevant variables would be unlikely, and (c) generalizability of results would be low. Moreover, the foci of the two are contrasting: the emphasis of research is on contributing to the development of knowledge in a field and the growth of theory, while program evaluation focuses primarily on providing useful information to assist stakeholders in making a judgement about the value of whatever is being evaluated (Fitzpatrick, Sanders, & Worthern, 2011). As the Phi Delta Kappa National Study Committee on Evaluation pointed out in its introduction to *Educational Evaluation and Decision Making* (1971): "The purpose of evaluation is not to prove but to improve" (p. v).

Examining alternative models for evaluating technology use in schools and classrooms is important, as the conclusions we reach or answers we obtain in educational research and evaluation are determined by the types of questions we ask, as well as by the methods we use to answer them. Unfortunately, an investigator's personal commitment to a given evaluation model or research methodology sometimes guides and shapes the research process, affecting the choice of design, instrumentation, and interpretation of data. In other words, the selection of the evaluation model is often related to the investigator's theoretical or ideological commitments and/or beliefs. An awareness of a variety of evaluation models or approaches can broaden our perspectives about research problems and change our ways of thinking about what we can study and how we can study it (Kerlinger, 1977).

The conceptual work on models of evaluation by House (1980); Madaus, Scriven, and Stufflebeam (1983); Stufflebeam, Madaus, and Kellaghan, (2000); Stufflebeam and Shinkfield (2007); Stufflebeam and Webster (1980); and Worthen and Sanders (1987) is an important starting point for examining alternative models of evaluation, as these encompass the most recent and comprehensive theoretical perspectives in the field of program evaluation. The following sections describe several alternative models that can be used to examine the effectiveness of technology use in schools. Additionally, this chapter will discuss key assumptions and the methodology for each of the evaluation models, as well as the strengths and weaknesses of each in regard to evaluating technology use in education.

Experimental Model

Historically, the experimental model for evaluation is probably the most prevalent. This model investigates whether or not there is a statistically significant difference on one or more dependent variables (e.g., students' or teachers' cognitive, affective, or behavioral outcomes) between the technology-enriched school and a control school. A typical question that this evaluation model would address is as follows: Are there significant differences between the technology-enhanced schools and control or comparison schools on (a) students' cognitive, affective, and behaviors outcomes; (b) teachers' classroom instruction; or (c) teachers' implementation of technology?

The strongest advantage of the experimental model is that it provides evaluators and researchers with the ability to make causal inferences relating the effects of the technology to a specified outcome variable(s). Conversely, although experimental evaluation models are often referred to as the gold standard in research and evaluation, a number of concerns are related to such designs. First of all, most experimental studies do not examine what happens in classrooms or in schools. The "black box" metaphor has been widely used to describe the experimental model of evaluation because it does not allow educators to examine *how* and *why* the treatment contributes to the outcomes (Cuban, 2013). Other pragmatic concerns with the experimental model include the fact that it is often very difficult to conduct "true" experiments in the field due to problems associated with random selection. Specifically, a researcher may experience difficulty in determining which schools should receive technology enhancements (or be identified as technologically enhanced) and which should serve as a control. For example, it can be difficult to identify schools evenly matched in regard to characteristics both of students (e.g., ethnicity, socio-economic status, or achievement level) and of teachers (e.g., level of education, ability to utilize technology, or instructional ability). Finally, in using the experimental model, researchers must be cognizant of other threats to validity when generalizing the results to a larger population.

Context-Input-Process-Product (CIPP) Model

One of the most widely recognized evaluation models focusing on program improvement is arguably the Context-Input-Process-Product (CIPP) model, originated by Egon Guba and Daniel Shufflebeam, but primarily refined and promoted by Daniel Stufflebeam (Popham, 1993). Based on systems theory, the CIPP model was conceived as a vehicle for using evaluation as a tool to inform program decision-making. Each step in the program cycle (i.e., planning, designing, implementing, and reviewing and refining decisions) is examined through one of the core concepts of the model: *context* evaluation, *input* evaluation, *process* evaluation, and *product* evaluation—hence the acronym CIPP (Popham, 1993). The definition of evaluation as "a process of delineating, obtaining, reporting, and applying descriptive and judgmental information about some object's merit, worth, probity, and significance in order to guide decision making" (Stufflebeam, 2003, p. 10) is implicit in the framework of the CIPP model. The model's flexibility and appropriateness for a wide variety of situations has led to its utilization in evaluations of programs and projects (Stufflebeam, 2000).

The CIPP model relies on a strong participatory role for concerned and involved stakeholders, although it maintains an implicit assumption that the evaluator is responsible for the integrity of the evaluation process and its findings (Stufflebeam, 2001, 2003; Stufflebeam & Shinkfield, 2007). Specifically, evaluators constructing an evaluation plan based on the CIPP model identify individuals (and groups) at all organizational levels who are affected by a program's services—or who make decisions about planning, funding, or implementing a program—and involve these stakeholders in (a) clarifying evaluation questions and criteria, (b) identifying and providing pertinent information, and (c) providing feedback on evaluation reports. Many change models advocate for involving stakeholder groups in an evaluation, identifying the practice as an ethically responsible one that gives a voice to those individuals whose voices often go ignored or unheard. Stakeholder participation is also recognized as a prudent practice, assisting the evaluator in collecting valuable information that might otherwise be overlooked and contributing to the acceptance, perceived value, and utilization of evaluation findings.

The CIPP model promotes the use of multiple methods in data collection and analysis. Both qualitative and quantitative methods can and should be utilized, including, but not limited to, surveys, interviews, focus group discussions, observations of program sites and processes, mining of archival documents, and quasi-experimental and experimental designs. Stufflebeam (2003) recommends engaging multiple informants with divergent viewpoints and advocates for independent review as well as member checking in the form of stakeholder review of draft reports, both interim and summative. Finally, triangulation procedures should be utilized to provide reliability, and the use of multiple methods for each of the four stages of an evaluation can offer crosschecks of findings.

Key strengths of the CIPP model are its utilization of a balance of qualitative and quantitative methods and a structure allowing for both internal and external evaluations (Stufflebeam, 2001). Although the focus of the CIPP model is program improvement (formative assessment), it provides a framework to encourage accountability for program personnel (summative assessment) and encourages program planners and managers to use evaluation as a tool to help systematically plan and execute a program that effectively meets the needs of clients. Effective utilization of findings has traditionally been a weakness of evaluation in general, but to a great extent, the CIPP model overcomes this barrier by involving stakeholders in the evaluation process and through its focus on the decision-making process at all program levels. Finally, a major strength of the CIPP model is its flexibility, as not all components of the model are required in every evaluative situation.

The CIPP model is not without its limitations, however (Stufflebeam, 2001). Some critics have described the model as unrealistic, claiming it fails to recognize the difficulties of achieving an informative relationship between evaluation and decision-making and tends to ignore the reality of the influence of organizational politics. The model's reliance on collaboration among the external evaluator and various stakeholder groups, for example, can be a two-edged sword, as stakeholders who are heavily invested in particular elements of a program may attempt to obstruct an evaluation or influence its findings. In addition, evaluators who are actively influencing a program's course may identify so closely with the program that they find it difficult to maintain the impartial detachment needed to produce an objective, unbiased report. A tendency can arise, moreover, for some individuals to emphasize formative evaluation at the expense of summative evaluation when utilizing the CIPP model. Finally, some have argued that the model is so strongly disposed to top decision-makers that it primarily serves their needs (Posavac & Carey, 1997), although Stufflebeam (2001) labels this charge as "erroneous" (p. 58).

The CIPP model is quite comprehensive and an appropriate model for use in evaluating technology initiatives. Few actual examples of this model being used to evaluate technology-based programs, specifically technology-based programs in schools, are found in the literature, however.

AEIOU Model

The accountability, effectiveness, impact, organizational context, and unanticipated outcomes (AEIOU) evaluation framework has been used in several evaluations of technology-based programs (Simonson, 1997; Sorensen & Sweeney, 1997). Similar to the CIPP model, the AEIOU evaluation framework incorporates both qualitative and quantitative methods, and comprehensively covers many significant facets of the evaluation. Also similar to the CIPP model, the AEIOU framework allows the evaluator to examine whether project goals and related outcomes are met, as well as to investigate the processes and contexts that support the project's work and final products. The AEIOU approach allows for both quantitative and qualitative methodologies and has two principal functions as an evaluation strategy: (1) it provides formative data to stakeholders regarding the project's implementation and (2) it provides summative data regarding the project's value (Simonson, 1997).

First, the accountability component of the evaluation framework seeks to determine whether the program completed its proposed activities and accomplished its stated objectives. Evaluation questions addressing accountability focus on the completion of activities and objectives, not on examining the quality, and may address specific information regarding numbers of people, equipment, and activities (Simonson, 1997). For the evaluation of a technology program, evaluators might collect data to provide evidence that all of the specific activities related to implementation of the technology were realized and objectives were achieved. This could include, for example, whether technology training was provided, numbers of teachers who participated in the training and demographic information about them, and numbers of computers and types of software available for students' use. This might also include the amount of time students actually use the technology. Data related to accountability might be obtained from sources such as program records, training materials, or surveys of participants.

The effectiveness component of the AEIOU framework looks beyond the actual completion of activities to determine how well program activities were accomplished and the extent to which objectives were achieved. The focus of this component is participants' attitudes and knowledge. For an evaluation focusing on a technology initiative, data might be collected to assess teachers' satisfaction with the technology training, teachers' integration of technology in their teaching practices, students' satisfaction with the quality of the software, or students' perceptions regarding user-friendliness of the hardware. Evaluation questions might also examine students' engagement and quality of learning when they use technology. Information related to the effectiveness component of a program could be obtained through participant surveys, participant interviews, classroom observations, or student grades.

The impact component specifically examines planned changes brought about by program activities in order to determine if the program achieved the desired results (Simonson, 1997; Sorenson & Sweeney, 1997). Determining impact is one of the most critical aspects of an evaluation. When, as often happens, direct measures of impact are not available, indirect indicators may be examined (Sorensen & Sweeney, 1997). In an evaluation of a technology program, data might be collected to provide evidence regarding whether or not, for example, significant increases were achieved in several student outcomes (e.g., student achievement or attitudes) as a result of the technology use. Other than standardized tests, data can be obtained from surveys, focus groups, or interviews. Since longitudinal data is often very helpful in determining impact, follow-up interviews or surveys might be utilized.

The organizational context component of the AEIOU framework helps evaluators identify policies, structures, or events that facilitated or detracted from a project's ability to reach its goals. Typically, these driving or restraining factors are features that are outside the control of the project. In order to effectively evaluate the organizational environment in which a program operates, an evaluator must be closely involved with the project, directly participating in project activities (Simonson, 1997). Evaluation of organizational context is particularly important for the evaluation of an innovative program, such as the implementation of a technology initiative. Qualitative data often help to paint a picture of the structures and framework that support a successful implementation of the program, and interviews with key project personnel and focus groups with those impacted by the program provide important data.

Finally, the unanticipated outcomes component of the evaluation framework is similar to the impact component in that the focus is both on discovering and examining consequences that occurred as a result of the program. While impact questions focus on planned change, however, unanticipated outcomes questions focus on unplanned, unexpected change (Sorensen & Sweeney, 1997). Unexpected program outcomes can be either positive or negative, and in some cases, unexpected consequences can be as important as ones that were anticipated. For evaluation of a technology project, questions focus on important and unexpected changes that can be attributed to the use or implementation of the technology. The data collected related to this component can help to determine the success of the project, as well as the direction the project should take in the future. Qualitative data (e.g., interviews, focus groups, or surveys) provide narrative information useful in determining unanticipated outcomes; however, the evaluator can rely on informal interactions and conversations with participants as well.

The AEIOU model is similar to the CIPP model in that it is quite comprehensive, as well as appropriate for use in evaluating technology initiatives. This model is also similar to the CIPP model in that few actual examples are found in the literature of this model being used to evaluate technology-based programs.

Logic Model

Logic models are most commonly used in theory-based evaluations (W. K. Kellogg Foundation, 2004). When using this specific tool, researchers base an evaluation on a theory of how the program works (Fitz-Gibbon & Morris, 1996). This theory, model, or philosophy demonstrates causal relationships within the program. Within this framework, a logic model serves as a "tool that describes the *theory of change* (emphasis in original) underlying an intervention, product, or policy" (Frechtling, 2007, p. 1). This section of the chapter will focus on how logic models can be used for evaluation purposes, although logic models can also be used during the planning and implementation stages of a program as well.

A logic model is typically a graphical representation, usually presented in the form of a diagram, that depicts the relationships between proposed actions and expected results (Fitzpatrick et al., 2011). In its most basic form, a logic model illustrates the logic of a program by illustrating the associations among resources available for the program, activities the program implements, and changes that result from the program. Moreover, in contrast to the experimental model, previously described as a "black box" model of evaluation, logic models "have influenced evaluation by filling in the 'black box' between the program and its objectives" (Fitzpatrick et al., 2011, p. 160).

The W. K. Kellogg Foundation is recognized as one of the leaders in promoting the use of logic models for program planning and evaluation. According to the *Logic Model Development Guide* (W. K. Kellogg Foundation, 2004), a basic logic model has five components: (1) inputs, (2) activities, (3) outputs, (4) outcomes, and (5) impacts (p. 1). The input component of a logic model is sometimes referred to as resources. Inputs include the assets that enable a program to reach its stated goals, such as funding, collaborating partners, staff, and facilities. Other factors, such as policies, attitudes, or regulations, might be identified as inputs that limit the program's success. Activities include products, services, or infrastructure contributing to the outputs or direct results of the program. Outputs, which indicate if the program was delivered properly to the anticipated audience, can include the number of pieces of technology provided, participation rates in professional development, or hours of professional development provided. In contrast, outcomes, which can be identified as short term, medium term, or long term, are described more at the individual level and include changes in participant attitudes, behaviors, knowledge, skills, and so on. Finally, impacts include changes that occur at the organizational or system level, such as increased capacity.

Using a logic model to design a program evaluation offers several advantages. A logic model can help to build a common understanding of a program among all the stakeholders (Wholey, Hatry, & Newcomer, 2010). This shared understanding facilitates the evaluation by expediting communication among stakeholders and the community, assisting evaluators in determining the data collection procedures, and increasing the usefulness of the data collected. The evaluation can also become more meaningful in providing formative and summative feedback related to improving the design of the program. Results from an evaluation utilizing a logic model also strengthen the case for funding, as a well-constructed logic model clearly depicts the process in which results will occur (W. K. Kellogg Foundation, 2004). Finally, proponents of this type of evaluation argue that by combining outcome data with an understanding of how the program works, researchers gain valuable information regarding the impact and influential factors of the program (Schorr & Kubisch, 1995).

In a recent study, for example, researchers utilized a logic model in the evaluation of a large-scale, statewide, multi-site program aimed at increasing science, technology, engineering, and mathematics (STEM) teacher quality (Brown, Alford, Stillisano, Rollins, & Waxman, 2013). The process of improving teacher quality typically requires a shift in practice or implementation of a professional program. The program evaluated in this study (a) focused on strengthening teacher subject matter knowledge and pedagogical skills; (b) integrated the areas of science, mathematics, and technology; (c) included problem-based learning in the classroom; and (d) instructed teachers on the infusion of technology into their lessons. Participants were engaged in either a teacher preparation program or a professional development program that was designed to change or improve their classroom instructional practices. The ultimate goal of the program was to improve student outcomes by enhancing teachers' classroom practices, and the logic model utilized in the evaluation depicted the process through which teacher change could occur for participants in the program. The evaluation was guided by the concept that participation in the program would positively impact pre-service and in-service teachers' beliefs and attitudes, leading to changes in classroom practices and, ultimately, improved student learning outcomes

Classroom Observation Model

The National Research Council (2011) argues that "the most useful way of identifying criteria for success relates to educational practices: What practices should be used to identify effective STEM schools?" (p. 18). This focus on practices rather than outcomes suggests the need for more observational evaluation approaches that specifically examine technology instruction and practices. Although observation is often incorporated as a method in many types of evaluations, it has a distinctive role in evaluating technology use or technology-based programs because it specifically examines the actual use of technology in schools and classrooms.

The classroom observation model addresses one of the important concerns regarding research and evaluation of technology use in schools: that is, the measurement of "technology use." Most studies and evaluations assessing technology use have relied on self-report data from administrators or teachers (e.g., McKinney, Chappell, Berry, & Hickman, 2009; Vannatta & Fordham, 2004). These types of data, however, are often unreliable and tend to be upwardly biased in the direction of over reporting the amount of technology use (Cuban, 2001). Few researchers have actually gone into classrooms to see how teachers and students use technology daily (Cuban, 2001). The observation evaluation model allows us to address the need to look "inside the black box of classroom practice" (Cuban, 2013, p. 10).

Generally, data that are collected via observations focus on the frequency with which specific behaviors or types of behavior occurred in the classroom and the amount of time over which they occurred. Several elements are common to most observational systems: (a) a purpose for the observation, (b) the operational definitions of all the observed behaviors, (c) the training procedures for observers, (d) a specific observational focus, (e) a setting, (f) a unit of time, (g) an observation schedule, (h) a method to record the data, and (i) a method to process and analyze data (Stallings & Mohlman, 1988). Although several types of observational procedures or techniques have been used to examine effective teaching (e.g., charts, rating scales, checklists, and narrative descriptions), the most widely used procedure or research method has been systematic classroom observation based on interactive coding systems. These interactive coding systems allow the observer to record nearly everything that students and teachers do during a given time interval (Stallings & Mohlman, 1988). The interaction systems are very objective and typically do not require the observer to make any high inferences or judgments about the behaviors observed in the classroom. In other words, these low-inference observational systems classify specific and easily-identifiable behaviors that observers can code (Stodolsky, 1990).

Historically, observational research has focused almost exclusively on the instructional behaviors of classroom teachers, offering minimal attention to the classroom behaviors of individual students or to the classroom learning environments. Classroom instruction is complex, however, and is best understood when examined from multiple perspectives (Waxman, 2003). In order to obtain a more comprehensive picture of classroom life, especially in classrooms where technology is integrated into instruction, researchers and evaluators need to utilize broader observational systems that allow them to look at classrooms from a variety of perspectives, including those of students, teachers, and the overall class (Waxman, Padrón, Franco-Fuenmayor, & Huang, 2009).

Some of the major strengths of using classroom observation methods are that they (a) permit researchers to study the processes of education in naturalistic settings, (b) provide more detailed and precise evidence than other data sources, and (c) can be used to stimulate change and verify that the change occurred (Anderson & Burns, 1989). The descriptions of instructional events that are provided by this method have also been found to lead to improved understanding and better models for improving teaching (Padrón & Waxman, 1999; Waxman & Huang, 1999).

Classroom observational evaluation is described in this chapter as a somewhat unique approach or evaluation model. This observational evaluation model focuses on the observed classroom processes and behaviors of students and teachers in technology-enriched programs (Waxman & Padrón, 1994). This model investigates how classroom instruction and student behavior change as a result of the technology-based program or are influenced by the technology. The following questions are typical of those that this evaluation model would address:

- How have teacher and student behaviors changed as a result of the implementation of technology?
- To what extent has technology been integrated into the existing curriculum?
- To what extent are students engaged in their academic work when using and when not using technology?

An advantage of the classroom observation approach is that it typically utilizes low-inference, observational instruments that provide reliable and valid measures of classroom processes and interactions among students and teachers. Utilizing the classroom observation model, however, is very costly in terms of time and money to collect observational data. Additionally, this method focuses on observed classroom behaviors without typically considering the intent of the behavior. This model is also useful because it can include the realities of multidimensional classrooms.

In one of the few studies that have focused on classroom observations of technology use, Waxman and Huang (1995) examined the extent to which computer technology was integrated into the curriculum of 200 elementary and middle school classrooms from a large, urban school district. The researchers found that there was no integration of computer technology in the elementary school classrooms, while middle school students were observed working with computers in the content areas only 2% of the time. In another observational study focusing on 1,315 students from 220 middle school mathematics classrooms, Waxman and Huang (1996) found that calculators were the most frequent type of technology used, but calculators were observed being used only about 25% of the time. In the same study, meanwhile, computers were observed being used less than 1% of the time in mathematics classrooms.

More recently, Padrón, Waxman, Lee, Lin, and Michko (2012) observed technology use in 27 fourth- and fifth-grade classrooms serving Hispanic English language learners (ELLs) who came from socially- and economically-disadvantaged circumstances. The researchers found that the use of technology in these classrooms was very limited and that direct instruction was the only instructional practice that was used extensively. Similarly, Waxman, Evans, Boriack, and Kilinc (in press) developed and used systematic observations to evaluate the effectiveness of a federally-funded technology grant that was designed to increase the availability and use of instructional technology in 64 middle school classrooms serving predominantly minority students from economically-disadvantaged families. The *T3 overall classroom observation measure,* a high-inference walkthrough instrument, was developed for this study to examine (a) types of technology present in the classroom and extent of use, (b) teachers' technology usage, (c) students' technology usage, (d) teachers' general instructional behaviors, and (e) students' general behaviors. The results revealed that instructional technology was widely available in the classrooms, but most teachers and students were only using it to "some extent." For the most part, instruction in these urban middle school classrooms was student-centered, with teachers actively engaging students in classroom activities by acting as a coach/facilitator. Although technology has been found to be a better fit with more constructivist approaches to teaching rather than with the traditional lecture, recitation, and drill-and-practice approaches that are most common in schools today (Collins & Halverson, 2009; Wenglinsky, 2005), constructivist approaches were rarely noted in classrooms observed for the present evaluation.

The findings from these observational studies also raise several other important questions that need to be addressed in future evaluations. Most of these questions center on determining (a) the skills and abilities that teachers need to effectively implement technology, (b) the factors that constrain teachers from using technology, and (c) the types of support teachers need to implement the use of technology throughout their instruction. Future researchers may also want to examine the use of walkthrough or walkabout data for providing feedback to teachers or administrators about the quality of technology use and classroom instruction. By providing the answers to these questions, results from future research may demonstrate how technology can help students achieve academic success both in the present and in the future.

DISCUSSION

One of the most serious problems related to the increased use of technology in schools is the proliferation of technology-based programs without adequate research and evaluation examining their effectiveness. Before technology-based programs and curriculums become more widely implemented across the country, they should be systematically and rigorously evaluated. In addition, reports from these evaluations should be widely disseminated so that their findings can be used to guide and improve practice.

This chapter focused on five common evaluation models that are useful for evaluating technology programs in schools and classrooms. It should be pointed out, however, that other evaluation approaches, such as developmental evaluation and collaborative evaluations, may also be applicable for such programs. Developmental evaluation is an especially useful evaluation approach for exploring innovative and dynamic programs where developers and administrators expect that the technology use may be continually developing and changing (Patton, 2011). Collaborative evaluations are appropriate when a great deal of collaboration exists between evaluators and stakeholders in the evaluation process (Rodriguez-Campos & Rincones-Gomez, 2013).

The most effective programs of educational research and evaluation reflect the intelligent deployment of a diversity of research paradigms applied to the appropriate research questions. The use of alternative evaluation models may enable us to extend our understanding of several aspects of technology use in schools that could then be incorporated in programs to monitor and improve policies and practices and their effects. Improving the research and evaluation on technology use in schools, however, will take more than just awareness of the problems and knowledge of some solutions. A commitment to quality research and evaluation from both stakeholders and evaluators is also essential. A broad, interdisciplinary research agenda will need to be collaboratively developed and implemented vigorously. Policy makers will similarly need to acknowledge the significant contribution that research and evaluation can provide in formulating policies and suggesting improvements for technology use in schools.

REFERENCES

Anderson, L. W. & Burns, R. B. (1989). *Research in classrooms: The study of teachers, teaching, and instruction.* Oxford, UK: Pergamon.

Brown, D. B., Alford, B. L., Stillisano, J. R., Rollins, K. B., & Waxman, H. C. (2013). Evaluating the efficacy of mathematics, science, and technology teacher preparation academies in Texas. *Professional Development in Education, 39*(5), 656–677.

Collins, A. & Halverson, R. (2009). *Rethinking education in the age of technology: The digital revolution and schooling in America.* New York, NY: Teachers College.

Collis, B. & Carleer, G. (1993). The effects of technology-enriched school intervention: A multiple case study analysis. *Computers and Education, 21*(1/2), 151–162.

Cuban, L. (2001). *Oversold and underused: Computers in the classroom.* Cambridge, MA: Harvard University Press.

Cuban, L. (2013). *Inside the black box of classroom practice: Change without reform in American education.* Cambridge, MA: Harvard Education Press.

Drew, D. E. (2011). *STEM the tide: Reforming science, technology, engineering, and math education in America.* Baltimore, MD: The Johns Hopkins University Press.

Fitz-Gibbon, C. T. & Morris, L. L. (1996). Theory-based evaluation. *Evaluation Practice, 17*(2), 177–184.

Fitzpatrick, J. L., Sanders, J. R., & Worthen, B. R. (2011). *Program evaluation: Alternative approaches and practical guidelines* (4th ed.). Boston, MA: Pearson.

Frechtling, J. A. (2007). *Logic modeling methods in program evaluation.* San Francisco, CA: Jossey-Bass.

Gayl, C. L. (2007). *Global competitiveness in the 21st Century* (National School Boards Association Policy Research Brief). Retrieved from www.nsba.org/na

House, E. R. (1980). *Logic of evaluative argument.* Thousand Oaks, CA: Sage Publications.

Kerlinger, F. N. (1977). The influence of research on education practice. *Educational Researcher, 6*(8), 5–12.

Madaus, G. F., Scriven, M., & Stufflebeam, D. L. (Eds.). (1983). *Evaluation models: Viewpoints on educational and human services evaluation.* Boston, MA: Kluwer-Nijhoff.

McKinney, S. E., Chappell, S., Berry, R. Q., & Hickman, B. T. (2009). An examination of the instructional practices of mathematics teachers in urban schools. *Preventing School Failure, 53,* 278–284.

National Academies of Sciences, National Academy of Engineering, & Institute of Medicine. (2007). *Rising above the gathering storm: Energizing and employing America for a brighter economic future.* Washington, DC: The National Academies Press.

National Research Council. (2011). *Successful K–12 STEM education: Identifying effective approaches in science, technology, engineering, and mathematics.* Washington, DC: The National Academies Press.

Padrón, Y. N. & Waxman, H. C. (1999). Effective instructional practices for English language learners. In H. C. Waxman & H. J. Walberg (Eds.), *New directions for teaching practice and research* (pp. 171–213). Berkeley, CA: McCutchan.

Padrón, Y. N., Waxman, H. C., Lee, Y.-H., Lin, M.-F., & Michko, G. M. (2012). Classroom observations of teaching and learning with technology in urban elementary school mathematics classrooms serving English language learners. *International Journal of Instructional Media, 39*(1), 45–54.

Patton, M. Q. (2011). *Developmental evaluation: Applying complexity concepts to enhance innovation and use.* New York, NY: Guilford.

Phi Delta Kappa National Study Committee on Evaluation. (1971). *Educational evaluation and decision-making.* Itasca, IL: Peacock.

Popham, W. J. (1993). *Educational evaluation* (3rd ed.). Needham Heights, MA: Allyn and Bacon.

Posavac, E. J. & Carey, R. G. (1997). *Program evaluation: Methods and case studies* (5th ed.). Upper Saddle River, NJ: Prentice-Hall.

President's Council of Advisors on Science and Technology. (2010). *Prepare and inspire: K–12 education in science, technology, engineering, and math (STEM) for America's future.* Washington, DC: Author.

Rodriguez-Campos, L. & Rincones-Gomez, R. (2013). *Collaborative evaluations: Step-by-step.* Stanford, CA: Stanford University Press.

Schorr, L. B. & Kubisch, A. C. (1995, September). *New approaches to evaluation: Helping Sister Mary Paul, Geoff Canada, and Otis Johnson, while convincing Pat Moynihan, Newt Gingrich, and the American public.* Presentation at the Annie E. Casey Foundation Annual Research Evaluation Conference: Using Research and Evaluation Information to Improve Programs and Policies, Baltimore, MD.

Simonson, M. R. (1997). Evaluating teaching and learning at a distance. *New Directions for Teaching and Learning, 71,* 87–94.

Sorensen, C. & Sweeney, J. (1997, November). *A-e-I-o-u: An inclusive framework for evaluation.* Paper presented at the annual meeting of the American Evaluation Association, San Diego, CA.

Stallings, J. A. & Mohlman, G. G. (1988). Classroom observation techniques. In J. P. Keeves (Ed.), *Educational research, methodology, and measurement: An international handbook* (pp. 469–474). Oxford, UK: Pergamon.

State Educational Technology Directors Association (SETDA), International Society for Technology in Education (ISTE), & Partnership for 21st Century Skills (P21). (2007, November). *Maximizing the impact. The pivotal role of technology in a 21st century education system.* Retrieved from www.setda.org/web/guest/maximizingimpactreport

Stodolsky, S. S. (1990). Classroom observation. In J. Millman & L. Darling-Hammond (Eds.), *The new handbook of teacher evaluation: Assessing elementary and secondary school teachers* (pp. 175–190). Thousand Oaks, CA: Sage Publications.

Stufflebeam, D. L. (2000). The CIPP model for evaluation. In D. L. Stufflebeam, G. F. Madaus, & T. Kellaghan (Eds.), *Evaluation models: Viewpoints of educational and human services evaluation* (2nd ed., pp. 279–318). Norwell, MA: Kluwer Academic Publishers.

Stufflebeam, D. L. (Ed.). (2001). *Evaluation models* (New Directions for Program Evaluation, No. 89). San Francisco, CA: Jossey-Bass.

Stufflebeam, D. L. (2003, October). *The CIPP model for evaluation.* Paper presented at the annual conference of the Oregon Program Evaluators Network, Portland, OR.

Stufflebeam, D. L., Madaus, G. F., & Kellaghan, T. (Eds). (2000). *Evaluation models: Viewpoints on educational and human services education* (2nd ed.). Norwell, MA: Kluwer Academic Publishers.

Stufflebeam, D. L. & Shinkfield, A. J. (Eds.). (2007). *Evaluation theory, models, and applications.* San Francisco, CA: Jossey-Bass.

Stufflebeam, D. L. & Webster, W. J. (1980). An analysis of alternative approaches to evaluation. *Educational Evaluation and Policy Analysis, 2*(3), 5–19.

Vannatta, R. A. & Fordham, N. (2004). Teacher dispositions as predictors of classroom technology use. *Journal of Research on Technology in Education, 36*, 253–271.

W. K. Kellogg Foundation. (2004). *Logic model development guide.* Retrieved from http://www.wkkf.org/knowledge-center/resources/2006/02/WK-Kellogg-Foundation-Logic-Model-Development-Guide.aspx

Waxman, H. C. (2003). Systematic classroom observation. In J. W. Guthrie (Ed.), *Encyclopedia of education* (2nd ed., pp. 303–310). New York, NY: Macmillan.

Waxman, H. C., Evans, R. T., Boriack, A. W., & Kilinc, E. (in press). Systematic observations of the availability and use of instructional technology in urban middle school classrooms. *Journal of Contemporary Research in Education.*

Waxman, H. C. & Huang, S. L. (1995). An observational study of technology integration in urban elementary and middle schools. *International Journal of Instructional Media, 22*, 329–339.

Waxman, H. C. & Huang, S. L. (1996). Classroom instruction differences by level of technology use in middle school mathematics. *Journal of Educational Computing Research, 14*(2), 147–159.

Waxman, H. C. & Huang, S. L. (1999). Classroom observation research and the improvement of teaching. In H. C. Waxman & H. J. Walberg (Eds.), *New directions for teaching practice and research* (pp. 107–129). Berkeley, CA: McCutchan.

Waxman, H. C. & Padrón, Y. N. (1994). Alternative models for evaluating technology-enriched professional development schools. In J. Willis, B. Robin, & D. A. Willis (Eds.), *Technology and teacher education annual* (pp. 199–202). Charlottesville, VA: Association for the Advancement of Computing in Education.

Waxman, H. C., Padrón, Y. N., Franco-Fuenmayor, S. E., & Huang, S.-Y. L. (2009). Observing classroom instruction for ELLs from student, teacher, and classroom perspectives. *Texas Association for Bilingual Education Journal, 11*(1), 63–95.

Wenglinsky, H. (2005). *Using technology wisely: The keys to success in schools.* New York, NY: Teachers College Press.

Wholey, J. S., Hatry, H. P., & Newcomer, K. E. (2010). *Handbook of practical program evaluation.* San Francisco, CA: Jossey-Bass.

Worthen, B. R. & Sanders, J. R. (1987). *Educational evaluation: Alternative approaches and practical guidelines.* New York, NY: Longman.

CHAPTER 12

FUTURE DIRECTIONS FOR IMPROVING TECHNOLOGY USE IN MULTICULTURAL SETTINGS

Anna W. Boriack, Tirupalavanam G. Ganesh, and Hersh C. Waxman

ABSTRACT

This chapter will briefly discuss additional research on the benefits of using technology in multicultural settings. Educational technology from a sociology of education perspective will also be discussed. Implications for practice and policy and directions for future research will be suggested. There is still much work to be done in using technology in multicultural settings, especially in the areas of access, skills, and student achievement.

INTRODUCTION

As the previous chapters in this book have shown, there are many benefits to using technology in multicultural settings. Those benefits do not come without their challenges. There is a persistent divide among ethnic groups in technology and Internet access and usage. In February 2011, the U.S. Department of Commerce

Research on Technology Use in Multicultural Settings, pages 225–236.

released a report on broadband Internet usage in homes across the United States. The results showed that there is still a "digital divide" between ethnic groups for broadband Internet usage, although the gap is narrowing. Asian Americans had the highest home broadband Internet usage (68.8%), followed closely by White, non-Hispanics (68.3%). Less than half of Black, non-Hispanics; American Indian/ Alaskan Native; and Hispanics reported using broadband Internet in their homes (49.9%, 46.1%, and 45.2%, respectively; U.S. Department of Commerce, 2011). Access to the Internet and technology may not be the only factor contributing to the digital divide.

Epstein, Nisbet, and Gillespie (2011) suggest that the "digital divide" has two different meanings depending on the audience and the context. The "digital divide" can mean a problem accessing technology or a lack of skills to use the technology when it is present (Epstein, Nisbet, & Gillespie, 2011). These two meanings have to be kept in mind when using technology in multicultural settings. The technology might be present, but if the students have limited access to technology (either during or outside of school), they might not have the skills necessary to use the technology to its full potential. This could be especially true when trying to use technology to increase student achievement. Students might spend so much time on basic skills (such as turning the computer on, using a mouse and keyboard, accessing the program, etc.) that they do not have an adequate amount of time to actually use the program. It might be beneficial for schools to set time aside to teach students basic technology skills before trying to use technology for academic purposes. This is especially true in areas where the students have a lack of access to technology, because academic achievement for these students can be increased through the use of technology. The following section will discuss research studies that have shown the benefits of using technology with students in multicultural settings.

TECHNOLOGY USE AND STUDENT ACHIEVEMENT

One study (Judge, 2005) used data from the Early Childhood Longitudinal Study-Kindergarten (ECLS-K) to examine academic achievement and access to computers for African-American students in kindergarten and first grade. It was found that computers were used in the vast majority of both kindergarten and first grade classrooms (91% and 97%, respectively). At home more students had access to computers in first grade (40%) than in kindergarten (29%). Additional results showed that high achieving students used computers to learn reading, writing, and spelling skills significantly more than average and low achievers (Judge, 2005). A possible explanation is that computer time is used as a reward for students who complete their work, therefore giving higher achievers more opportunities for computer use. Teachers should make sure that all students have equal opportunities to use computers in the classroom. This could increase the academic achievement of average and lower achievers (Judge, 2005).

Data from the ECLS-K was also used to investigate students' access to computers, both at school and home, from kindergarten through third grade (Judge, Puckett, & Bell, 2006). The results showed that high-poverty schools had more computers than low-poverty schools, but only 60% of high-poverty and 53% of low-poverty third grade classrooms had a student to computer ratio of at least five to one. Furthermore, it was found that 96% of upper income households had a computer, while only 45% of low-income households had computer. This lack of home computer access could be a disadvantage to low-income students considering that mathematics and reading achievement were found to be significantly correlated to home computer use (Judge et al., 2006).

Jackson, von Eye, Biocca, Barbatsis, Zhao, and Fitzgerald (2006) studied home Internet use in low-income children over a 16-month period. The participants were mostly African American males 12–14 years old, although the full age range of participants was 10–18 years old. The study found that older children used the Internet more than younger children, and European American children used the Internet more than African American children. No difference in Internet usage between genders was found. The participants did not log on to the Internet daily, spent only 27 minutes a day on the Internet, and were more likely to use the Internet for information gathering rather than communication (Jackson et al., 2006). Furthermore, participants who used the Internet had higher GPAs after one year and higher scores on reading achievement tests after six months. Internet usage did not have an effect on mathematics achievement. The increased GPAs and reading achievement continued throughout the 16-month project. One explanation for increased reading achievement and GPAs but not mathematics achievement is that participants were spending time reading information on the Internet. Students who did not have Internet connections might not have been spending any time reading at home, which could account for lower reading achievement and GPAs for these students (Jackson et al., 2006). These results indicate that it could be beneficial for low-income students, especially African-American students, to have Internet access at home.

Other studies have examined how technology usage in school can increase student achievement. A study of middle school students found that students' GPAs increased if they spent less than three hours a day on computers (Lei & Zhao, 2007). If students spent more than three hours a day on computers, their GPAs decreased over the course of a school year. Additionally, certain types of technology use were found to have positive educational impacts. These uses included: (a) using Microsoft Word to take notes; (b) learning with Geometer's Sketchpad, Aleks (a mathematics program), or science probes; (c) creating websites; (d) working with desktop publishing; and (e) doing computer programming (Lei & Zhao, 2007). Further results indicated, however, that the technology uses that had positive educational impacts were among the least frequently used (Lei & Zhao, 2007). These findings indicate that there are certain types of technology that can increase student achievement, and teachers should be encouraged to frequently use these technologies in their classrooms.

Technology can also be used to help English language learners (ELLs) and struggling readers to increase their vocabulary knowledge and reading comprehension. Proctor, Dalton, and Grisham (2007) explored the use of a universal literacy environment (ULE) with fourth grade students who were struggling readers, including ELLs. The ULE that was used included eight hypertexts for students to read in a digital reading environment. Each text included pre-reading, during reading, and post-reading activities that were designed to help students develop their vocabulary knowledge along with cognitive and metacognitive strategies for reading comprehension. It was found that the use of the vocabulary and comprehension-based supports were associated with increased vocabulary and reading comprehension. Additionally, students who scored lower on the pre-test were more likely to use the supports (Proctor et al., 2007). These results suggest that the use of a ULE may help both struggling readers and ELLs increase their reading comprehension and vocabulary knowledge.

Another study examined the use of interactive whiteboards (IWB) technology to increase the mathematics and reading achievement of third and fifth grade ELLs (Lopez, 2010). ELLs in a third grade classroom with an IWB had a higher pass rate on the state mathematics test than ELLs in a traditional classroom (82% and 69%, respectively); however, there was not a statistically significant difference between the scores for the two classroom types. For third grade reading, the converse was true; ELLs in a traditional classroom had a higher pass rate than ELLs in an IWB classroom (85% and 78%, respectively). The least squares mean estimate showed that ELLs in an IWB classroom scored 75.6 points more than ELLs in a traditional classroom, which was a statistically significant difference. This indicates that even though the pass rates were not higher, having an IWB significantly increased ELL third graders' reading achievement (Lopez, 2010).

Similar results were found for ELL students in regards to fifth grade mathematics. ELL students in an IWB classroom had a higher pass rate for mathematics than those in a traditional classroom (89% and 66%, respectively), but there was no statistically significant difference between the two classroom types. For reading, fifth grade ELLs in an IWB classroom had a 100% pass rate, while the pass rate for ELLs in a traditional classroom was 73%. There was no statistically significant difference between the two classroom types for reading, which indicates that having an IWB did not significantly increase ELL fifth graders reading achievement (Lopez, 2010). The results of this study suggest that having an IWB might help to increase ELLs passing rates on standardized tests and perhaps their reading achievement. Teachers, however, need to be trained on how to effectively use the IWB and have support to successfully integrate the IWB into their classrooms.

The studies discussed previously show that technology can be beneficial to students in multicultural settings. Examining educational technology from a sociology of education perspective can help us better understand technology integration in multicultural settings.

EDUCATIONAL TECHNOLOGY FROM A SOCIOLOGY OF EDUCATION PERSPECTIVE

The tradition of instruction that is student-centered and experiential has its foundations in the curricular and psychological research work of Dewey (1902), Freudenthal (1973), Fröbel and Hailmann (1901), Kilpatrick (1918, 1921), Montessori (1964, 1965), Piaget (1969, 1970), Stevenson (1928), and Vygotsky (1978, 1986). As education scholars developed theories of learning over time, von Glasersfeld's (1974) work advocating for constructivism as a theory of knowledge essentially diverged from behaviorism (e.g., Skinner, 1954). This distinction is important for the study of educational technology, as it also marks a different way of thinking about the use of technology as a "machine that teaches and tests" to change student behavior (e.g., Lumsdaine, 1959; Pressey, 1932; Skinner, 1958) in comparison with the use of technology as a "tool to construct" learning (e.g., Dede, 1987; Papert, 1980). Since the advent of computers into classrooms (Saettler, 1990) "technology integration" into K–12 education has become a goal for many educators, policy makers, and education technology industries. However, Cuban (1986, 2001, 2013) has thoroughly established through his study of technology integration into education that the many new technologies can only impact learning in the classroom to the extent that teaching practices change to accommodate the unique affordances of the technologies.

Research describing conditions of technology integration pedagogy in classrooms ranging from dissertation studies (e.g., Ganesh, 2003; Pierson, 2001) to research reports in peer-reviewed journals dedicated to the topic (e.g., *British Journal of Educational Technology, Educational Technology Research and Development, Journal of Research on Technology in Education*) began to appear to inform the field. To mitigate the perceived concern that teachers were the primary barriers to successful integration of technology into education, funding efforts focused on teacher preparation. New research emerged when the U.S. Department of Education (1999) funded over 400 grants to prepare teachers to integrate technology into teaching and learning through the Preparing Tomorrow's Teachers to Use Technology Program (PT3). For instance, Howland and Wedman (2004); Ludwig and Taymans, (2005); Polly, Mims, Shepherd, and Inan (2010); and Thompson (2005), among others, found that the PT3 efforts had facilitated greater confidence in teacher education faculty to integrate technology and that teachers had developed facility in integrating technology with teaching and learning. Furthermore, education technology researchers developed a framework, technological pedagogical content knowledge (TPACK), for examining the types of teacher knowledge needed to achieve technology integration (Abbitt, 2011; Koehler & Mishra, 2005; Koehler, Shin, & Mishra, 2011; Voogt, Fisser, Pareja, Tondeur, & van Braak, 2013). TPACK is based on Shulman's (1986) idea of pedagogical content knowledge, which included understanding of content knowledge and pedagogical knowledge, in other words, what makes learning content easy or challenging for students. However, there has been criticism that TPACK is too intricate and too vague (Brantley-Dias & Ertmer, 2013) and that teacher education needs to support 21st century learning (see http://www.p21.org/).

While there has been a focus on research related to technology integration pedagogy, there has also been interest in research on the impact of educational technology on student learning. Meta-analysis (e.g., Cheung & Slavin, 2012, 2013; Li & Ma, 2011; Pearson, Ferdig, Blomeyer, & Moran, 2005) and second-order meta-analysis (e.g., Tamin, Bernard, Borokhovski, Abrami, & Schmid, 2011) have been useful to help us better understand the impact of technology on student learning. These studies clearly indicate that gains in student learning in content areas like mathematics and reading as a result of educational technologies, such as computer-aided instruction, are modest at best.

Rushby (2013), who had a 40-year investment in the field of educational technology and served as editor of the *British Journal of Educational Technology,* noted that it is necessary to have a healthy dose of skepticism with regard to predictions about the role technology can have on education. He stated:

> Our learners make extensive use of the new technologies—but less so for their formal education....The greater part of formal learning continues to follow the traditional lecture-based model and is only slowly responding to the innovations of the past twenty years. Technology is neither the problem nor the answer. (Rushby, 2013, p. 54)

He advocated for a grand challenge and research direction for the field that focuses on the sociology of education and of educational technology.

According to the National Research Council (2012), "Over a century of research on transfer has yielded little evidence that teaching can develop general cognitive competencies that are transferable to any new discipline, problem or context, in or out of school" (p. 7). While classroom learning has been found to be lacking in relevance and value, failing to transfer knowledge and skills necessary for everyday life and future work, success in K–12 schools has continued to be tied closely to life opportunities. Gutiérrez, Izquierdo, and Kremer-Sadlik (2010) found that students from privileged families were spending more time on school-related and out-of-school activities that were carefully and strategically managed by their parents. Such experiences were also extending the achievement gap for students who did not have these same advantages as their privileged peers.

As public schools have lacked interest-driven learning experiences for their students, along with a recent rise in interest in digital fabrication (Gershenfeld, 2012) and making (cf. Maker Faire see http://www.makered.org), educational technologists have begun advocating for making, tinkering, and engineering as ways of knowing that should be visible in every classroom, regardless of disciplinary silos or student level (e.g., Martinez & Stager, 2013). Furthermore, the

Next Generation Science Standards (NGSS Lead States, 2013) advanced science and engineering practices as a cross-cutting concept in teaching and learning in grades K–12. The idea of integrating technology into education when advances in technology (e.g., digital fabrication) occur is not merely about the technology, it is also about the social aspect of invention. Regrettably this social aspect of invention often manifests itself as interest-driven activities—for example evident in the "do it yourself" culture prevalent outside of school (Kafai & Peppler, 2011). Nevertheless, opportunities for students to engage in interest-driven activities at school are not prevalent.

A large group of researchers have advocated for "connected learning—an approach to learning and educational reform that leverages the opportunities afforded by new media in the service of a more equitable educational system" (Ito et al., 2013, p. 87). This is especially important for populations of our society who lack economic opportunity, who lack organized support structures in and out of school, and who also find schoolwork disjointed from the meaningful social contexts in their daily lives. "Connected learning" encourages for expanded access to interest-driven and socially embedded learning that is concerned with life opportunities—educational, economic, and political.

If educational technology is to be successfully integrated into multicultural classrooms, better policies and practices need to be put into place. Additionally, further research is needed to advance our understanding of the use of educational technology in multicultural settings.

IMPLICATIONS AND FUTURE RESEARCH

Implications for Policy and Practice

Home Internet usage may increase students' GPAs and reading achievement (Jackson et al., 2006; Judge et al., 2006). Many low-income and minority students do not have a computer or broadband Internet access (Judge et al., 2006; U.S. Department of Commerce, 2011). This suggests that more programs need to be developed to provide computers and the Internet to low-income and minority households. This would increase the access to technology and the Internet; however, these households also need to be taught the skills necessary to use technology and the Internet. Programs could be funded that require parents and students to attend classes on basic technology skills. Once they complete the program they could receive a computer and Internet access at either a minimal or no cost. This could help decrease the "digital divide" both in terms of access and skills (Epstein et al., 2011).

Students also need to have access to computers at school; however, both high-poverty and low-poverty schools do not have an adequate computer to student ratio (Judge et al., 2006). Policies need to be developed to provide all schools with technology for their students. The technology needs to be put in the classrooms so that students have access to it at all times and do not have to wait to go to a computer lab to use it. This could also help to increase student achievement, especially for ELLs and lower achieving students (Lei & Zhao, 2007; Lopez, 2010; Proctor et al., 2007). In order for student achievement to increase, teachers need to be trained on how to effectively use the technology in their classrooms.

Lei and Zhao (2007) showed that there were at least five types of technology that had positive education impacts, but these technologies were among the least frequently used in classrooms. One probable cause is that teachers were not adequately trained on how to use the technologies. Time and money need to be invested in training teachers on how to use the technologies that have been shown to be beneficial to students. This would also include training teachers on the use of universal literacy environments and interactive white boards since both of these technologies have also been shown to increase reading achievement for ELLs or struggling readers (Lopez, 2010; Proctor et al., 2007). Once the teachers are trained, they need to be provided support so that they can successful implement these new technologies in their classrooms.

Future Research

There is still much research to be done on the use of technology in multicultural settings. The "digital divide" is narrowing, but it is still not clear how much of an impact this truly has on student achievement. The most recent report from the U.S. Department of Commerce (2011) looked only at broadband Internet usage in the home, not at home computer access. This data needs to be updated to include other pieces of technology, such as tablets and smart phones. Once this data is collected, future studies need to reexamine how home technology usage impacts student achievement. These studies need to examine difference by ethnic groups, geographical location, and grade level.

Many of the studies that have been done focus only on elementary and middle school students (Judge, 2005; Judge et al., 2006; Lei & Zhao, 2007; Lopez, 2010; Proctor et al., 2007), so it is unclear what influence technology usage has on high school student achievement. Students in high school use technology to research and write reports, create presentations, and communicate with friends. They are also active in social networking. Future research needs to focus on high school students, their use of technology (how and why they are using it), and the impact on their achievement. This could also provide insight into if high school students are being adequately prepared with the technology skills that they need for college or careers.

CONCLUSION

Technology is a fast growing field. The students in schools today have always been surrounded by technology, whether at home or school. Technology can increase student achievement if it is used in the correct manner. Low-income, minority students need to have access to technology and the Internet both at home and school. Programs need to be developed that can help them and their parents have access to technology and develop the skills necessary to use that technology. Future research needs to delve further into how technology impacts student achievement at all grade levels and for all ethnic groups. This will allow for a deeper understanding of how the powerfulness of technology can be harnessed to benefit students and prepare them for the future.

REFERENCES

Abbitt, J. T. (2011). Measuring technological pedagogical content knowledge in preservice teacher education: A review of current methods and instruments. *Journal of Research on Technology in Education, 43*, 281–300.

Brantley-Dias, L. & Ertmer, P. A. (2013). Goldilocks and TPACK: Is the construct "just right"? *Journal of Research on Technology in Education, 46*(2), 103–128.

Cheung, A. C. & Slavin, R. E. (2012). How features of educational technology applications affect student reading outcomes: A meta-analysis. *Educational Research Review, 7*(3), 198–215.

Cheung, A. C. & Slavin, R. E. (2013). The effectiveness of educational technology applications for enhancing mathematics achievement in K–12 classrooms: A meta-analysis. *Educational Research Review, 9*, 88–113.

Cuban, L. (1986). *Teachers and machines: The use of classroom technology since 1920.* New York, NY: Teachers College Press.

Cuban, L. (2001). *Oversold and underused: Computers in the classroom.* Cambridge, MA: Harvard University Press.

Cuban, L. (2013). *Inside the black box of classroom practice: Change without reform in American education.* Cambridge, MA: Harvard Education Press.

Dede, C. (1987). Empowering environments, hypermedia and microworlds. *The Computing Teacher, 15*(3), 20–24, 61.

Dewey, J. (1902). *The child and the curriculum.* Chicago, IL: University of Chicago Press.

Epstein, D., Nisbet, E. C., & Gillespie, T. (2011). Who's responsible for the digital divide? Public perceptions and policy implications. *The Information Society: An International Journal, 27*, 92–104.

Freudenthal, H. (1973). *Mathematics as an educational task.* Dordrecht, Netherlands: Reidel.

Fröbel, F. & Hailmann, W. N. (1901). *The education of man.* New York, NY: D. Appleton.

Ganesh, T. G. (2003). *Practices of computer use in elementary education: Perceived and missed opportunities.* (Doctoral dissertation). Retrieved from Dissertation abstracts international (3166092).

Gershenfeld N. (2012). How to make almost anything: The digital fabrication revolution. *Foreign Affairs, 91*(6), 43–57.

Gutiérrez, K., Izquierdo, C., & Kremer-Sadlik, T. (2010). Middle class working families' ideologies and engagement in children's extracurricular activities. *International Journal of Learning, 17*, 633–656.

Howland, J. & Wedman, J. (2004). A process model for faculty development: Individualizing technology learning. *Journal of Technology and Teacher Education, 12*(2), 239–263.

Ito, M., Gutiérrez, K., Livingstone, S., Penuel, B., Rhodes, J., Salen, K.,...Watkins, S. C. (2013). *Connected learning: An agenda for research and design.* Irvine, CA: Digital Media and Learning Research Hub.

Jackson, L. A., von Eye, A., Biocca, F. A., Barbatsis, G., Zhao, Y., & Fitzgerald, H. E. (2006). Does home Internet use influence the academic performance of low-income children? *Developmental Psychology, 42,* 429–435.

Judge, S. (2005). The impact of computer technology on academic achievement of young African American children. *Journal of Research in Childhood Education, 20,* 91–101.

Judge, S., Puckett, K., & Bell S. M. (2006). Closing the digital divide: Update from the Early Childhood Longitudinal Study. *The Journal of Educational Research, 100,* 52–60.

Kafai, Y. & Peppler, K. (2011). Youth, technology, and DIY: Developing participatory competencies in creative media production. *Review of Research in Education, 35*(1), 89–119.

Kilpatrick, W. H. (1918). The project method. *Teachers College Record, 19,* 319–335.

Kilpatrick, W. H. (1921). Dangers and difficulties of the project method and how to overcome them: Introductory statement: Definition of terms. *Teachers College Record, 22,* 282–288.

Koehler, M. J. & Mishra, P. (2005). What happens when teachers design educational technology? The development of technological pedagogical content knowledge. *Journal of Educational Computing Research, 32,* 131–152.

Koehler, M. J., Shin, T. S., & Mishra, P. (2011). How do we measure TPACK? Let me count the ways. In R. N. Ronau, C. R. Rakes, & M. L. Niess (Eds.), *Educational technology, teacher knowledge, and classroom impact: A research handbook on frameworks and approaches* (pp. 16–31). Hershey, PA: IGI Global.

Lei, J. & Zhao, Y. (2007). Technology uses and student achievement: A longitudinal study. *Computers & Education, 49,* 284–296.

Li, Q. & Ma, X. (2011). A meta-analysis of the effects of computer technology on school students' mathematics learning. *Educational Psychology Review, 22,* 215–243.

Lopez, O. S. (2010). The digital learning classroom: Improving English language learners' academic success in mathematics and reading using interactive whiteboard technology. *Computers & Education, 54,* 901–915.

Ludwig, M. & Taymans, J. (2005). Teaming: Constructing high-quality faculty development in a PT3 project. *Journal of Technology and Teacher Education, 13*(3), 357–372.

Lumsdaine, A. A. (1959). Teaching machines and self-instructional materials. *Audio-Visual Communication Review, 7,* 163–181.

Martinez, S. L. & Stager, G. (2013). *Invent to learn: Making, tinkering, and engineering in the classroom.* Torrance, CA: Constructing Modern Knowledge Press.

Montessori, M. (1964). *The advanced Montessori method.* Cambridge, MA: R. Bentley.

Montessori, M. (1965). *Spontaneous activity in education.* New York, NY: Schocken Books.

National Research Council. (2012). *Education for life and work: Developing transferable knowledge and skills in the 21st Century.* Washington, DC: National Academies Press.

NGSS Lead States. (2013). *Next generation science standards: For states, by states.* Washington, DC: National Academies Press.

Papert, S. (1980). *Mindstorms: Children, computers, and powerful ideas.* New York, NY: Basic Books.

Pearson, P. D., Ferdig, R. E., Blomeyer, R. L., & Moran, J. (2005). *The effects of technology on reading performance in the middle-school grades: A meta-analysis with recommendations for policy.* Naperville, IL: Learning Point Associates.

Piaget, J. (1969). *The psychology of the child.* H. Weaver (Trans.). New York, NY: Basic Books.

Piaget, J. (1970). *Science of education and the psychology of the child.* New York, NY: Viking Press.

Pierson, M. E. (2001). *Technology integration practice as a function of pedagogical expertise* (Doctoral dissertation). Retrieved from Dissertation abstracts international (9924200).

Polly, D., Mims, C., Shepherd, C. E. & Inan, F. (2010). Evidence of impact: Transforming teacher education with Preparing Tomorrow's Teachers to Teach with Technology (PT3) grants. *Teaching and Teacher Education: An International Journal of Research and Studies, 26*(4), 863–870.

Pressey, S. L. (1932). A third and fourth contribution toward the coming "industrial revolution" in education. *School and Society, 36*(934), 668–672.

Proctor, C. P., Dalton, B., & Grisham, D. (2007). Scaffolding English language learners and struggling readers in a universal literacy environment with embedded strategy instruction and vocabulary support. *Journal of Literacy Research, 39,* 71–93.

Rushby, N. (2013). The future of learning technology: Some tentative predictions. *Educational Technology & Society, 16*(2), 52–58.

Saettler, P. (1990). *The evolution of American educational technology.* Englewood, CO: Libraries Unlimited.

Shulman, L. S. (1986). Those who understand: Knowledge growth in teaching. *Educational Researcher, 15*(2), 4–14.

Skinner, B. F. (1954). The science of learning and the art of teaching. *Harvard Educational Review, 24,* 86–97.

Skinner, B. F. (1958). Teaching machines. *Science, 128*(3330), 969–977.

Stevenson, J. A. (1928). *The project method of teaching.* New York, NY: Macmillan.

Tamin, R., Bernard, R., Borokhovski, E., Abrami, P., & Schmid, R. (2011). What forty years of research says about the impact of technology on learning: A second-order meta-analysis and validation study. *Review of Educational Research, 81,* 4–28.

Thompson, A. (2005). Scientifically based research: Establishing a research agenda for the technology in teacher education community. *Journal of Research on Technology in Education, 37*(4), 331–337.

U.S. Department of Commerce. (2011). Digital nation: Expanding Internet usage. Retrieved from http://www.ntia.doc.gov/report/2011/digital-nation-expanding-Internet-usage-ntia-research-preview

U.S. Department of Education. (1999). Preparing tomorrow's teachers to use technology. *Federal Register, 64*(248), 72801–72804.

von Glasersfeld, E. (1974). Piaget and the radical constructivist epistemology. In E. von Glasersfeld & C. D. Smock (Eds.), Epistemology and education: The implications of radical constructivism for knowledge acquisition (pp. 1–26). Athens, GA: Follow Through Publications.

Voogt, J., Fisser, P., Pareja, N., Tondeur, J., & van Braak, J. (2013). Technological pedagogical content knowledge (TPACK): A review of the literature. Journal of Computer Assisted Learning, 29, 109–121.

Vygotsky, L. S. (1978). Mind in society: The development of higher psychological processes. M. Cole, V. John-Steiner, S. Scribner, & E. Souberman (Eds.). Cambridge, MA: Harvard University Press.

Vygotsky, L. S. (1986). Thought and language. A. Kozulin (Ed.). Boston, MA: MIT Press.

EDITOR AND AUTHOR BIOGRAPHIES

BOOK EDITORS

Dr. Tirupalavanam G. Ganesh is an engineer, educator, and education researcher who designs, implements, and studies "learning environments" that offer opportunities for mastery learning in K–12 and university settings. He is assistant dean for K–12 education in the Ira A. Fulton Schools of Engineering at Arizona State University.

Dr. Anna W. Boriack is a senior research associate for the Education Research Center at Texas A&M University. Her research interests include teacher professional development in the areas of mathematics, science, and technology and implementation of what is learned during professional development. She is also interested in how to help English language learners be successful in mathematics and science through the use of technology.

Dr. Jacqueline R. Stillisano is the co-director of the Education Research Center at Texas A&M University. Stillisano's research primarily incorporates qualitative

Research on Technology Use in Multicultural Settings, pages 237–243.
Copyright © 2015 by Information Age Publishing
237

case study methods, focusing on college access, particularly for under-represented and non-traditional students; online teaching and learning; and evaluation of educational programs and initiatives.

Dr. Trina J. Davis is an assistant professor at Texas A&M University. Her research includes investigations related to teaching and learning in 3-D virtual environments and statewide school technology studies. She is a past president of the International Society for Technology in Education (ISTE) and continues to champion digital equity issues nationally.

Dr. Hersh C. Waxman is director of the Education Research Center at Texas A&M University and a professor in the Department of Teaching, Leaning, and Culture at College of Education and Human Development. He has authored or co-authored more than 100 research articles in the areas of urban education, classroom learning environments, and students at risk of failure.

CHAPTER AUTHORS

Chapter 1

Dr. Anna W. Boriack is a senior research associate for the Education Research Center at Texas A&M University. Her research interests include teacher professional development in the areas of mathematics, science, and technology and implementation of what is learned during professional development. She is also interested in how to help English language learners be successful in mathematics and science through the use of technology.

Dr. Hersh C. Waxman is director of the Education Research Center at Texas A&M University and a professor in the Department of Teaching, Leaning, and Culture at College of Education and Human Development. He has authored or co-authored more than 100 research articles in the areas of urban education, classroom learning environments, and students at risk of failure.

Chapter 2

Dr. Pérez-Granados is an associate professor of human development at California State University, Monterey Bay, and served as an assistant professor in the Stanford University School of Education. Her research focuses on cognitive, language, and literacy development from infancy through early childhood; and socio-cultural approaches to teaching and learning in family and early schooling contexts.

Lynne C. Huffman, MD, is a developmental-behavioral pediatrician (board certified, 2002) and associate professor of pediatrics at Stanford School of Medicine. Her research focuses on the early identification and treatment of behavioral problems; emergent literacy and school readiness; and community-based mental health/educational program evaluation and outcomes measurement.

Chapter 3

Barbara Hug is a clinical assistant professor at the University of Illinois, Urbana-Champaign in the Department of Curriculum and Instruction. Her current research focuses on understanding the development and use of curriculum materials that support inquiry learning in science. Through her work, she has participated in the development of project-based science materials that allow students to engage in extended inquiry investigations. She is currently investigating what inquiry practices develop as students participate in learning science with these reform-oriented materials.

Elizabeth Gonzalez received her Master of Education degree from the University of Illinois, Urbana-Champaign in the Department of Curriculum and Instruction. Her research interests include developing and using curriculum materials that support inquiry learning in science, integrating technology for teaching science, investigating how materials are adapted in different settings, and the types of support needed by teachers and students engaged in these activities.

Chapter 4

Doug Clark's research investigates the learning processes through which people come to understand core science concepts. This work focuses primarily on conceptual change, explanation, collaboration, and argumentation. Clark's research often explores these learning processes through the design of digital learning environments and games in middle and high school classroom settings.

Brian Nelson is an associate professor of educational informatics at Arizona State University. His research focuses on the theory, design, and implementation of immersive learning and assessment environments. He has published and presented extensively on the viability of immersive environments for situated, collaborative learning and embedded assessment.

Robert K. Atkinson is an associate professor with a joint appointment in the School of Computing, Informatics and Decision Systems Engineering in the Ira A. Schools of Engineering and the Division of Educational Leadership and Innovation in the Mary Lou Fulton Teachers College at Arizona State University.

Frank Ramirez-Marin is a fulltime professor and the director of the language center at Universidad Veracruzana—Campus Veracruz, Mexico. He holds a PhD degree from Arizona State University. His research interests focus on foreign/

second language education and second language learning from socio-cultural perspectives to language and literacy.

Dr. William Medina-Jerez is an associate professor in science education and teaches undergraduate science methods courses, as well as graduate level courses on science teaching in bilingual classrooms. His research explores science education for students from diverse backgrounds and science education in less developed countries.

Chapter 5

Dr. Brooke E. Kandel-Cisco is an assistant professor and director of the Master's in Effective Teaching and Leadership Program at Butler University in Indianapolis, IN. Her research focuses on the education of English learners and immigrant students and the preparation of teachers to work with diverse students.

Dr. Jacqueline R. Stillisano is the co-director of the Education Research Center at Texas A&M University. Stillisano's research primarily incorporates qualitative case study methods, focusing on college access, particularly for under-represented and non-traditional students; online teaching and learning; and evaluation of educational programs and initiatives.

Dr. Trina J. Davis is an assistant professor at Texas A&M University. Her research includes investigations related to teaching and learning in 3-D virtual environments and statewide school technology studies. She is a past president of the International Society for Technology in Education (ISTE) and continues to champion digital equity issues nationally.

Dr. Hersh C. Waxman is director of the Education Research Center at Texas A&M University and a professor in the Department of Teaching, Leaning, and Culture at College of Education and Human Development. He has authored or co-authored more than 100 research articles in the areas of urban education, classroom learning environments, and students at risk of failure.

Chapter 6

Cecelia Merkel is an information specialist at Penn State University. She coordinates the Media and Learning Design Initiative, a partnership between World Campus and Penn State Public Media. The group is charged with finding ways to strategically enrich online programs, courses, and student services through the infusion of rich media.

Chapter 7

Kimberley Gomez is an associate professor of urban schooling in the Graduate School of Education and Information Studies at UCLA. Her research explores how cognitive and social interaction elements of learning environments serve to make STEM content more accessible for non-English background students and those with low levels of literacy skills.

Louis M. Gomez is the MacArthur Chair in Digital Media and Learning at UCLA's Graduate School of Education & Information Studies and senior fellow at the Carnegie Foundation for the Advancement of Teaching. Professor Gomez' primary interest is in working with school communities to create social arrangements and curriculum that support school reform.

Samuel Kwon is an assistant professor of instructional design and technology at Concordia University Chicago. His research looks into the design of computer-mediated activities to support teaching and learning in traditional and blended learning environments.

Jennifer Zoltners Sherer is a designer and online instructor for The Institute for Learning at the University of Pittsburgh. Her work focuses on improving teacher practice and designing effective learning environments, particularly for K–12 at risk populations.

Chapter 8

Dr. Héctor H. Rivera obtained his degree in developmental psychology from UC Santa Cruz. He conducted his post-doctorate fellowship at CREDE and worked as a scientific advisor for TIMES at the University of Houston. Currently, he is an assistant professor in the Department of Educational Psychology at Texas A&M University.

Dr. David J. Francis is a Hugh Roy and Lillie Cranz Cullen Distinguished Professor and chairman of the Department of Psychology at the University of Houston, where he also directs the Texas Institute for Measurement, Evaluation, and Statistics. He is an inaugural fellow of the American Educational Research Association.

Chapter 9

Dr. Tirupalavanam G. Ganesh is an engineer, educator, and education researcher who designs, implements, and studies "learning environments" that offer opportunities for mastery learning in K–12 and university settings. He is assistant dean for K–12 education in the Ira A. Fulton Schools of Engineering at Arizona State University.

Chapter 10

Finbarr (Barry) Sloane serves as chair of the Knowledge Building Cluster in the Division of Research on Learning at the National Science Foundation. His research interests include the understanding of student growth in mathematics and how such growth can be measured, modeled, and better understood.

Jennifer Oloff-Lewis is an assistant professor of mathematics education at CSU-Chico. Her research interests include the study of gifted students and how their mathematical knowledge develops over time.

Antony (Eamonn) Kelly is a professor of educational psychology at George Mason University. Dr. Kelly is interested in the intersection of the creative space of innovative practices and where it meets the pruning function of research methods (i.e., design-based research). He also works to promote research intersecting mathematics cognition and cognitive neuroscience.

Chapter 11

Dr. Jacqueline R. Stillisano is the co-director of the Education Research Center at Texas A&M University. Stillisano's research primarily incorporates qualitative case study methods, focusing on college access, particularly for under-represented and non-traditional students; online teaching and learning; and evaluation of educational programs and initiatives.

Dr. Danielle B. Brown is an assistant professor in the Department of Teaching and Learning at the University of Nevada, Las Vegas. Previously, she worked as an assistant research scientist at the Education Research Center at Texas A&M University, where she served as co-principal investigator for three research grants and participated in numerous program evaluations.

Dr. Hersh C. Waxman is director of the Education Research Center at Texas A&M University and a professor in the Department of Teaching, Leaning, and Culture at College of Education and Human Development. He has authored or co-authored more than 100 research articles in the areas of urban education, classroom learning environments, and students at risk of failure.

Chapter 12

Dr. Anna W. Boriack is a senior research associate for the Education Research Center at Texas A&M University. Her research interests include teacher professional development in the areas of mathematics, science, and technology and implementation of what is learned during professional development. She is also interested in how to help English language learners be successful in mathematics and science through the use of technology.

Dr. Tirupalavanam G. Ganesh is an engineer, educator, and education researcher who designs, implements, and studies "learning environments" that offer opportunities for mastery learning in K–12 and university settings. He is assistant dean for K–12 education in the Ira A. Fulton Schools of Engineering at Arizona State University.

Dr. Hersh C. Waxman is director of the Education Research Center at Texas A&M University and a professor in the Department of Teaching, Leaning, and Culture at College of Education and Human Development. He has authored or co-authored more than 100 research articles in the areas of urban education, classroom learning environments, and students at risk of failure.